The Superpowers and the Middle East

The Superpowers and the Middle East

Tarun Chandra Bose
Jadavpur University

ASIA PUBLISHING HOUSE
BOMBAY · CALCUTTA · NEW DELHI · MADRAS
LUCKNOW · BANGALORE · LONDON · NEW YORK

© 1972 Tarun Chandra Bose

Tarun Chandra **Bose** (1931)

All rights reserved. No part of this publication may be reproduced, stored in a retrieval system, or transmitted, in any form or by any means, electronic, mechanical, photocopying, recording or otherwise, without the prior permission of the Publisher.

ISBN 0.210.22345.6

PRINTED IN INDIA

BY G. G. PATHARE AT THE POPULAR PRESS (BOM.) PRIVATE LTD., BOMBAY 34 WB. AND PUBLISHED BY P. S. JAYASINGHE, ASIA PUBLISHING HOUSE, BOMBAY-1

To

A. APPADORAI

Distinguished scholar and educationist, the founder of the Indian School of International Studies and a pioneer in promoting instruction, research and publication in international affairs and area studies in India.

Preface

The Middle East, which stands at the crossroads between the East and West, is the birthplace of three of the world's great religions and the home of some 60 million people. This region, where civilization flourished more than 5,000 years ago, has been the scene of turmoil and violence since the creation of Israel in 1948. The establishment of the Jewish state resulted in an immediate conflict between it and the Arab states — a conflict that has been raging for over two decades. The involvement of the two superpowers — the United States and the Soviet Union — in the region has made matters more complicated. In view of the importance of the Middle East to both the United States and the Soviet Union, and the stake which both have in the region, they have not remained impartial observers of the Arab-Israeli conflict. In an effort to check the extension of each other's influence in the area, both the superpowers have become involved in the region. This study attempts to describe the important events in the Middle East since the end of the Second World War and to analyse the reasons for the involvement of the two superpowers — their interests and objectives in the region and the policies pursued by them in furtherance of the same.

A research grant by the American Studies Research Center, Hyderabad, in the summer of 1969, made it possible for me to do the initial research for the present study. However, the completion of this study was made possible by the award of a Fulbright-Hays Senior Professor Grant during the academic year 1969-70, which enabled me to conduct further research at the Harvard University, Cambridge, Massachusetts, USA. I wish to express my gratitude for the above grants.

At Harvard, I had the privilege of using the facilities of the Widener Library, the library of the Russian Research Center and of the Center for International Affairs which made it possible for me to carry out research for the major portion of the present study. In this connection I wish to thank Professor Merle Fainsod, Carl H. Pforzheimer University Professor and Director of the Widener Library, Harvard University; Dean Ernest R. May of Harvard University; Professor Donald Fleming of the Charles Warren Center, Harvard University; Professor Benjamin H. Brown of the Center for International Affairs, Harvard University; and Professor Adam B. Ulam of the Russian Research Center, Harvard University, for the kindness and assistance that were extended to me. My thanks are due also to Mr. John F. Stewart, Director of the John F. Kennedy Library in Waltham, Massachusetts, USA, for granting me permission to use transcripts of the oral history interviews at the above library, to Mrs. Sylvie Turner, Research Archivist at the Kennedy Library, for the prompt assistance that was extended cheerfully, and to Professor M. S. Rajan, Director of the School of International Studies, Jawaharlal Nehru University, New Delhi, for going through my manuscript and offering me encouragement for the publication of this book. Finally, I owe more than I can readily express to my wife Zinnia, who helped me in a variety of ways and made it possible for me to bring this study to early completion.

Calcutta
September, 1970

TARUN CHANDRA BOSE

Contents

Preface   vii

Chapter One

THE POST WAR DECADE: 1945-1956   1

THE SOVIET UNION, IRAN AND TURKEY 2; THE BIRTH OF ISRAEL 6; ARAB REFUGEES 9; DELINEATION OF BOUNDARY LINES 13; THE BAGHDAD PACT 15; SOVIET PENETRATION IN THE MIDDLE EAST 20; ASWAN DAM AND NATIONALIZATION OF THE SUEZ CANAL 24; SOVIET ECONOMIC ASSISTANCE 27; THE FIELD OF CULTURE AND EDUCATION 30; AFTERMATH OF SUEZ CANAL NATIONALIZATION 32; THE SUEZ CRISIS 35; SOVIET GAINS 42.

Chapter Two

PERIOD OF TRIAL AND HOPE: 1957-1965   45

THE EISENHOWER DOCTRINE 45; JORDAN AND SYRIA 49; CRISIS IN LEBANON AND IRAQ 52; WASHINGTON SEEKS NASSER'S FRIENDSHIP 57; ISRAEL'S APPREHENSIONS 60; KENNEDY'S MIDDLE EAST POLICY 64; SHARING OF THE JORDAN RIVER WATERS 71; SOVIET

Contents

MIDDLE EAST POLICY SINCE KHRUSHCHEV 74; RENEWED SOVIET INTEREST IN IRAN AND TURKEY 82.

Chapter Three

THE THIRD ARAB-ISRAELI WAR: PRELUDE AND AFTERMATH — 87

ERUPTION OF BORDER CONFLICTS BETWEEN ISRAEL AND THE ARAB STATES 87; TRIGGERING THE CRISIS 91; SOVIET MOTIVES 99; U.S. POSITION 102; THE SIX DAY WAR 107; AFTERMATH OF CEASEFIRE 113; UNITED STATES FEELS CONCERNED 118; POLITICAL AND ECONOMIC CONSIDERATIONS 122; SEARCH FOR A FORMULA 128; ARAB POSITION 132; ISRAELI VIEW 135; PERILS OF CONTINUING CONFRONTATION 139; INTERESTS OF THE SUPERPOWERS 141; PROSPECTS OF PEACE 144.

Appendixes — 152

Index — 203

LIST OF MAPS

Arab-Israeli War 1956 — 38

Territory occupied by Israel after the June 1967 hostilities with the Arabs — 109

CHAPTER ONE

The Post War Decade: 1945-1956

The end of the Second World War witnessed the breakdown of the old international political order in the Middle East and led to a change in the relative position of the great powers in that area. British and French influence declined progressively after 1945, and a series of events eventually brought about a rivalry between the United States and the Soviet Union in the Middle East. With the collapse of the British and, almost simultaneously, the French power in that region after World War II, it fell to the United States[1] to step into the breach to prevent the influx of communism[2]

---

[1] Before the Second World War, United States' contact with the countries of the Middle East were limited chiefly to missionary, cultural and educational activities. American oil companies moved into the region in 1920, but they succeeded in making formidable penetrations only after the war. They obtained a quarter share of the Iraq Petroleum Company, the entire concessions of Saudi Arabia and Bahrein, one half of the concession of Kuwait and 40 per cent share in Iranian oil after 1945

[2] The necessity for preventing Soviet dominance or control of the countries of the Middle East appeared to be particularly important to the United States in view of the large U.S. investments in oil and also the enormous income obtained therefrom. According to the *New Times*, Moscow, the net profit earned by the American oil companies on every ton of crude oil varied between $10 and $14, out of which $5-$7 was paid to the oil producing countries. The crude oil was then exported,

through direct or indirect aggression especially in view of Soviet threat to the countries that lay to the south of her borders. As a matter of fact, during the past two and a quarter decades since the Truman Doctrine was enunciated in 1947, the United States set as its major task in the Middle East the blocking of the expansion of Soviet power into that area and the prevention of Soviet dominance or control over one or more states in the Middle East.

The Soviet Union, Iran and Turkey

Although Soviet penetration in the Middle East did not begin in an active manner till after the death of Stalin in 1953, yet the Russians harboured territorial aspirations in this region especially during the first phase of the "cold war". Between 1945 and 1947, Soviet Middle Eastern policy makers fastened on Iran and Turkey both of which lay to the south of the Soviet border and could be used as forward military bases by the West.

During World War II, Soviet forces had moved into Northern Iran in 1941 to protect a major supply route for the U.S. lend-lease materials. At the end of the war, Moscow presented the Iranian government with a series of demands that centered on oil concessions in Northern Iran. The presence of the Soviet forces served as an eloquent threat; not content, Moscow created a communist led movement and set up puppet regimes in Persian Azerbaijan and Kurdish Republic with the intention of using these as bases for a subsequent drive against Iran. Iran, however, stood fast against the Soviet pressure and early in 1946, brought the issue before the United Nations where she was strongly supported by the United States. Eventually, the United States with the

refined and sold at prices ranging from $12 to $40 per ton of petrol and $100 or more for lubricants, petrochemicals, etc. None of the profits from these went to the oil producing countries in the Middle East. *The Times,* Moscow, 14 June 1967, p. 3.

threat of United Nations intervention forced the Red Army to withdraw from Iran in May 1946.

In the immediate post-war years the Soviet Union also cast her eyes toward Turkey and asked for the return of the provinces of Kars and Ardahan which had been ceded to her in 1921. The Soviet Union also reached for a base at the Dardanelles and sought to impose on Turkey a bilateral revision of the Montreux Convention of 1936 to give Russia a privileged position in the Bosphorous and the Dardanelles. It was also designed to exclude the Western Powers, especially Great Britain, France and the United States from all future participation in the Straits question, and to place the Straits exclusively under the control of the Black Sea Powers. The United States actively and successfully fought against this plan and thereby enabled Turkey to stave off the Soviet pressure.[3] The United States could not allow Turkey to come under Soviet influence since it was of obvious strategic importance to her. Its geographic position afforded a command of land, sea and air communications in much of the Balkans and the Middle East and, moreover, it also formed an obstacle to Soviet expansion towards the Mediterranean and the oil lands of the Middle East.

After having failed in her attempt to pressurize Iran and Turkey, the Soviet Union turned to outflanking these two nations by concentrating her attention on Greece. It was believed that if Greece collapsed, it would be only a question of time before Iran and Turkey crumbled to Soviet power. The inability of Great Britain to continue its role of providing military and economic aid to Greece and Turkey in order to strengthen them against Soviet pressures compelled the United States to act in this situation. It was realized that inaction might result in the collapse of

---

[3] U.S. Department of State, *Issues in Foreign Policy, The Middle East*, Washington, D.C., 1968. p. 13.

Europe's flank in the Eastern Mediterranean and the establishment of communist dominance in the Middle East.

President Harry S. Truman was quick to recognize this stark fact. In an address before a joint session of the Congress on 12 March 1947, he emphasized that the United States could survive only in a world in which freedom flourished. And this objective would not be realized unless she was "willing to help free peoples to maintain their institutions and their national integrity against aggressive movements that seek to impose totalitarian regimes". He further pointed out that "totalitarian regimes imposed upon free peoples, by direct or indirect aggression, undermine the foundation of international peace and hence the security of the United States".[4] By May 1947, Congress had approved the extension of military and economic aid to Greece and Turkey and, by undertaking to arm these countries, the United States successfully forestalled Russian advances southward.

At the time of the Anglo-Iranian oil crisis, following the nationalization of the oil company in 1951 by the Iranian government headed by Mohammed Mossadegh who had undercut the power of the Shah of Iran, there was some evidence that the Soviet Union had planned to occupy northern Iran in case the British landed troops to protect the Abadan refinery.[5] This contingency

---

[4] *Department of State Bulletin* (Washington, D.C.), vol. 16 (23 March 1947), pp. 536-37. According to George F. Kennan, who was at that time about to assume charge as the Chief of the Policy Planning Division in the U.S. Department of State, the Soviet threat to Greece in 1947 was "primarily a political one and not a threat of military attack." Kennan was unhappy about the "sweeping" nature of some of the passages of Truman's address before the joint session of the Congress in March 1947, and had some reservations about the Truman Doctrine itself. George F. Kennan, *Memoirs*, 1925-1950, Boston, 1967, pp. 317-321. For the text of Truman's message to the Congress, see Appendix I.

[5] Richard P. Stebbins, *The United States in World Affairs, 1951*, New York, 1952, p. 280. Hereafter cited as *U.S. in World Affairs*.

did not arise, but Washington was perturbed over the increased Communist influence in Iran,[6] and brought pressure on Britain and Iran to work out a compromise. In 1953 Mossadegh was overthrown and in 1954, a compromise settlement was arranged through the good offices of American diplomats. It resulted in the establishment of an international consortium giving the British 40 per cent, five American oil companies (Gulf, Socony Vacuum, Standard Oil of California, Standard Oil of New Jersey and Texaco) 40 per cent, and Dutch Shell and French Petroleum the remaining 20 per cent of Iranian oil production. Iran was securely brought within the Western camp and British monopoly over Iranian oil production was broken. The Russians claimed that the coup which overthrew Mossadegh was maneuvered by the Americans. Available evidence seems to indicate that the United States did provide the Shah of Iran with guns, trucks, armoured cars and radio communications when he staged the successful coup to regain power.[7]

The Soviet Union, however, made no serious attempt to take advantage of the Anglo-Iranian oil crisis. It remained largely quiescent except for a few dubious hints to Iran that it could provide the new nationalized oil company with both markets and oil technicians. The explanation lies, perhaps, in Moscow's unwillingness to risk a showdown with the Western powers at a time when its larger world policy was somewhat uncertain. Its earlier attempts to intervene directly in Iranian affairs had not been particularly rewarding. As a matter of fact, following Soviet failures in Iran, Turkey and Greece just after the Second World War, Moscow showed only a limited interest in the Middle East till about the mid-fifties. Most of its political moves, in the meanwhile, came as a response to Western attempts to organize the

[6] Dwight D. Eisenhower, *The White House Years: Mandate for Change, 1953-1956*, New York, 1963, pp. 160-66.
[7] Robert Engler, *The Politics of Oil*, New York, 1961, p. 206.

military defense of the area. Thus the Soviet Union regarded Turkey's membership of the North Atlantic Treaty Organization (NATO) and, *ipso facto* its extension to the Middle East with grave misgivings and branded Turkey as "a base for Western aggression". But the effect of such attacks was to make Turkey more apprehensive about Soviet designs and to drive her further into the Western alliance.

THE BIRTH OF ISRAEL

After the end of the Second World War, a powerful nationalist upsurge swept through the Arab countries. The United States sympathized with the Arab nationalist aspirations and attempted to reach an accord with the Arab states with a view to building up positions of strength in the Middle East against the threat of Soviet external aggression or internal subversion. But these efforts were largely frustrated as a result of Arab hostility towards the United States on account of the active role played by her in the creation of the state of Israel which was regarded by the Arabs as a foreign intrusion into their land and a future threat to their territories. As a matter of fact, American support for the establishment of Israel[8] was largely responsible for alienating Arab sympathy for the United States.

In 1947, the United States along with the Soviet Union played a leading role in securing approval of the U.N. General Assembly

[8] According to Professor Hans J. Morgenthau, "the creation of the State of Israel was not the result of a positive act by the West favouring such a State, but of two embarrassments which could be most conveniently eliminated by allowing it to come into existence: (a) the breakdown of British rule due to the activities of the Israeli underground, and (b) the existence of a couple of hundred thousand Jews whom Hitler had not gotten around to exterminating and whom nobody wanted as permanent residents". Hans J. Morgenthau, "The U.S. and the Mid-East", *The New Leader*, 19 June 1967, p. 4.

The Post War Decade

resolution recommending partition of Palestine into a Jewish state, and an Arab State. The two big powers, however, supported the partition plan for different reasons. To the United States it seemed to offer the only practical solution to the problem. The Soviet Union, on the other hand, favoured partition because it promised the prompt withdrawal of the British and because it offered the best means to increase Soviet influence in the Middle East. The prospect of the establishment of a Jewish homeland in Palestine naturally aroused the hostility of the Arabs, and, when it became evident that they would not acquiesce in its partition, the United States suggested an international trusteeship for Palestine. But this proposal was turned down by both the Arabs and the Jews. Left with no alternative, the Jewish leaders, on the eve of the British departure from Palestine on 14 May 1948, carried out the intent of the U.N. General Assembly resolution and proclaimed the independence of the State of Israel. American recognition was at once announced by President Truman[9] who had all along favoured the goal of the General Assembly resolution but was hoping to see it peacefully implemented.[10] This was followed by Soviet recognition of the State of Israel three days later. The Soviet Union, however, looked upon the Palestine problem as a secondary issue[11] and her friendly attitude toward Israel lasted for only a short while. A deterioration in the relation between the two countries set in toward

---

[9] The United States extended its *de facto* recognition of Israel on 14 May 1948, and *de jure* recognition on 31 January 1949. Harry S. Truman, *Memoirs, Years of Trial and Hope*, New York, 1956, pp. 164-65.

[10] *Ibid.*, pp. 163, 166.

[11] Competent observers have expressed some doubt whether the decision to support the establishment of a Jewish State was taken at top level? In view of subsequent developments, it is possible that this course of action was recommended by some Foreign Ministry advisers and approved by Stalin in a fit of absent-mindedness. See Walter Z. Laqueur, *The Soviet Union and the Middle East,* London, 1959, p. 147. Hereafter cited as Laqueur, *USSR and Middle East.*

the end of 1948 and reached its climax within four years. The Soviet Union charged that Israel had turned out to be a "tool" of the United States. But apart from this accusation, factors of global strategy and intensification of the "cold war" were responsible for the change in Soviet attitude towards Israel.

The newly formed Jewish state did not get even a "breathing spell" for Arab retaliation against it took place almost immediately after its formation was announced. On 15 May 1948, the armies of Egypt, Lebanon, Syria, Iraq and Jordan invaded Israel and a full scale war immediately erupted. The armies of the Arab states, with the exception of the British trained Jordan's Arab Legion, were however ignominiously defeated by the Israelis. The Soviet government was indignant about this "act of aggression" against Israel and called upon the Arab governments to desist.[12] Initially, at least, the Soviet Union had shared the attitude of the United States toward Israel and, indeed, the latter's survival in the war against the Arabs was due in a large measure to the arms which was supplied to her from Soviet dominated Czechoslovakia.[13] The United States was also greatly perturbed and used her influence through the United Nations to halt the

---

[12] The official Soviet attitude at the time was that the Arab war against Israel had been an act of aggression. But after 1950, when relations with Israel had deteriorated, a different version was adopted: the reactionary governments of both Israel and the Arab countries, instigated by Anglo-American imperialism, had been responsible for the 1948 war. In 1957, following the extension of Soviet influence in Egypt and other Arab states, yet another version was given currency: Israel had been the attacker in 1948, taking advantage of the weakness of the young Arab national movement. *Ibid.*

[13] The Arab States later bitterly remarked that there was no opposition from the West to the supply of Czech arms to Israel, but in 1955 when the Czech arms deal was concluded with Egypt, there was an uproar in the West. Richard H. Nolte and William R. Polk, "Toward a Policy for Middle East", *Foreign Affairs*, July, 1958, p. 654.

Arab-Israeli war, an effort which was crowned only with the limited success of the armistice agreements of 1949. But this did not end the turmoil in the middle East. If anything, the creation of Israel gave rise to new tensions in the region.

ARAB REFUGEES

One of the consequences of the Arab-Israeli war was the displacement of more than 800,000 Arabs who fled from Palestine and created a refugee problem. In September 1948, the U.N. mediator Count Folke Bernadotte reported to the U.N. Security Council of the existence of a serious refugee problem. Following this, the U.N. General Assembly on 11 December 1948 resolved that:

> The refugees wishing to return to their homes and live at peace with their neighbours should be permitted to do so at the earliest practicable date, and that compensation should be paid for the property of those choosing not to return, and for loss or of damage to property which, under the principles of international law or in equity, should be made good by the governments or authorities responsible.[14]

In view of the urgent need of the Palestine refugees a U.N. Relief for Palestine Refugees (UNRPR) was established on 1 December 1948 to provide short-term relief. This was succeeded by the U.N. Relief and Works Agency for Palestine Refugees (UNRWA) in May 1950, to carry out relief and work projects in collaboration with the local governments.[15] The United States'

---

[14] *Middle East Journal*, vol. 18, Winter, 1964, p. 9.

[15] The rehabilitation functions of the UNRWA were limited to offering elementary and secondary education and vocational training as a means of making the refugees eventually self supporting. Limited grant aid was also extended to those refugees who wished to go into business

contribution to the UNRWA amounted to almost 70 per cent of the total.

Israel had initially offered the refugees compensation for their land but had refused to accept the return of the embittered and hostile Arabs who, it was argued, would be a security risk to the new nation. Israel, moreover, had no room for the Arab refugees since she was taking in Jewish immigrants from the Arab countries. She contended that the solution of the refugee problem rested in the settlement of the refugees in Arab countries.

The Arabs on the other hand, looked upon increased Jewish immigration into Israel as a threat to their security. They feared that as more people came into Israel, the state will perforce burst its bounds and attempt to expand its boundaries.[16] In regard to the refugees, the Arabs rejected anything but the collective, unconditional return of all of them to their former homes in Israeli territory. They opposed all schemes for the resettlement of refugees in Arab states since they apprehended that it might prejudice the refugees' right to repatriation and also deprive them of one of the principal arguments against the continued existence of Israel. They insisted on maintaining a state of war with Israel and refused to participate in any plan for the solution of the refugee problem short of the dismemberment and destruction of the state of Israel. The resettlement of the refugees was also refused by the Arab governments even after funds had been appropriated for this purpose by the United Nations, and they were deliberately maintained "as a vested interest in the Arab cause against Israel".[17]

---

for themselves. U.S. House of Representatives, Congress 85, Session 2, Committee on Foreign Affairs, Hearings, *Mutual Security Act of 1958*, Washington, D.C., 1958, Pt. XIII, p. 1670.

[16] *Congressional Record,* Congress 86, Session 2, Vol. 106, 1960, p. 12619.

[17] *Ibid.,* Congress 86, Session 1, Vol. 105, 1959, p. 18221.

The Post War Decade

In 1953, Senator Taft, Chairman of the Senate subcommittee on Foreign Relations to examine the problem of Arab refugees stated:

> The American people are moved by strong humanitarian motives, but they cannot be expected to bear indefinitely a large share of the burden involved in this situation when Israel and the Arab states show so little initiative in helping to settle the matter among themselves.[18]

In the same vein, the Chairman of the Near Eastern subcommittee of the U.S. Senate Foreign Relations Committee commented in June 1957:

> The Arab states have . . . used the Palestine refugees as political hostages in their struggle with Israel. While Arab delegates in the United Nations have condemned the plight of their brothers in the refugee camps, nothing has been done to assist them in a practical way lest political leverage against Israel be lost. The Arabs have consistently refused to make any effort to find a solution because they fear that any concerted effort of resettlement will mean the abandonment of the principle of return to Palestine.[19]

In 1956, when a U.S. Study Mission to the Middle East met with a group of refugee leaders from some of the refugee camps, none of them expressed even a modicum of gratitude for United States assistance to the U.N. Relief and Works Agency for Palestine Refugees which amounted to almost 70 per cent of the total.

[18] *Ibid.*, Congress 86, Session 2, Vol. 106, 1960, p. 12621.
[19] Walter Laqueur, ed., *The Israel Arab Reader: A Documentary History of the Middle East Conflict,* New York, 1969, p. 158. Hereafter cited as Laqueur, *Documentary History.*

Instead, they held the United States responsible for their plight on two counts: first, for assisting Israel which took away their property; and, second, for United States' failure to help them get their property back.[20]

The Arab states, on their part, insisted that the solution to the problem lay in carrying out the repatriation-compensation provisions of the General Assembly resolution of 11 December 1948. President John F. Kennedy agreed to it when in a letter addressed to the heads of Arab States on 11 May 1961, he wrote in part: "We are willing to help resolve the tragic Palestine refugee problem on the basis of the principle of repatriation and compensation of property."[21] This statement, however, evoked strong protest from Senator Jacob Javits of New York and Senator Scott of Pennsylvania. They were critical of the President's omission to mention resettlement of the refugees in the territories where they were residing as a means of solving the refugee problem.[22] Senator J. William Fulbright of Arkansas, Chairman of the Senate Foreign Relations Committee, pointed out that "to get the [refugee] problem in proper perspective for settlement, it is essential that the Arabs reconsider the view that the refugees are a political asset to be used against Israel but an economic liability in Arab lands. The Arabs must realize that to seek to make refugees serve a political purpose will in time become counter productive". At the same time he warned that the longer the refugee problem remained unsolved, the greater was the likelihood that the responsibility for the problem would be viewed as resting on Israel re-

---

[20] U.S. House of Representatives, Congress 84, Session 2, Committee on Foreign Affairs, *Report of the Special Study Mission to the Middle East, South and Southeast Asia and the Western Pacific*, Washington, D.C., 1956, p. 44.

[21] *Congressional Record*, Congress 87, Session 1, Vol. 107, 1961, p. 13010.

[22] *Ibid.*, p. 13028.

gardless of what one may conclude with respect to the facts.[23] Senator Thomas B. Curtis of Missouri, on the other hand, believed that no settlement of the Arab refugee problem could be achieved without a final political settlement between Israel and her Arab neighbours.[24] This point of view had a certain validity and it was shared by a number of informed observers of the Middle Eastern situation.

DELINEATION OF BOUNDARY LINES

Apart from the refugee problem, the Arab-Israeli conflict gave rise to another complication resulting from the haphazard delineation of boundary lines under the armistice agreements. The armistice terms had greatly revised the U.N. Partition Plan[25] to the disadvantage of the Arab states who now insisted that the boundaries be settled on the basis of the partition plan. Israel, on the other hand, held that the armistice terms should be the basis for peace negotiations since it was the Arab states that went to war for the specific reason of destroying the partition plan. But the Arab states ignored the Israeli argument and refused to convert the 1948 armistice into treaties of peace, maintaining that they were still at war with Israel.

Fundamental to the crisis in the Middle East was the fact that the Arabs could not reconcile themselves to the existence of the Israeli state and they chafed over the humiliation of their military

[23] *Ibid.*, 16n., p. 12621.
[24] *Ibid.*, 21n., p. 16754.
[25] Under the armistice terms, which greatly revised the U.N. partition plan, the proposed Arab State disappeared. The Arab countries received about 2,000 sq. miles of land formerly in mandatory Palestine, and Israel got a major portion of the Negev Desert territory that had not been allotted to it under the partition plan. Control of Jerusalem was divided between Israel and Jordan. *Ibid.*, Congress 84, Session, 2, Vol. 102, 1956, p. 2273.

defeat. They imposed an economic blockade against Israel and, in the case of Egypt, refused passage through the Suez Canal to ships carrying goods despatched from or to Israel. The Arab leaders proclaimed constantly their intention to take revenge by destroying Israel as soon as they could. This was also a theme which Cairo Radio blared out incessantly.[26]

Pending the day of vengeance, Israel was subjected to almost daily attacks from Egypt and Jordan, especially from the six mile wide Gaza Strip between Israel and the sea which sheltered quarter of a million refugees many of whom were trained to systematically raid Israel. The constant attacks made life unsafe around most of Israel's boundary. Israel's reaction was to reply occasionally with big raids, designed to punish and discourage the little ones. These retaliations often led to strong condemnation by the United Nations following minor chidings of the Arabs for the small raids.[27] The Israelis in the meanwhile became increasingly impatient at the refusal of the Arab states to accept the armistice settlement as permanent or to agree to the establishment of normal relations.

In an attempt to preserve the precarious balance of power established by the armistice agreements, the United States, Great Britain and France issued a tripartite declaration on 25 May 1950,[28] claiming unilaterally the prerogative of governing the balance of armaments in the Middle East and of preventing, by action taken "both within and outside the United Nations", any violation of frontiers and armistice lines. In the years that followed, the United States sought to preserve peace along the armis-

---

[26] *New York Times*, 11 November 1956.

[27] Thus for instance the U.N. Security Council admonished Israel and Syria on two occasions in May 1951. See *Department of State Bulletin*, vol. 24, 14 May 1951, p. 797; & 4 June 1951, pp. 916-17.

[28] For the text of the Tripartite Declaration of 25 May 1950, see Appendix II.

tice lines, while trying to promote a final settlement of the dispute which would ensure the survival of Israel and at the same time do something to allay the bitterness of the Arabs over what they regarded as the theft of Arab territory. This was in American interest for the unrest in the Middle East during the early cold war period impinged on U.S. policy in two ways. Firstly, in view of the strategic significance of the area and the tremendous petroleum reserves of Iran, Iraq, Saudi Arabia and the sheikdoms in the Persian Gulf, it was the policy of the United States not to allow this region to come under Soviet influence and control. Secondly, the United States realized that crisis in any area along the Russian periphery might offer an opportunity for exploitation by the Soviet Union, and hence she sought to bring about a swift and peaceful end to the disputes that occurred in the Middle Eastern region.

THE BAGHDAD PACT

The intense anti-American sentiments that prevailed all over the Arab world for a period after the United States supported the creation of the State of Israel and recognized her in May 1948, gradually waned until shortly after the coup d'etat in Egypt that deposed King Farouk and brought first General Mohammed Naguib, and subsequently Colonel Gamal Abdel Nasser into power. It was fondly hoped by the United States that the rise of Nasser to power in a republican Egypt would usher in a period of economic and social reform within the country and that the strong nationalistic sentiments of the Egyptians would spur them to resist any Russian attempt at penetration. At the same time it was hoped that Nasser would cooperate with the United States and with the West generally, on reasonable terms.

In an effort to win over Nasser, the United States threw its weight in order to secure a resolution of the Anglo-Egyptian deadlock over the Suez and Sudan, and succeeded in bringing about an agreement with regard to both the issues. Sudan was launched on its course toward independence, and by an agreement signed in July 1954, the British withdrew from the Canal zone[29] within twenty-eight months with only a tenuous right of return in case of attack by a foreign power on a member of the Arab League or on Turkey. This was interpreted by Moscow as a victory of American diplomacy and the Soviet press bitterly reproached the Egyptian leaders for having "jumped on the American bandwagon" and for their "shortsightedness and weakness".[30] The Soviet leaders even became convinced that the Suez agreement had merely been the "first step toward the inclusion of Egypt in the Western bloc". This, however, proved to be a wrong assessment for while Egypt accepted American economic help, she rejected military aid as limited by the requirements of the Mutual Security Program, and refused to consider any sort of alliance with the United States and the West.

Recognizing the tenuous nature of the 1954 Suez agreement and to counterbalance the withdrawal of Britain as well as to check Soviet designs, the United States decided to stabilize the situation with a Middle East version of NATO (North Atlantic Treaty Organization). The apparent success of the NATO in counteracting Russian power in Europe, followed by Communist threat in Korea, led the United States to believe that Russia was prepared to employ military aggression along its peripheries whenever it was not opposed by adequate military force[31] and,

[29] Withdrawal of the British Canal Zone Force meant the loss of a vital potential buffer between Israel and the largest of the Arab states—Egypt—and, consequently, it increased Israeli concern for its security.

[30] *Izvestia*, 8 August 1954.

[31] On this point see Tarun C. Bose, "American and Soviet Interests in Asia: Conflict and Cooperation", *International Studies*, vol. 10, July-October, 1968, p. 51.

therefore, it might be expected to seek to outflank NATO through the Middle East. This realization prompted the United States to make an effort early in the fifties to set up a Middle East Defense Organization with the local countries and the Western powers participating on an equal basis. It was to be linked with the NATO and was to serve as a bulwark against Soviet aggression in the Middle East.

The Arab states, however, did not share the West's estimation of the Soviet Communist threat. Instead they viewed Britain, France and the United States as "colonial powers" trying to use "anti-communist strategy as a means of establishing their control over the region."[32] Thus Egypt interpreted the plans to set up a Middle East Defense Organization as an effort to substitute NATO control for British domination in the country and promptly rejected the proposal. The Soviet Union also lashed out at the attempt to establish a military alliance in the Middle East. In a note presented to the United States, Great Britain, France and Turkey on 28 January 1952, the Soviet Government pointed out that there was no need for the MEDO since the security of the Middle Eastern countries was not being threatened from any quarter, and charged that its proposed establishment was "closely linked with the aggressive plans of the Anglo-American grouping of powers . . . to serve the purpose of encircling the Soviet Union".[33]

Egypt's refusal to participate in the proposed Middle East Defense Organization (in October 1951) forced the United States to hold the scheme in abeyance. The idea was, however, not abandoned and Secretary of State John Foster Dulles after a visit to the Middle East in 1953, returned with the belief that while most of the Middle Eastern peoples and governments were

[32] *Congressional Record*, Congress 87, Session 2, Vol. 108, 1962, p. 11294.
[33] *Pravda*, 28 January 1952. The United States did not reply to this note. See *Department of State Bulletin*, vol. 27, 15 December 1952, p. 937.

unwilling to associate themselves with the West in a common defensive organization, the states of the "Northern Tier" bordering the Soviet Union were more aware of the Soviet threat and ready to cooperate.[34] With this background there came into being, in the course of 1955, the Baghdad Pact[35] linking Turkey, Iran, Iraq, Pakistan and Great Britain in a defensive alliance. The United States, the chief architect of the Pact, did not formally join it but associated itself with its major functioning committees and provided economic and arms aid to its members. The United States' decision to "cooperate with" but not to become a member of the organization was largely due to her desire to avoid the charge made by Arab nationalists that she was merely interested in establishing a puppet organization to further Western aims in the Middle East. "The purpose of the pact", as Dulles explained, "is not in any way to disrupt the Arab world [but] . . . to create a solid band of resistance against the Soviet Union".[36]

Unfortunately, the Baghdad Pact aroused the antagonism of nearly all Arab nationalists because of Britain's presence in the alliance. Dynastic rivalries between Iraq and Saudi Arabia were embittered because of Iraq's participation in the alliance, and Egypt was angered along with her other allies, Syria and Yemen, since they regarded the Pact to be contrary to the national inter-

---

[34] *Department of State Bulletin*, vol. 28, 15 June 1953. Dulles assumed that the common threat in the region lay only in Soviet aggression. This was wishful thinking. Turkey was probably the only country that fitted into this category. The other "Northern Tier" countries largely desired western support to buttress their position not against the Soviet Union but against their neighbours. See *Middle Eastern Affairs*, vol. 12, May, 1961, p. 132.

[35] For the text of the Baghdad Pact, see Appendix III.

[36] U.S. Senate, Congress 84, Session 2, Committee on Foreign Relations, *Hearing on the Situation in the Middle East*, 24 February 1956, Washington, D.C., 1956, p. 23. Hereafter cited as Senate Committee on Foreign Relations, Hearings, *Middle East Situation*.

ests of the Arab world. It appeared that the Pact had "stirred up the hornet's nest and heightened local tensions all around".[37]

Egypt, in the meanwhile, had pressed the Arab states to ratify the Arab League Collective Security Pact which had been drafted in 1950 to integrate the Arab military forces in case fighting with Israel flared up again. This pact, which by 1953 had been ratified by almost all the League members, was quite different from the Baghdad Pact insofar as its *raison d'etre* was the threat from Israel, not from the Soviet Union. But Iraq's participation in the Baghdad Pact in 1955, which indicated Iraq's abandonment of neutrality in favour of a pro-Western alignment, was considered as a setback to Egypt's aspirations since it was likely to make it difficult for Nasser to carry out his plans for the unification of the Arab world. However, the accession of Iraq to the Baghdad Pact did not mean her defection from the Arab cause, and Iraq made this point clear by "reiterating her pledge to come to Egypt's aid if Israel should attack her".[38]

The formation of the Baghdad Pact also alarmed Israel considerably since she believed that any arms aid earmarked for the Northern Tier countries would be ultimately turned against her. She asserted that even with the weapons supplied by the United States "Iraq could not stand up against a single Russian division", while on the other hand, "the weapons could prove to be weighty if turned against Israel".[39] Despite this possibility, the United States turned a deaf ear to Israel's request to provide her with compensatory arms.

Ironically, the Baghdad Pact which was intended to form a *cordon sanitaire* against further Soviet expansion into the Middle East, produced the opposite result and precipitated the Soviet

---

[37] J. C. Hurewitz, "Our Mistakes in the Middle East", *Atlantic* (December, 1956), p. 49.
[38] *New York Times*, 15 August 1955.
[39] *Congressional Record*, 25n. p. 2274.

drive for penetration into the Middle East. The Soviet government had already warned that it could not remain indifferent to the formation of blocs and establishment of foreign military bases on the territory of the Middle Eastern countries since they have "a direct bearing on the security of the U.S.S.R."[40] This prompted the U.S. government to declare, with a view to reassuring the members of the newly formed Baghdad alliance, that any threat to the territorial integrity or political independence of the nations which had joined the Baghdad Pact would be viewed by the United States with the utmost gravity.[41]

SOVIET PENETRATION IN THE MIDDLE EAST

Confronted by a Pact which constituted a bulwark against her expansion in the Middle East, the Soviet Union promptly took measures to outflank the new alliance by strengthening its ties with Afghanistan. Following a visit by Khrushchev and Bulganin to Kabul, the Soviet government on 18 December 1955 announced a loan of $100 million to Afghanistan. The Soviet-Afghan rapprochement appeared to give the Soviet Union a foothold there which served a two-fold purpose. In the first place, it enabled the Soviet Union to maintain the gap in the Baghdad Pact chain of defence along the southern Soviet frontier; and, in the second place, it afforded her with an opportunity to outflank Iran (as well as Pakistan). At the same time an earnest effort was made by Russia to acquire a foothold in Egypt. It was believed that if she succeeded in doing so, she would be able to outflank the Baghdad Pact grouping of powers in the West as she did via Afghanistan in the East. She could thus hold the Middle East in a pincer grip that could constitute a direct threat to Western defence of that area. Moscow realized that its task of penetrating the Middle East could be served best by exploiting "Arab nation-

[40] *Current Digest of the Soivet Press*, 1 June 1955, pp. 18-19.
[41] *Department of State Bulletin*, vol. 35, 10 December 1956, p. 918.

alism". Accordingly, the Soviet leaders started cultivating the more radical variety of Arab nationalism and supported all elements whose weight could be thrown onto the scales against the West. They saw Egypt as the best means of blocking Western attempts to organize the Middle East, and they saw in Nasser a leader who had become a symbol and an inspiration to Arab nationalists everywhere and who perhaps could be made to serve the Soviet cause.

Events seemed to conspire to provide the Soviet Union with the necessary opportunity. In 1955 Egypt was hard hit by a decline in world cotton prices. This decline was brought on in part by rumours that the United States intended to dump about ten million bales of its surplus cotton into Western Europe at considerably reduced prices. Since cotton made up 85 per cent of Egyptian exports, the mere expectation of lower cotton prices temporarily dried up Egypt's European markets and confronted her with an exceedingly difficult situation. The cotton crisis provided the Soviet Union with an opportunity to step into the Middle East. She offered to buy some of the Egyptian cotton and to get her East European satellites and Communist China to purchase the rest of the cotton that had been turned down by the West.[42]

---

[42] In the case of the sale of certain items as arms, oil, etc., Soviet offers, particularly to the developing countries of Asia and Africa, were nearly always politically inspired. Their objective was to pull such countries into the Soviet economic orbit and then to use government to government trade contacts to extend and strengthen their political influence. When an underdeveloped country in Asia or Africa had a surplus of some commodity which Russia was able to dispose of in its domestic economy, the Kremlin could hold out an offer which few countries could resist, since the country concerned received the Russian product for practically nothing. It thereby could not only realize substantial foreign exchange savings, but also trade in a commodity which otherwise would have to be destroyed or dumped on world markets. This kind of deal put great pressure on a government to acquiesce to any Soviet demands.

Nasser welcomed Russia not only as a profitable ally, but as a country from where he could obtain arms shipments which had become especially important since Israel had launched a big military attack against Egyptian forces in the Gaza strip in February 1955. The Israeli attack had clearly demonstrated Egypt's weakness and compelled Nasser to search frantically for arms. The United States had previously promised to supply arms to Egypt upon the conclusion of the Anglo-Egyptian agreement regarding the Canal Zone. But even though the agreement was signed in July 1954, the United States maintained, especially after the Arab-Israeli clash in February 1955, that under the existing legislation it could provide arms only for cash in dollars—which Egypt lacked,[43] or accompanied by a U.S. Military Mission—which Egyptian nationalism could not tolerate. Under the circumstances, the offer for arms from the Soviet Union came as a god-send to Nasser especially since they were payable in cotton of which Egypt then had an unsold surplus. The Soviet Union, on the other hand, was only too happy to provide Egypt with arms to counteract the Baghdad Pact. Moscow believed that with the arms, Nasser would be able to organize "a counteralliance in opposition to the Baghdad Pact".[44] In fact, the cotton-for-arms deal in September 1955 [45] between Egypt and the Soviet

---

[43] The United States had, as a matter of fact, offered to sell to Egypt early in 1955, certain types of weapons to the tune of $27 million. However, all of Egypt's request for arms had not been acceded to since she had "demanded types of weapons that the United States just could not send to the area if the regional military balance was to be maintained". But Egypt turned down the U.S. offer pleading a shortage of foreign exchange although this plea was not tenable since, according to informed observers, "Egypt's foreign exchange position at that time was not really critical". Uri Ra'anan, *The USSR Arms the Third World: Case Studies in Soviet Foreign Policy*, Cambridge, Mass., 1969, p. 56.

[44] *Ibid.*, p. 27.

[45] Actually, the arms deal was concluded in May 1955, between Egypt

Union—by which Nasser mortgaged the Egyptian crop for several years into the future in return for the purchase of military equipment—ignited the Middle East powder keg. The arms deal not only opened the door to Russian penetration of the Middle East, but also upset the balance of military power between Egypt and Israel since the Soviet Union delivered large quantities of weapons, bombers and tanks which Egypt desired. Moscow however made it clear that the arms had been given "in order to strengthen the Arabs' bargaining power", and that it did not at all favour the prospects of a war since it believed that the Arabs would gain nothing thereby while it might give the West "an opportunity to regain a foothold in the area".[46] Israel pleaded with Washington for arms to counterbalance the Soviet shipments. But Secretary of State Dulles refused to heed to this request on the ground that it would give impetus to an arms race. In a testimony before the Senate Foreign Relations Committee in February 1956, he stated that if the U.S. Government bowed to domestic political pressure to send arms to Israel in response to the supply of Communist arms to Egypt, it would lead to an all-out arms race in which the Arabs would triumph because "thirty-odd million Arabs [have] far greater . . . absorptive capacity" than 1.7 million Israelis.[47] United States' refusal to restore the arms balance came as a great disappointment to the Israelis. They however succeed-

---

and Czechoslovakia although it was officially made known only in September 1955. This fact as well as other pertinent information concerning the whole episode was revealed by Hassanein Haykel, the Editor of the influential Egyptian newspaper, *Al Ahram*. See *Summary of World Broadcasts*, Pt. 4, 14 April 1967, Cairo Radio Broadcast.

[46] *The Reporter*, 6 September 1956, p. 33.

[47] Senate Committee on Foreign Relations, Hearings, *Middle East Situation* (n. 36), p. 43. It might be noted, however, that Dulles considered the Soviet arms deal with Egypt in 1955 as "the most serious development since Korea, if not since World War II". See Herman Finer, *Dulles Over Suez*, Chicago, 1964, p. 28.

ed in obtaining some arms from France after the latter had become alarmed at Nasser's support for the Algerian nationalists.

The United States' first and somewhat hasty reaction to the Soviet bid for Egypt's friendship was to ponder a quick way for giving arms to Nasser before the Russians could do so. But this strategy was quickly abandoned since it would have been "tantamount to submitting to blackmail", as the British Prime Minister Anthony Eden put it. After a diplomatic pause, Secretary of State Dulles advanced a much more suitable proposal, namely, a guarantee of the Arab-Israeli border against any violations. This proposal which circumvented the non-negotiable character of the Arab-Israeli dispute offered the best practical hope for minimizing the explosive tensions in the Middle East. Egypt however paid no heed to this proposal and stepped up her raids into Israel after September 1955, with the help of the irregular commando forces, and the situation in the Middle East became increasingly critical.

Aswan Dam and Nationalization of the Suez Canal

The United States and Great Britain tried to divert Nasser from his expansionist ambitions by offering in December 1955, to help him finance the huge Aswan Dam on the Nile, a ten year $1.3 billion project. It was expected that the dam would help to add two million more acres to the total of irrigated land, generate 750,000 more kilowatts of electrical energy per year and facilitate general development by permitting the construction of a much needed fertilizer plant and a steel mill to process the iron ore deposits near Aswan.[48] Nasser wanted the huge project to serve as a symbol of how his regime was triumphantly taking Egypt along the path of progress. The Anglo-American offer, which was made to "forestall a possible Soviet offer", was based on one

[48] *Middle East Journal*, vol. 9, Autumn, 1955, p. 383.

condition, that Egypt would have to forego any assistance from the communist countries.[49] An initial grant of $70 million was promised by Britain and the United States of which the latter's contribution was to be 80 per cent. While Egypt was assured that aid would also be forthcoming for later phases of the work, she was to be responsible for the payment of a major portion of the money—$900 million—over the long run. The Anglo-American aid was intended to supplement a $200 million loan which the International Bank for Reconstruction and Development was ready to make.[50]

Complications, however, arose when in May 1956, Nasser recognized Communist China. This immediately led the supporters of the Nationalist China 'Lobby' in Washington to denounce Nasser. At the same time they formed an alliance with Southern Congressmen who demanded to know "why the United States was offering to build a dam which would allow huge crops of Egyptian cotton to compete with American cotton". It was also contended that Nasser neither had the technicians nor the industry to use the dam. Secretary of State Dulles was aware that Nasser would suffer a "disastrous political blow" if the United States withdrew its offer. But he was advised by the World Bank President Eugene Black to "go through with the deal" since he feared that otherwise serious consequences might follow.[51] The proposed American offer to assist in the construction of the Aswan dam had been negotiated over a period of steadily declining Egyptian-American relations during which Nasser had strengthened econo-

[49] *New York Times,* Weekly Review, 22 July 1956.
[50] *New York Times,* 17 December 1955.
[51] Walter LaFeber, *America, Russia and the Cold War,* 1945-1966, New York, 1967, pp. 188-91. Also see Finer, (47n), pp. 45-47. The French Ambassador in Washington at that time, Couve de Murville, also warned that "a most likely consequence" of a refusal to provide the loan for the building of the Aswan Dam would be "the seizure of the Suez Canal". But nobody took him seriously when he uttered the warning.

mic and political ties with the Soviet bloc. And during all this time there had been rumours of Soviet aid offers. But, as a matter of fact, the Soviet government was not very enthusiastic about the Aswan Dam scheme, and the Soviet Foreign Minister Shepilov, during his visit to Cairo in June 1956, was reported to have told Nasser that "though the Soviet Union would make a great contribution towards Egypt's industrial development,[52] it could not commit itself with regard to the Aswan Dam."[53]

Dulles felt that it was necessary "to call Russia's hand in the game of economic competition"[54] and to demonstrate to Egypt that she could not insult the United States—by recognizing Communist China—and get away with it easily. This led to the decision to withdraw precipitiously the U.S. offer of assistance. Publicly, however, it was stated that it was "not feasible in present circumstances" to participate in the Aswan project, that the Nile riparian states had not agreed to the project and that because of the arms purchase Egypt apparently would not be able to devote sufficient financial resources to it. To make matters worse, the American decision was announced on 19 July 1956,[55] just when the Egyptian Ambassador to the United States, Dr. Ahmed Hussein, had come to Dulles' office to accept the offer. The offer, in other words, was withdrawn in such a brusque maner as to appear as an insult to Nasser, and the phrase in the Dulles rejection which caused most resentment was the one which cast doubt on Egypt's

---

[52] The Russians did promise large scale assistance for Egyptian industrial development which resulted in a $175,000,000 aid agreement late in 1957. *Foreign Affairs*, 13n., p. 655.

[53] Laqueur, *USSR & Middle East*, 11n., p. 232.

[54] John R. Beal, *John Foster Dulles,* New York, 1957, p. 258.

[55] *Department of State Bulletin,* vol. 35, 30 July 1956, p. 188. America's withdrawal of financial support for the Aswan Dam on 19 July 1956, was followed by Britain's withdrawal the next day, and as a result the World Bank cancelled its loan. See Appendix IV for the Press Release of 19 July 1956.

ability to back the project economically. Nasser was stunned at the maner in which Dulles announced the rejection. As he said: "America was perfectly entitled to refuse us aid despite all her promises. It is her right because it is her money. But to create doubt about our economy, to cast suspicion on the soundness of our financial policies at a time when we are striving hard to raise our standard of living, could only be interpreted as a move to destroy world confidence in our economic position".[56] In other words, Nasser interpreted the American rebuff not only as an effort to humiliate him, but also as a deliberate attempt to undermine world confidence in the Egyptian economy, and he retaliated by announcing the nationalization of the Suez Canal on 26 July 1956, seven days after the withdrawal of the U.S. offer. Nasser promised the Egyptian people that the Aswan Dam would be built from the money obtained from the operations of the Suez Canal. He also gave the assurance to the world that there would be free and open transit through the canal without discrimination and that the operation of the canal would be insulated from the policies of any country. But he failed to honour this pledge. Some observers believe that Nasser would not have "defied" the West so "recklessly" without "full assurance of Soviet support", and it does not seem improbable that the Soviet Foreign Minister Shepilov might have given some such assurance when he visited Cairo in June 1956, since Moscow had long regarded the Suez Canal Company as "an important bulwark of colonialism".[57]

SOVIET ECONOMIC ASSISTANCE

From the moment Egypt took action to nationalize the Suez Canal Soviet Union's support of that action was unqualified, but she did not use the opportunity, resulting from U.S. refusal to give

[56] *The Reporter,* 46n., p. 32.
[57] *Current History,* February 1957, p. 87.

Egypt the promised aid, to come forward immediately with an offer to help in the construction of the Aswan dam. As a matter of fact, there was no immediate Soviet interest in the project.[58] This attitude, however, underwent a change two years later—in 1958—in the light of fresh political developments when a rift developed between Cairo and Baghdad that affected the Arab Communist Parties. Since this was undesirable from the Soviet point of view, Moscow became eager to keep Nasser happy and decided to offer Egypt its assistance for the construction of the Aswan High Dam after more than two years of hesitation to commit iself.

In the same year a new dimension was added to Soviet Egyptian friendship when the communist oriented Afro-Asian Peoples' Solidarity Movement set up its organization in Cairo. The fact that the Russians and the Egyptians could agree to cooperate in such a "patently obvious communist front organization", indicated the extent to which the Russians had succeeded in extending their influence on Nasser. In October 1958, the Soviet Union granted a loan of $100 million to finance the first stage of the Aswan Dam[59] and also agreed to provide Soviet technicians and machinery needed for the construction of the dam. Egypt also accepted the Soviet offer in January 1960, to build the second stage of the dam on the same basis as the first, using Soviet men and equipment.

In so far as trade between the Soviet Union and the countries of the Middle East were concerned, they were relatively insignificant before 1954, but started increasing after that year and rose sharply in 1957 and 1958. Simultaneously, a number of countries in the region, particularly Egypt, Syria, Iraq and Yemen started receiving appreciable economic and technical assistance from the Soviet Union. In providing economic assistance, the

---

[58] *Izvestia,* 12 August 1956.
[59] *Mizan,* Vol. 10, (6), November-December, 1968, p. 219.

Russians did not call for the economic justification of the projects desired by the recipient countries nor did they pass any judgement on the economic feasibility of the projects. This feature of the Soviet program had an obvious advantage especially in view of the practice of the United States to refuse loans for projects or programs that she considered "uneconomic or wasteful".[60] Unhampered by the built-in checks and balances or the pressure of an effective public opinion, the Soviet Union could use its economic resources to penetrate into the Middle East (as well as in other parts of the underdeveloped world). Thus it could offer credits to the Middle Eastern countries at rates of interest ranging from 2 to 2.5 per cent where the United States charged rates ranging from 3.5 to 6 per cent.[61] Furthermore, the credits were extended over a long period—from ten to thirty years—and repayments were often accepted in the form of local export goods, which on many occasions happened to be domestic agricultural surpluses which the credit receiving countries were eager to dispose off.

Moscow also assisted the Middle Eastern countries in setting up big enterprises. Thus in the case of Egypt, the Soviet Union assisted her in constructing six enterprises in the ferrous and non-ferrous metal industry, six machine building plants, and twelve enterprises in the oil and chemical industry. Besides these, she also assisted in the construction of a shipyard, three food processing plants, a railroad of 650 kilometres length, and irrigation systems.[62] Another country in the Middle East, Iraq, also received valuable Soviet assistance in the construction of more than fifty enterprises, including a metallurgical re-rolling plant, a nitric fertilizer plant, an antibiotics and drugs plant, an agricultural machinery, implements and spare parts plant, a glass plant, an electro-bulb plant, etc. Soviet agencies, moreover, helped in organizing

[60] *Middle Eastern Affairs*, vol. 10, August-September, 1959, p. 288.
[61] *Congressional Record*, 17n., p. 10971.
[62] *Middle Eastern Affairs*, vol. 11, June-July, 1960, p. 206.

four state farms in Iraq and also rendered assistance to research in irrigation works, in training medical personnel and in the establishment of a medical college.[63] In addition to Egypt and Iraq, Moscow also provided assistance to Yemen,[64] and between 1955 and 1959, the total Soviet economic aid to these three countries amounted to $696 million of which Egypt alone received $515 million. This was in addition to the aid provided for the construction of the Aswan Dam. Soviet objectives in providing assistance to the countries of the Middle East were to convince them of the peaceful character of her intentions, thereby encourage their "neutralist" orientation; and to demonstrate to them that it had more to offer than the West for their transition to a modern, industrialized society.

THE FIELD OF CULTURE AND EDUCATION

Apart from providing aid and assistance to the countries in the Middle East, the Soviet Union has been also active in the educational and cultural fields. Of the Soviet cultural program, the ballet performances have received warm welcome in the Middle Eastern countries. Moreover a number of countries in that region have been stimulated by them to develop ballet troupes of their own, turning to the Soviet Union for help and support. But Soviet films have not met with the same kind of success. They are rarely seen on local television or in commercial cinemas and Russian film techniques have not exercised any influence on the local film

---

[63] *Ibid.*, p. 207.

[64] Apart from economic assistance substantial military assistance was also provided to Egypt, Syria, and Yemen during 1955-59, by the Soviet bloc countries. Iraq also received military assistance after her withdrawal from the Baghdad Pact. Till 1959, she had received Soviet bloc arms to the extent of $120 million, while the UAR and Yemen received arms in the amount of $443 million and $17 million respectively. *Congressional Record*, 16n., p. 6347.

makers. In certain cases, Soviet cultural activities have been accepted by some of the countries in the Middle East not because they stood to benefit from them, but because of political reasons. The countries receiving Soviet assistance often considered it incumbent upon themselves to accept cultural programs since giving public display to cultural activities often served as "a useful way of keeping political fences mended". In the educational field, the Soviet Union has not been very effective in the Middle East. After the first surge of students going to study in Soviet Universities, educational missions to the Communist world dwindled. They are now supported chiefly by the need for training technicians to operate Soviet equipment, or to work with Soviet advisers in administering national programs. There has been no continuing stream of students seeking to study medicine, law, engineering, science, history, business, or general culture in Soviet Universities. Although Soviet publications are often within the reach of the urban middle class and student groups, there is little popular interest in Soviet literature. There is also little evidence that Soviet literary patterns are being widely copied or are furnishing models for the new national writers, except possibly in political pamphlets.

In contrast to the paucity of permanent cultural influence emanating from Soviet programs, it would appear that the programs of the United States have had a lasting impact on cultural developments in the Middle East. Students and exchange professors are eager to proceed to U.S. universities whenever they find an opportunity. American universities have also served as models for a number of new universities in the Middle East. Thus when the Asyut University was opened in Egypt early in the 1960's, it sought to introduce the American system of engineering education. New technical universities in Turkey and Iran have also copied elements of the American university pattern, and American films and television programs are widely popular and are copied by local producers. This has been true not only in countries which are considered to be politically pro-Western, but also in those with close connection with the Soviet Union such as, Egypt and Syria.[65] To a large extent, the impact which the United States has made on the cultural development in the countries of the Middle East has been due to the character of the modernizing process which the latter has chosen to follow.

Aftermath of Suez Canal Nationalization

To return to the events following the nationalization of the Suez Canal Company, Nasser's decision took Secretary of State Dulles completely by surprise. He obviously did not expect Nasser to react so violently despite the warning by the World Bank President Eugene Black that the consequences of U.S. failure to "go through with the deal" to finance the Aswan Dam might be serious. Reaction in Britain and France to Nasser's action was one of consternation and anger. Besides the financial loss, great alarm arose over the possibility that retaliation might extend to interference in the free flow of traffic through the Suez Canal, especially in view of Nasser's record (between 1948 and 1956) of illegally closing the Canal to Israel's ships and to any cargo bound for her ports, in defiance of United Nations orders. Since the free use of the Canal was a matter of vital importance to both Great Britain and France, these two countries were inclined from the first to adopt strong measures aimed at reasserting their rights.

[65] It was significant that even when American-Syrian diplomatic relations were near the breaking point in the sixties, the American cultural program in the country flourished and was eagerly sought out, especially by the university community. Again, although the UAR broke its relations with the United States during the Six-Day war in June 1967, it has continued to send students to the United States to study, has allowed the American University in Cairo to function, and has been eager to have the Fulbright exchange program revived.

The United States, on the other hand, sought to bring about a compromise settlement of the issues raised by Egypt's action. As the basic problem seemed to center on the control and operations of the Suez Canal, Dulles frantically looked around for a formula that would establish an "international system" to protect the interests of all Canal users by insulating the operations of the Canal from "the influence of the politics of any nation".[66] Nasser, was, however, suspicious that this plan sought to deprive Egypt of her "essential rights and sovereignty". Dulles' idea, as a matter of fact, was to get the Suez Canal out of Nasser's hands and establish a user's association to manage the canal. Britain and France had sensed that no such proposal would be acceptable to Nasser. At the same time, they were unwilling to take risks regarding their vital petroleum imports that had to pass through the Suez. Hence they started consultations for joint intervention and military preparations were undertaken quickly. On 3 August 1956, the French Premier Mollet warned that force would be used if necessary and, on 8 August 1956, the British Prime Minister Anthony Eden made the same statement.[67] It soon appeared, however, that there were various obstacles to effective military action. Suitable forces were not immediately available. French manpower was pretty fully employed in Algeria and Great Britain was already feeling the effects of its emphasis on reduced standing forces and "strategic deterrance". Moreover, the United States had made known her opposition to the use of force against Egypt. President Eisenhower

---

[66] *U.S. in World Affairs,* 1956, p. 272.

[67] As early as the end of July 1956, the British Foreign Secretary, Harold MacMillan revealed to Dulles Britain's plans for military action if the problem was not quickly settled. Dulles however refused to exercise excessive pressure on Nasser and announced that the United States would abide by the 1950 Tripartite Declaration which condemned the use of force in the area. Interview with Robert Murphy, Dulles Oral History Project, Dulles Papers, Princeton University Library, cited in LaFeber 51n., p. 192. Also see Finer 47n., p. 67.

had put his foot down on any military action. As he stated on 12 October 1956: "American motives, purposes and policies were formulated at the beginning of this thing. We sat down and as we were determined to pursue a course that would not lead to war, we were certain a negotiation could settle this problem".[68]

The unequivocal position thus assumed by the United States at the very outset reflected her comparative independence of the Suez Canal, and her preference for negotiation arising from her realization of the damage that would be done to Western interests if hostilities against Egypt were started by Britain and France. Throughout the troubled weeks that followed Nasser's action of nationalizing the Suez Canal, the primary American objective appeared to be that of preventing the conflict from degenerating into armed hostilities. The *London Daily Telegraph* complained that the United States in attempting to play the middleman had "shirked risks inherent in her loyalty to her allies and her leadership of the West", and called upon her to "refrain from blowing now hot, now cold," in matters that concerned the very existence of the British people.[69] What particularly irritated the British and the French was Washington's seeming indifference to their views regarding their dispute. Dulles had "indicated by his actions that he did not believe that the vital interests of the United States were involved" at Suez. The United States was more concerned about the control of the Middle East oil fields, and it was not so much the possible loss of the Canal which perturbed her (and the U.S. oil companies in the Middle East), but the loss of oil itself. Pipelines and installations could be blown up and company personnel massacred. Dulles' predicament was that the Middle East crisis had come in the midst of a presidential election and was a source of tremendous embarrassment to him. As a matter of fact with his eyes on the election, Dulles tried frantically to dissuade the

[68] *U.S. in World Affairs*, 1956, p. 260.
[69] *Daily Telegraph*, London, cited in 66n., p. 271.

British and the French from resorting to force and, at the same time, exerted diplomatic pressure on Egypt to make Nasser more compliant. But his efforts went in vain. Israel had become impatient with the commando raids by the irregular forces across her border from Egypt, and had also watched with anxiety the latter's formidable accumulation of Soviet arms. In August 1956, London, Paris and Tel Aviv secretly agreed upon a plan—carefully concealed from Washington—for an attack on Egypt which envisaged an Israeli invasion that would be quickly followed by Anglo-French occupation of the Suez Canal zone.

THE SUEZ CRISIS

On 29 October 1956, the Israeli army made a lightning attack which within a short while almost crippled the Egyptian army and conquered much of the Sinai peninsula. In close cooperation with Israel, England and France then delivered ultimatums to Israel and Egypt on 30 October 1956, to keep away their forces from the canal zone since the outbreak of hostilities threatened to disrupt the freedom of navigation through the canal. Egypt was, moreover, asked to "accept the temporary occupation by Anglo-French forces of key positions at Port Said, Ismailia and Suez." On Egypt's refusal to bow to these demands, British and French planes started aerial bombardment of Egyptian military targets on 31 October 1956. On the same day, the Egyptians blocked the Suez Canal by scuttling a number of ships and thereby stopped the flow of approximately 1,650,000 barrels of oil per day to Europe and the U.S.A.

Israel was considered by the Soviet Union to have played a "treacherous" role in the Suez crisis. Since Britain and France had no legal grounds for armed attack on Egypt, Israel by starting hostilities provided them with an opportunity to join the war "on the pretext of protecting the Suez Canal from destruction".[70]

[70] *New Times*, Moscow, 2n., p. 4.

When the Anglo-French forces launched their attack, they probably expected quick military success, whereby they would be able to seize the Suez Canal without much opposition. But in doing so, they underestimated the reaction of the Soviet Union to take action in favour of Nasser, and overestimated the unwillingness of the United States—on the eve of the 1956 Presidential election —to take any strong action at all.

The United States, in fact, was "greatly irritated" by the Anglo-French-Israeli action which did not fit in with her "long term objectives" in the Middle East region, especially in relation to the intentions of the Soviet Union. The United States felt that her association with Britain, France and Israel at that juncture would discredit her in the eyes of the Arabs and might force them to draw closer to the Soviet Union. On the other hand, vigorous American disavowal of the Anglo-French-Israeli action, coupled with measures that would have the appearance of "penalizing the disturbers of peace" would serve at least to stem the steady decline in her popularity in Arab countries and, at the same time, prevent any Soviet attempt to "fish in troubled waters".

The Soviet Union, however, did not remain quiet even though a rebellion had erupted in Hungary[71] simultaneously with the de-

---

[71] It was argued in Moscow that the West had "staged" the Hungarian revolution in order to cause difficulties for the Russians, and to be free to act against Egypt. But this point of view hardly appears to be plausible since nobody could possibly have known about the dramatic events that were to occur in Hungary soon when Britain, France and Israel were preparing for action against Egypt. On the other hand, it has been contended by Western observers that Soviet intervention in Hungary only became possible because Moscow could use the "Western aggression" in Egypt as a pretext. Subsequent developments have, however, made this argument appear unconvincing, since all the available evidence indicates that Soviet forces would have invaded Hungary in any case, once power in Budapest had passed into "enemy" hands. Laqueur, *USSR and Middle East*, 11n., p. 239.

terioration of the situation in the Middle East. The confrontation in the Middle East, in fact, provided the Soviet Union with a perfect opportunity to crush the rebellion which was accomplished about the same time as the Anglo-French forces moved into the Suez Canal area on 4 and 5 November 1956. Having smashed the Hungarian rebellion, the Soviet Union intervened in the Suez crisis in a dramatic way by indicating her intention to send "volunteers" to fight for Egypt and by threatening Britain, France and Israel with missile warfare if they did not withdraw from Egypt. Whether or not the Soviet threat would have been carried out is conjectural, but it served as a sobering influence on the three countries. Although President Eisenhower quickly warned Russia that such action would lead to American retaliation, Soviet Union's maneuver succeeded in emphasizing that she would not abandon the Arab states and would fight for them, if necessary, while the United States would not. But some competent observers believed that the Russians were, in fact, bluffing.[72] The question whether the Russians really intended to send "volunteers" to fight in Egypt and blast London, Paris and Tel Aviv with missiles if they did not stop the war immediately is, as I have pointed out above, conjectural. Soviet timing, however, makes it appear as if "the threats were made only after it was virtually certain that there would be no need to follow them up with military actions".[73] Thus it was only after it had become clear that the United States would not intervene in the Suez crisis did the Soviet Union send threatening letters to Great Britain, France and Israel indicating her resolve to use force to destroy them unless they terminated

---

[72] After the June 1967 Arab-Israeli War, Israeli leaders declared that their fear of Russian threat during the 1956 Suez Crisis was a gross miscalculation on their part. They are now convinced that the Russians were then bluffing. See David Kimche & Dan Bawly, *The Sandstorm*, London, 1968, p. 285.

[73] Laqueur, *USSR and Middle East*, 11n., p. 239.

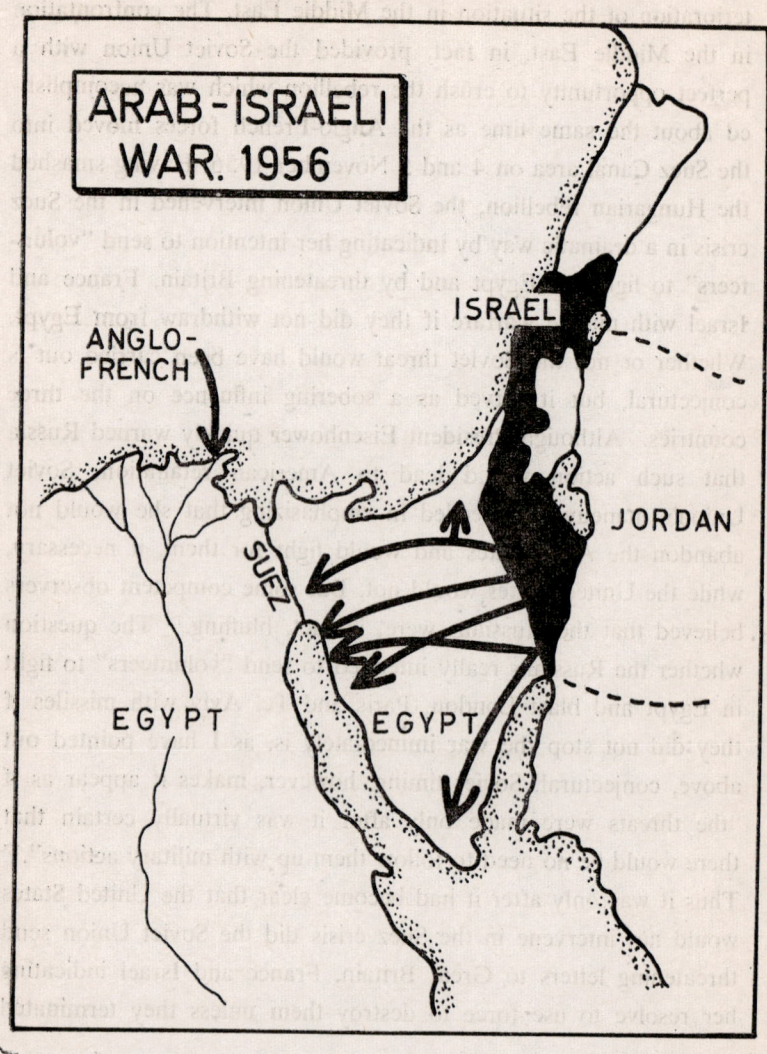

hostilities forthwith. Similarly, the "official Soviet statement about the dispatch of volunteers came only after the armistice in Egypt had already come into force."[74]

However, it might be mentioned here that during their offen-

[74] *Ibid.*

sive in the Sinai peninsula, the Israelis came across a large amount of war material. To their amazement, they found huge stocks of about two million pairs of boots and blankets as well as many millions of gallons of petrol and lubricants "vastly exceeding the most extravagant requirement of Egyptian forces". This gave rise to a presumption that the stores might have been set up by the Russians—in collusion with Egypt—for the "volunteers" from the Soviet bloc countries, in case hostilities had lasted longer.[75]

The United States, on her part, was unwilling to let the Soviet Union reap all the benefits of acting on behalf of the Arab peoples in a case in which the "aggression" was clear. She was apprehensive that the Russians might take advantage of the situation to inveigle their way into negotiating a settlement and thereby "interject Soviet power in an area which for centuries Western Europe had fought to keep free of Russian influence".[76] To forestall this eventuality, the United States brought pressure to bear on London, Paris and Tel Aviv by passing a resolution through the General Assembly, in which it voted together with the Soviet Union, calling for an immediate cease-fire and withdrawal of forces from Egypt. By another resolution they approved the sending of a U.N. Emergency Force to police the boundary between Egypt and Israel. The British Prime Minister Anthony Eden was taken aback at this action and felt that the United States at that time "seemed to be dominated by one thought only, to harry its allies";[77] but Vice-President Richard M. Nixon treated United States' break with her traditional allies as an accomplishment rather than a setback. He stated in part:

> For the first time in history [as a result of the Suez crisis] we

---

[75] E. Hinterhoff, "The Soviet Penetration into the Middle East", *Contemporary Review*, February 1960, p. 68.
[76] LaFeber, 51n., p. 193.
[77] Anthony Eden, *Memoirs, The Full Circle*, London, 1960, p. 569.

have shown independence of Anglo-French policies toward Asia and Africa which seemed to us to reflect the colonial tradition. That declaration of independence has had an electrifying effect throughout the world.[78]

However, the "electrifying effect", insofar as United States' allies were concerned, was closer to dismay than to rejoicing. To compel the evacuation of Anglo-French forces out of Egypt, the United States exerted additional pressure by cutting off oil supplies from the Western Hemisphere which Great Britain and France needed to replace the oil they were hitherto obtaining from the Middle East. This was accomplished by refusing to authorize the operation of the Middle East Emergency Committee[79] of 13 U.S. oil companies to expedite petroleum supplies to Europe.[80] According to Professor M. S. Venkataramani, the main intention of the United States was "not to impose oil sanctions against her European allies", but "to give the appearance of such a policy". "American authorities", according to him, "had to balance the temporary unpopularity that such a stand might evoke in Western Europe against significant gains . . . in the Arab world".[81]

[78] *Congressional Record*, 16n., p. 19334.

[79] The Middle East Emergency Committee was set up in August 1956, composed of 13 American oil companies engaged in foreign petroleum operations. Its task was (i) to make investigations and obtain pertinent information relating to foreign petroleum operations; (ii) to estimate the petroleum requirements of foreign countries and supplies available; and (iii) to make recommendations in respect of stocks of petroleum to be maintained in friendly countries.

[80] Despite this, private companies on their own had shipped some 15 million barrels of oil products to Europe during November 1956. See U.S. House of Representatives, Congress 85, Session 1, Commitee on Interstate and Foreign Commerce, Preliminary Report, *Petroleum Survey*, Washington, D.C., 1957, pp. 18-22.

[81] M. S. Venkataramani, "Oil and U.S. Foreign Policy during Suez Crisis", *International Studies*, vol. 2, October, 1960, p. 136.

The Post War Decade

This point of view appears to be substantially correct since one of the main reasons behind the reluctance of the United States to make arrangements "too quickly" to supply the oil urgently needed by Europe was her apprehension that she might thereby infuriate the Arab nations "which held huge reservoirs of oil leased to Americans".[82] The supply of oil to Europe was restored only after the U.N. resolution had been obeyed and the troops withdrawn. The British and French forces were almost within the reach of their goal—which was the seizure of the Suez Canal area—when they were ordered to pull back and the two governments agreed to a ceasefire. Israel also pulled back her troops from the Gaza strip and the Gulf of Aqaba as a 6,000-man U.N. peace-keeping force moved into positions to police the boundary between Egypt and Israel. But she received no guarantees that there would be no resumption of raids by the irregular commando forces across the Gaza strip or the blockade of the Suez Canal once again by Egypt. Israel, however, made it clear that she would be entitled to exercise the right of self-defence in case of interference with her ships in the Gulf of Aqaba. To assure Israel of her right of navigation across the Gulf, Secretary of State Dulles stated in an aide memoire that "the United States believes the Gulf of Aqaba comprehends international waters and that no nation has the right to prevent free and innocent passage in the Gulf and through the Straits giving access thereto".[83] The United States also made a commitment not to allow any interference in navigation over the Suez Canal.[84]

[82] Engler 7n., pp. 261-63.

[83] *Department of State Bulletin*, vol. 36, 11 March 1957, p. 393. For the text of the Aide Memoire see Appendix VI.

[84] This undertaking was given by President Dwight D. Eisenhower at a television appearance in February 1957. Yet, when Nasser reimposed the blockade of the Suez Canal in 1959 for Israeli ships and goods, neither the United States nor the United Nations could muster sufficient courage or resolve to deter him.

The Superpowers and the Middle East
SOVIET GAINS

While the pressure exerted by the United States appeared to many Western observers to have been responsible for the Anglo-French capitulation; some others and, practically everybody in the Arab world, believed that without Russia's threat of military intervention and missile warfare against the "aggressors", the U.N. would not have achieved a ceasefire in Egypt so quickly, and Britain, France and Israel would not have agreed to withdraw from Egyptian territory in favour of the U.N. peace-keeping force "once they were in a position to assume effective control". Soviet action during the Suez crisis, as a matter of fact, made a very strong impression in the Arab world where events in Hungary passed practically unnoticed. Nasser officially thanked the Soviet people and government stating that the Soviet help "reflected Soviet-Egyptian friendship".[85] As pointed out earlier, the risk of Soviet involvement as a result of her intervention in the Suez crisis was very little indeed, and yet she succeeded, in Arab eyes, in getting most of the credit for stopping the war. The crisis in the Middle East, in short, while accentuating Arab distrust of Western motives, strengthened the position of the Soviet Union as a self-styled defender of "Arab nationalism". It also resulted in the consolidation of Nasser's position in the Arab world.

The firm stand taken by President Eisenhower against the Anglo-French-Israeli invasion of Egypt had, however, helped the United States to regain at least some of the lost ground in the Arab world. But the opportunity thus gained was soon dissipated by some of her actions which seemed to "give lie to the President's stand". Thus after the outbreak of fighting, the Egyptian government had asked the United States for kerosene—the principal fuel used by the Egyptians. But this was refused and eventually supplied by the Soviet Union. Again, when the Egyptian government re-

---

[85] Laqueur, *USSR and Middle East* 11n., p. 241.

quested for the release of $14,000 of its frozen funds[86] for the purchase of medicines badly needed for the victims of the war, it was also turned down by the U.S. government. Subsequently, the medicines were supplied by the Soviet Union. Yet another action that made the United States unpopular was her refusal to renew the CARE program in Egypt. Through CARE's feeding program, nearly three million Egyptian school children were receiving free school lunches by September 1956. However, when the supplies were exhausted soon thereafter, the U.S. government refused to renew the program. Senator Hubert H. Humphrey of Minnesota considered this action to be a "blunder."[87] The United States also made a "blunder" when she refused to sell Egypt her surplus wheat at a time when the latter's reserves were almost exhausted. As a result Egypt was compelled to turn to Russia to meet her wheat needs. Russia's handling of the Egyptian wheat deal showed more astuteness than had been displayed by the United States. As Senator Humphrey stated:

> When we sell wheat, we talk unimaginatively of our surplus, our disposal program etc. When Russia was asked to sell wheat to Egypt, Soviet officials at first played coy, saying in effect, 'Well, we will see, we need all we have, but we want to help if we can'. A week later they were back saying in effect: 'We really cannot spare it [our wheat], but we are willing to share what we have with you'. The result had a real propaganda impact. The Soviet Union did not provide much wheat but everybody apparently knew about the wheat they did send.[88]

[86] The United States had frozen $40 million of Egyptian Government funds when Nasser nationalized the Suez Canal Company.

[87] U.S. Senate, Committee on Foreign Relations, *The Middle East and Southern Europe,* Report of Senator Hubert H. Humphrey, Washington, D.C., 1957, p. 14.

[88] *Ibid.*

The Superpowers and the Middle East

The above actions taken by the United States offset any temporary goodwill she might have gained in the Arab world for opposing the Anglo-French-Israeli invasion of Egypt. It should be noted that both the United States and the Soviet Union, while putting up a common front in the United Nations as "defenders of the victim of aggression", and "upholders of the Charter", did their best to capitalize on that role in the Middle East and to forestall each other's moves there. What the United States did not realize was that in undertaking joint action with its "cold war" adversary, it was acting against its own vital interests. By helping to destroy the power and jeopardize the interests of Great Britain and France, the United States destroyed the power of its strongest and most reliable supporters in the area and strengthened the position of the Soviet Union which convinced the Arabs that she was their firm ally. Furthermore, since the United States was not willing to substitute effective power of its own for that of Great Britain and France, the political and military vacuum created by the destruction of the British and French power in the Middle East was filled up by the power of Egypt and the Soviet Union which militated against the interests of the United States. The objective which the United States had sought to attain through the Baghdad Pact—namely, containment of Soviet expansion in the Middle East—was thus nullified by her attitude during the Suez crisis.

CHAPTER TWO

Period of Trial and Hope: 1957-1965

The decline of British and French power in the Middle East after the Suez Crisis created a "power vacuum" in that region and provided the Soviet Union with an excellent opportunity for penetration. The Soviet Union, as a matter of fact, emerged as a dominant power in the Middle East after the Suez Crisis and it was believed that she would attempt to expand her foothold in the Arab countries with a view to eventually bringing the entire area under its influence. The United States was compelled to take note of this grave danger in view of her strategic and economic stake in that area.[1] She deemed it to be her responsibility to deter the Soviet Union from possible aggression and also to prevent subversive activities on its part in the countries of the Middle East. What was needed, under the circumstances, was a declaration informing the Kremlin that the U.S. government was ready and willing to oppose by military might any Soviet attempt to penetrate in that region.

THE EISENHOWER DOCTRINE

With this end in view, President Eisenhower addressed a joint

[1] U.S. Department of State, *United States Policy in the Middle East*, September 1956-June 1957, Washington, D.C., 1957, pp. 419-20.

45

session of the Congress on 5 January 1957, in which he stressed the predatory nature of international communism and called upon the Congress to adopt a resolution to provide him with authority for giving military and economic aid to those countries or "group of nations" which desired such assistance, and to use the armed forces of the United States to protect the territorial integrity and political independence of such nations requesting military help which were endangered by the "overt armed aggression" of international communism.[2] The proposals put forward by President Eisenhower encountered some sharp criticism during Congressional hearings. It was contended that the proposals offered no sure defense against the real danger, subversion; while the possibility of conflicts arising in other ways was overlooked. It was also pointed out that the proposals were anti-Israeli, vague and injurious to Western alliance.[3]

However, after prolonged hearings lasting for two months, the Congress finally adopted a joint resolution—that came to be known as the Eisenhower Doctrine—and was approved by the President on 9 March 1957. The economic provisions of the Eisenhower Doctrine permitted the President to spend free of existing restrictions, upto $200,000,000 of previously appropriated foreign aid funds for special military and economic projects in the area. The new doctrine was actually an extension of the Truman Doctrine to the nations south of those on the Soviet

---

[2] *Public Papers of the Presidents of the United States, Dwight D. Eisenhower,* 1957, Washington, D.C., 1958, pp. 6-16. For the text of the Eisenhower Doctrine, see Appendix V.

[3] U.S. Senate, Congress 85, Session 1, Committee on Foreign Relations, *The President's Proposal on the Middle East, Hearings on S. J. Res,* 19, Washington D.C., 1957, pp. 48-50; 264-65. U.S. House of Representatives. Congress 85, Session 1, Committee on Foreign Affairs, *Economic and Military Cooperation with Nations in the General Area of the Middle East, Hearings on H.J. Res.* 117, Washington, D.C., 1957, pp. 13-17.

periphery, in an effort to "contain" the Soviet Union in that region, stem the advance of Egyptian influence and establish United States' own dominant position there.

The Eisenhower Doctrine, however, received a "chilly" reception abroad and, at the same time, split the Arab world into two camps. The British government did not foresee any immediate danger of Soviet armed attack and feared that military aid under the new doctrine might result in an arms race in the Middle East. Moreover, it was felt that the United States was seeking to take advantage of a power vacuum that, to a large extent, she herself had created by demanding the withdrawal of the British and French forces from Egypt. It was contended that while the United States had denounced the Anglo-French intervention in Egypt, she was now herself seeking, through the Eisenhower Doctrine, a cover for intervention in the Middle East region to protect her oil interests there.

Insofar as the countries of the Middle East were concerned, the Eisenhower Doctrine instead of unifying them produced just the opposite effect. Those countries that had already supported the West, such as Turkey, Iraq, Iran—the Baghdad Pact countries, and Lebanon, announced their strong support for the Doctrine. But Egypt and Syria denounced it as an "imperialist plot". The Soviet Union also joined with an attack against the new American "colonialism" and the gross interference in the domestic affairs of the Middle Eastern countries. She contended that the doctrine was intended "to turn the Middle East into an American colony". The Soviet Union also took advantage of the feeling of "injured pride" among the Arab nations resulting from the doctrine's pointed reference to the existence of a "military vacuum" in the Middle East and the inability of the Arab states to defend the area against communist aggression. In fact, "the American reference to the vacuum became the chief motif in Soviet propaganda" whose main object was to undermine the standing of the United States in the Arab world.[4] Further, in a strongly worded declaration on 18 January 1957, the Soviet Union (along with China) pledged support to all the countries of the Middle East against "aggression or interference" by the Western Powers. It was Moscow's answer to the Eisenhower Doctrine. In a few weeks time, however, the Soviet Union climbed down from the militant posture and reassured the West that it did not "wish to possess military bases or any kind of concessions in countries of the Near and Middle East . . . nor does it seek to obtain any kind of privileges in that area". Its primary concern was to promote peace in the region "situated in direct proximity to its borders". These observations, contained in a Soviet Note handed over to the United States, Britain and France on 11 February 1957, were also accompanied by Draft Proposals[5] which stipulated that the Four Powers jointly guarantee (a) peaceful settlement of disputes in the region; (b) non-interference in its internal affairs; (c) abolition of military alignments; (d) withdrawal of foreign forces; (e) ban on supply of arms to Middle Eastern countries; and (f) economic assistance without strings. The Soviet Union, in other words, wanted the Western Powers to recognize her interests in the Middle East as well since they no longer enjoyed the monopoly in that region after the Suez crisis. The Soviet proposals were, however, rejected by the United States which felt that in view of Russia's past record of infiltration and its record of broken treaty promises, it would be extremely risky for her to pledge to a mutual "hands off" policy. The close proximity of the Soviet Union would have then placed the countries of the Middle East at her mercy. The United States made it clear that she was not interested in dominating the coun-

---

[4] Walter Z. Laqueur, *The Soviet Union and the Middle East*, London, 1959, p. 243. Hereafter cited as Laqueur, *USSR and Middle East*.

[5] For text of the proposals see *News and Views from the Soviet Union*, New Delhi, vol. 16, 14 February 1957, pp. 2-4.

Period of Trial and Hope

tries of the Middle East, but merely in keeping them out of Russia's orbit. She further contended that Russian charges of intervention would be proved "spurious" as long as American aid was not forced on the countries of the Middle East, but was given on request to victims assaulted by aggressor nations "controlled by international communism".[6] The Eisenhower Doctrine, however, proved to be largely irrelevant to the real challenges to American policy in the Middle East. Its limitation in taking action under the doctrine except in cases of "overt aggression" by states "controlled by international communism", was clearly demonstrated in the case of Jordan and Syria in 1957.

JORDAN AND SYRIA

Although the Eisenhower Doctrine provided a basis for more active American intervention in Middle Eastern affairs, it proved scarcely more suited than the Baghdad Pact to meet the problems of the area. The immediate threat to stability in the Middle East was not the danger of Communist aggression, but the continued growth of radically anti-Western and increasingly pro-Soviet tendencies of indigenous origin. This was particularly noticeable in Egypt which had become the fountainhead of an intensive propaganda and subversive campaign against any Arab government that continued to display Western sympathies. Events in Jordan soon put the Eisenhower Doctrine to test. In early 1957, certain forces suspected of communist ties and sympathies attempted to overthrow King Hussein of Jordan. Syria and Egypt tried to bring the small kingdom into the pro-Nasser and anti-Western camp. At the same time, Iraq and Israel stood poised to intervene and possibly to partition the country. To forestall such an eventuality, King Hussein suddenly dismissed his pro-Egyptian

---

[6] For the reply of the U.S. Government see *Department of State Bulletin*, vol. 36, 1 April 1957, p. 523.

government and exiled the pro-Nasserist officers in the Arab Legion. Meanwhile, anticipating the need for U.S. help, he publicly denounced international communism and its followers and charged that they were responsible for the crisis. President Eisenhower responded by announcing on 24 April 1957 that the United States regarded "the independence and integrity" of Jordan as "vital", and the next day the U.S. Sixth Fleet—including the aircraft carrier Forrestal and 1,800 marines—were dispatched to the Eastern Mediterranean ostensibly for the purpose of evacuating American citizens in case of need.[7] What the United States failed to explain was why a whole "armada" (the Sixth Fleet) was considered necessary to accomplish so simple a task and why this particular occasion was chosen to put over 1,000 marines ashore at Beirut in Lebanon. The real reason for the naval maneuvers were, however, obvious. The United States wanted to make it clear to King Hussein's enemies who were being bolstered by Soviet aid, that she stood ready to intervene as a last resort, if the King should be unable to deal with the crisis. It might be noted, however, that this action in support of King Hussein did not come within the scope of the Eisenhower Doctrine since no "aggression" by any communist state had been committed against Jordan.

Fortunately, King Hussein was able to retain control of his kingdom without American assistance. He weeded out the pro-Soviet elements, dissolved political parties and installed a cabinet of unquestioned loyalty. Thereupon, the United States quickly granted Jordan "without any strings" a sum of $10 million to help the country's economic development and its political stability.[8] This amount was not appropriated pursuant to the Eisenhower Doctrine, for in that case it would have been impossible for Hussein to accept the money since it would have implied submission

[7] *New York Times*, 25 April 1957.
[8] *Ibid.*, 30 April 1957.

to American political leadership. Jordan's extreme fear of becoming a pawn of the Great Powers and a battleground in the East-West conflict was typical of the attitudes of other Arab states, and this became apparent to the United States a few monhs later in the case of Syria.

During the summer of 1957, pro-Nasser and pro-Soviet groups in the Syrian army seized control of the government. At the same time, Syria began to receive substantial Soviet military and economic aid. Though Syria's neighbours were concerned at the extension of communist influence in Syria, they refused to cooperate with the United States in bringing political or economic pressure on her. The reason for this was the determination of the Arab states to stand united against foreign pressure of any sort. Since Syria's leftward conversion had been accomplished without the force of arms, military counter measures were also not legally justifiable. There was, however, an apprehension that Russia might instigate Syria against Turkey. The United States therefore issued a warning that it would defend Turkey. Fortunately, the war scare died down quickly and in February 1958, Egypt and Syria formally joined together and formed the United Arab Republic (UAR).[9] This was hailed as a prelude to complete Arab unity. The Syrian case had shown that Secretary of State Dulles' prediction that communism could not gain a permanent foothold in the Middle East without the use of armed force was wrong and the Eisenhower Doctrine was a blunt tool to deal with communist subversion. After the formation of the United Arab Republic, the United States' hold on the Arab world weakened rapidly and she realized that her major difficulties in the region stemmed from

---

[9] The formation of the United Arab Republic meant that Nasser's pro-Russian, pan-Arab nationalism had gained in prestige and that he was in a better position to bring his influence to bear on Lebanon, Jordan and Iraq. Events in the Middle East proved this to be correct. *Middle Eastern Affairs*, vol. 10, May, 1959, p. 184.

pro-Nasser groups and Egyptian agents who appeared intent on overthrowing the pro-Western governments in Lebanon, Jordan and Iraq. The dilemma became most acute during the crisis in Lebanon and the Iraqi revolution. In both cases, it was alleged that pro-Nasser elements were the prime instigators.

Crisis in Lebanon and Iraq

When armed rebellion broke out in Lebanon in May 1958, in protest against President Camille Chamoun's pro-Western policies and his support for the Eisenhower Doctrine, he promptly alleged that foreign agents were behind it and appealed to the United States to save the country. Lebanon also complained to the U.N. Security Council of "massive infiltration" into its territory and charged the UAR with intervention in its internal affairs. A U.N. observation commission that was dispatched to Lebanon shortly afterwards, however, denied that there had been more than a trickle of foreign support from neighbouring Syria and, possibly, also from Egypt. But the United States believed otherwise on the basis of her own intelligence reports, and she was extremely anxious to keep Lebanon in the Western camp. Hence she moved the Sixth Fleet once again into the Eastern Mediterranean and arms aid to Lebanon was speeded up. It was hoped that the show of force coupled with the arms aid would enable President Chamoun to pacify his country and would discourage foreign support of Lebanese rebels.

The alleged intrigue by the UAR had threatened the security not only of Lebanon but also of Jordan whose King had become acutely aware of this fact. In these circumstances, it was not surprising that both Lebanon and Jordan became alarmed when on 14 July 1958, pro-Nasser faction in the Iraqi army led by General Abdel Karim Kassim overthrew the Iraqi government and established a regime friendly to the UAR. The coup in Iraq resulted in the elimination of the pro-Western leadership in that country and its removal from active participation in the Baghdad Pact.[10] President Chamoun of Lebanon thereupon requested for urgent help from the United States so that the tidal wave of revolution begun at Baghdad might not swamp the neighbouring countries. Despite the contention of some Congressmen that the Eisenhower Doctrine could not be applied in this case since the communist threat was only "dimly apparent", and despite the opposition of the Pentagon, President Eisenhower[11] on 15 July 1958, ordered 14,000 American marines to land in Lebanon to preserve the sovereignty and independence of the country which had been deemed "vital to United States national interests".[12] The size of the force served as a warning to General Kassim and his supporters that any threat to Western oil resources in the area would not be tolerated. On 17 July 1958, in response to a request from the Jordanian government, British paratroops landed in Jordan while the United States sent military supplies to her.

Although no military activities were engaged in by the American or British forces, and assurances had been given that the troops would be withdrawn as soon as the U.N. took adequate steps for the security of Lebanon and Jordan, the Soviet Union charged the United States and Britain with aggression and demanded the prompt withdrawal of their troops. This demand was turned down by both the United States and Britain, but they agreed to a "summit meeting" provided it was held at the U.N. Khrushchev backed away from this proposal and he urged instead, the calling of a special emergency meeting of the U.N. General Assembly. The U.N. pressed for the "early withdrawal" of the

---

[10] *U.S. in World Affairs*, 1959, p. 218.

[11] President Eisenhower was convinced that the revolt in Iraq had been "fomented by Arab leaders under the domination of Moscow". *New York Times*, 16 July 1958.

[12] *Department of State Bulletin*, vol. 39, 4 August 1958, pp. 182-83.

American and British forces. By October 1958, the situation became somewhat stabilized. Thereupon, the United States withdrew its forces from Lebanon, and the following month, the British followed suit in Jordan.[13] The Soviet Union looked upon the U.S. action in Lebanon as "an act of armed aggression violating all norms of international law and the most elementary concepts of responsibility of the Great Powers for international security."[14] The real reason for the armed intervention, the Soviet Union contended, was "the desire of the oil monopolies of U.S.A. . . . to retain its colonial hold on the Middle East countries and to preserve their colossal profits extracted by robbing the national wealth of those countries".[15]

The United States, however, defended herself against the charge of illegal intervention in Lebanon by pointing to the right of the Lebanese government to ask for aid from its friends in self defense when the United Nations could not act promptly enough.[16]

---

[13] *Ibid.*, 27 October 1958, p. 650.

[14] *News and Views from the Soviet Union,* New Delhi, vol. 8, 22 July 1958, p. 5.

[15] *Ibid.*, p. 7. Peking, on the other hand, looked upon the uprising in Lebanon as a war of liberation. The Chinese contended that the colonial people could liberate themselves only by resort to violence and hence the need to support wars of liberation. But while Communist China gave vocal support to the Lebanese rebels, she did not give any material aid to them. Peking, however, earnestly sought to bring about Soviet military intervention. See M. S. Agwani, "The Soviet Union, China and West Asia", International Studies, vol. 6, April, 1965, pp. 354-55.

[16] Examining the legality of the intervention from the standpoint of International Law, Professor Quincy Wright held that the United States in sending its armed forces in Lebanon would be "guilty of aggression unless it can prove that it acted... in individual or collective self-defence" or "on the invitation of Lebanon". He could not find any justification for the intervention as an act of American self-defence and held that a government gravely beset by internal revolt could not legally invoke armed aid from abroad. See Quincy Wright, "United States Intervention in the

Period of Trial and Hope

From the point of view of the U.S. government, moreover, there were sufficient political reasons to justify her action. The fires of a revolt which had broken out in Iraq in July 1958 were almost certain to spark a revolution in Lebanon and Jordan whose strong pro-Nasser elements were ready to seize any opportunity to install new regimes. The United States, furthermore, had committed herself so firmly to the defense of Lebanon that she could not refuse the Lebanese President's urgent appeal for help without losing the confidence of her other friends in the Middle East to whom support had been pledged. Above all, by her action, the United States attempted to demonstrate the effectiveness of the Eisenhower Doctrine. But, unfortunately, Lebanon was a poor example. Less than two years after the Suez crisis, the United States found itself resorting to the use of force to achieve "stability" in the Middle East, a tactic which it had condemned as morally reprehensible. The net result of America's intervention in Lebanon was that she forfeited whatever goodwill she had gained in the Arab countries for her role during the Suez crisis.

Arab resentment against the United States was, however, smoothed to some extent by Washington's prompt recognition of the new regime in Iraq headed by General Kassim. The revolt in Iraq was considered to be a popular rebellion, local in its origins and the product of internal discontent. No attempt was therefore made to reverse events in Iraq especially since General Kassim promised to cooperate with the United States and other Western powers and also gave an assurance that there would be no interference in the shipment of oil to Western Europe. Moreover, Kassim's government soon moved away from Nasserite pan-Arabism to an insistence on full Iraqi independence.

During the first few months following the Iraqi revolt, it is probable that the Soviet Union could have imposed its own dummy

Lebanon", *American Journal of International Law,* January, 1959, pp. 112-25.

regime upon Iraq since the pro-Soviet elements represented the only coherent force in the country and they had quickly penetrated into Iraq's main political and social institutions. The prize, it seemed, was theirs for the taking. But the Soviet Union hesitated to make a single power play that would have been required. There were several possible reasons for this. The Soviets were trying to identify themselves with nationalist movements throughout Asia and Africa. To crush one would have cost them immeasurably in trust, friendship, and prestige among other societies bent on transforming themselves. Iraq, moreover, was not worth that prize. The West would not have missed Iraq's oil seriously; its loss could have been balanced by increased production in Kuwait, Saudi Arabia, and other places. On the other hand, the example of a Soviet controlled Iraq would have deeply alarmed neighbouring Arab states which live on oil revenues. And the impact on Egypt—the key nation in the Arab world—would have been at least as great. Perhaps, for these reasons the Soviet Union did not consider that its gamble in taking over Iraq would be worthwhile.

For the United States, the Iraqi revolution constituted a serious blow to her strategic policies in the Middle East since it left a gaping hole in the Baghdad Pact. In March 1959, Kassim withdrew from the Pact and during the same month signed a comprehensive agreement on economic and technical cooperation with the Soviet Union embodying a 12-year Soviet credit of $137.5 million.[17] At the same time, Iraq made known her intention to terminate her military and economic aid agreements with the United States on the ground that they were inconsistent with her new policy of "positive neutrality".[18] However, although Kassim had sought help from the Soviet Union, he was not prepared to allow the Iraqi communists to control the government. He resist-

[17] *Current Digest of the Soviet Press*, 15 April 1959, p. 10.
[18] *New York Times*, 2 June 1959.

ed their efforts in this direction, and with the cooperation of other parties succeeded in curbing their activities.

On the other hand, the Baghdad Pact countries, weakened by the defection of Iraq from their ranks, were bolstered by the United States with an assurance that she would cooperate with them for their security and defense even "at great risk" if they faced a threat similar to that of Lebanon.[19] The United States had earlier (in March 1957) joined the military committee of the Baghdad Pact, enabling her to deploy air power to help hold certain mountain passes and to give an undertaking on the scope and character of military assistance to the Pact members in the event of their becoming involved in war. But after the coup in Iraq and the Lebanese crisis, the United States committed herself to defend a 3,000 frontier extending from Turkish Caucasus to the Khyber Pass against both direct and indirect aggression.[20] Upon Iraq's withdrawal, the United States attempted to replace the Baghdad Pact by immediately signing new bilateral military assistance treaties with Pakistan, Turkey, and Iran and forming a new organization named the Central Treaty Organization (CENTO). Moscow claimed that the new organization (CENTO) could not prevent the Arab states from drawing closer to the Soviet Union.[21] But as a matter of fact after the coup in Iraq, Nasser had backed away from excessive dependence on the Soviet bloc and had increased his precautions against communist infiltration in the Arab world. Other Arab countries, including Iraq, tended to follow UAR's example.

WASHINGTON SEEKS NASSER'S FRIENDSHIP

From the time the United Nations and the United States turned

[19] *Ibid.*, 30 July 1958.
[20] *Ibid.*, 31 July 1958.
[21] *New Times*, Moscow, 21 June 1967, p. 4.

Nasser's military defeat in the Sinai into a diplomatic triumph at Suez, Nasser's influence throughout the Middle East[22] had made him immensely attractive to the United States. During the Anglo-French-Israeli attack on Egypt in 1956, when President Eisenhower pressed for the withdrawal of Israeli troops from the Sinai region, he made a solemn pledge that if the Suez Canal were blocked in the future, such action would be dealt with firmly by the family of nations.[23] Despite this assurance, the United States failed to take any action when Nasser, soon after the 1956 conflict, sought to strangulate Israel economically by refusing transit through the Suez Canal to Israeli vessels as well as to foreign vessels carrying cargoes to or from Israel. The United States also did not oppose a loan of $56 million given to the UAR in December 1959, by the International Bank for Reconstruction and Development (IBRD) for widening and deepening the Suez Canal. Strong protest was, however, voiced by some Senators like Senator Ernest Gruening of Alaska who demanded that the UAR should, as *quid pro quo,* be compelled to give an assurance of free transit for all vessels through the Suez Canal.[24] But generally speaking, the United States had by that time recovered from her earlier fears that Nasser might turn out to be a communist tool, and she began to respond favourably to Nasser's overtures for increasing the scale of her economic aid to the UAR. The United States subsequently furnished substantial quantities of wheat to the UAR and resumed her technical assistance to help the UAR in its highway development and other programs. The U.S. government also released $21 million of Egypt's frozen balances. The

---

[22] Nasser's sway over the Arab nations beyond Egyptian frontiers reached a peak in 1958 with the union of Egypt with Syria in a United Arab Republic.

[23] *Congressional Record,* Congress 86, Session 2, Vol. 106, 1960, p. 19333.

[24] *Ibid.,* p. 19334.

Period of Trial and Hope

United States did not expect Nasser to join the Western camp when she decided to restore the aid that had been stopped during the Suez crisis. The decision was made because the United States could not refuse indefinitely to have normal relations with the man who not only headed the one stable Arab regime in the Middle East, but also dominated the Arab scene. The State Department realized that U.S. aid would inevitably strengthen Nasser; but the assumption was that he was United States' best guarantee against the extension of Soviet influence in the area. Moreover, he was considered most likely of all the Arab leaders to handle the Israeli problem with restraint. Also, since the roots of United States' policy lay in her determination to deny the Middle East to the communists,[25] it was felt necessary to foster strong and independent governments in the area to check Soviet encroachment. At the same time it was realized that to have bolstered other Middle Eastern governments while ignoring that of the UAR would have been self defeating, for nothing was likely to force Nasser to move quickly into external adventure than frustration at home. Hence the United States' decision to grant Nasser the necessary assistance to enable him to tackle his country's overwhelming social and economic problems.[26] This revised policy

[25] It should be noted, however, that communism has never been the main issue in the eyes of the Arab people. To them, the curbing of Communist advances in the Middle East have appeared far less important than the struggle to free their lands from the influence of the West, principally the United States, and its so called "Zionist appendage", the state of Israel. The resentment on the part of the Arab states for U.S. partiality towards Israel has, to a large extent, been responsible for nullifying the friendly feelings that might otherwise have been inspired by the extensive food-for-peace, technical assistance and development aid programmes in Arab countries.

[26] Between 1958 and 1964, the United States provided Egypt with over $1 billion worth of aid, mostly in cheap long term loans under P. L. 480 arrangement for the sale of surplus American foodstuffs. Peter Mansfield, *Nasser's Egypt*, Baltimore, 1965, p. 87.

of the United States towards the UAR was carried further after the election of President John F. Kennedy, who came close to establishing cordial relations with Nasser.

Israel's Apprehensions

Israel was extremely unhappy at the resumption of U.S. economic aid to the UAR. She argued that this enabled Egyptian funds to be released for new arms purchase from the Soviet Union. As an example, Israel pointed out that in the second half of 1963, Egypt had secured tanks, transport aircraft and spare parts to build up UAR forces after the losses suffered in the fighting in Yemen.[27] Israel contended that Nasser would have found it har-

[27] When fighting broke out in Yemen toward the end of 1962 between the royalist forces and the supporters of one Colonel Abdallah al-Salal who had usurped power, Nasser threw his support in favour of the latter with 30,000 troops, tanks and planes. Jordan and Saudi Arabia—Nasser's enemies—thereupon threw their support in favour of Yemen's dispossessed royal family to prevent Yemen from becoming an outpost of Egyptian influence and a base for subversive action against them. The U.S. government recognized the republican regime in Yemen, hoping that her recognition would speed the end of foreign intervention in Yemen and dilute Soviet influence; but these hopes were not realized. Nasser's objectives in Yemen were to impose a "revolutionary socialist" government there and to extend his influence southward by taking hold of Aden—as the British prepared to leave—and then sweep on to grab control of the whole oil rich Persian Gulf area; and finally to drive Israel into the sea. His troops in Yemen were rotated regularly, and it was expected that before he was finished he would have a battle-hardened army to be used against Israel backed up by a substantial amount of Soviet armour and aircraft. The Soviet Union supported Nasser's war effort in Yemen in the fond hope that if Nasser succeeded in gaining a stranglehold on the Yemen republican regime, she could hope for facilities for her Navy not only in Hodeida in Yemen, but also in Aden, and in due course, in the Persian Gulf. *Congressional Record*, Congress 88, Session 2, Vol. 110, 1964, pp. 10700-11041.

der to re-stock his arsenal had American aid not been flowing. Senator Kenneth Keating of New York also strongly objected to the U.S. decision to resume aid to Egypt. "The United States", he said, "should not increase aid to Egypt until she had definite assurances that Nasser would not use any of this assistance, directly or indirectly, to supply himself with additional Soviet weapons and thereby increase tension in the Middle East."[28] Assistant Secretary of State Frederick G. Dutton sought to allay Senator Keating's apprehension by stating that the U.S. assistance was directed toward the orderly development of Egypt which was a large, populous and strategically located country in an important area of the world. He also pointed out that the people of the UAR were determined to search for progress and they were likely to turn elsewhere if they could not obtain from the United States the help which they needed.[29]

However, the U.S. State Department's assumption that Nasser was likely to handle the Israeli problem with restraint soon turned out to be wishful thinking. This was evident from Nasser's action in detaining a Danish and a Greek ship—the Inge Toft and Astypalea—at Port Said because they were involved in trade with Israel.[30] Despite President Eisenhower's earlier commitment to

---

[28] *Congressional Record,* Congress 87, Session 2, Vol. 108, 1962, p. 12237.

[29] *Ibid.*

[30] Arab states had also started blacklisting of American ships and when this assumed ever growing dimensions, New York's longshoremen began to picket the Egyptian steamer Cleopatra on 13 April 1960, and refused to unload her. The UAR government and labour unions declared a counter-boycott, a stoppage of services to all American ships in UAR ports from 29 April 1960. The New York longshoremen ended their demonstration on 6 May 1960, after the State Department had stated that it would continue actively to oppose all boycotts, blacklistings and similar political restriction on the freedom of trade and movement. *Middle Eastern Affairs,* vol. 12, February, 1961, p. 38.

ensure freedom of passage through the Suez Canal, he preferred not to take any initiative at that time and left it to the U.N. Secretary General Dag Hammarskjold, to try to straighten out the matter with Nasser. "I don't know what you can do unless you want to resort to force in such affairs", said Eisenhower, "and I'm certain that we're not trying to settle international problems with force".[31]

This attitude was not encouraging to Israel which felt that force ought to be used if there was no other way of compelling a recalcitrant state (UAR) to comply with its obligations.[32] Certain dangers were, however, inherent in any such measure. Ever since Nasser had turned to the Soviet bloc for military assistance, an arms race had been going on between the Arab states and Israel, and there was a risk that the use of force by any one side might spark off a full scale war.

While Soviet arms flowed in freely into the UAR and also into Iraq after the 1958 coup, Israel had little luck in securing arms from the United States even though she had impressed upon the U.S. government its importance to prevent a deterioration in her security position. The Eisenhower Administration was reluctant to become a "major supplier" of arms to Israel for fear of antagonizing the Arab states. Israel had long been getting arms from Great Britain and France, and Eisenhower felt that they should "carry a little responsibility", especially since the United States was already sending arms to "enough nations".[33] But the arms which Israel had received from Britain and France were, unfortunately, not adequate enough for her to meet the challenge posed

---

[31] *New York Times,* 28 April 1960.

[32] The right of free and open transit through the Suez Canal was first laid down in the Convention of Constantinople, 1888. It was also provided in the declaration of the United Nations, 1951. Finally, it was pledged by President Nasser in 1956 when he nationalized the Suez Canal.

[33] *New York Times,* 18 February 1960.

Period of Trial and Hope

by the rapid build up of UAR's airforce, navy and ground forces by virtue of their Soviet acquisitions.

Thus in 1962-63, the UAR had 10 Russian W-class submarines, 7 destroyers, and a fleet of motor torpedo boats equipped with guided missiles. In comparison, Israel had only two outmoded submarines, two destroyers and a flotilla of smaller craft. The UAR airforce had approximately 20 squadrons of Soviet MIG-19 and MIG-21 jet fighters equipped with air-to-air missiles. She also possessed several Soviet TU-16 medium bombers as well as long range Soviet "Badger" bombers. In addition, the Soviet Union had provided the UAR with several transport planes and helicopters.[34] Against these, Israel had succeeded in obtaining from France only several squadrons of jet fighters and bombers, including Mysteres, Super-Mysteres, Mirages and Vautours. For her ground forces, the UAR had received from the Russians a large number of recoilless guns, other items of artillery, a number of TU-54 medium tanks, armoured personnel carriers, as well as small arms.[35] Israeli acquisitions in this field from Britain and France were far from satisfactory.

Israel was gravely concerned in view of the arms disparity, and her feeling of insecurity increased when in July 1962, it became known that with the help of German scientists and technicians, many of them diehard Nazis,[36] the UAR was in the process

---

[34] U.S. Congress, Congress 89, Session 2, Joint Economic Committee, *New Directions in the Soviet Economy. Pt. 4, The World Outside; Soviet Foreign Aid to the Less Developed Countries,* Washington, D.C., 1966, p. 965.

[35] *Congressional Record,* Congress 88, Session 1, Vol. 109. 1963, p. 15521. In 1963 it was estimated that the military and economic aid obtained by the UAR from the Soviet Union amounted to approximately $920 million. *Ibid.,* p. 20571.

[36] It was believed that nearly 400 German scientists and technicians, most of them from the wartime German V-2 missile center at Penemunde, worked on the first Egyptian made rocket missile. In March 1963, the

of developing a ground-to-ground missiles with a range of nearly 400 miles and with warheads containing radio-active materials. Israel felt especially perturbed when launching sites for the missiles were spotted throughout the Sinai Peninsula. Although she was confident of her ability to turn back any attack by Arab tank and infantry units, she had no comparable ground-to-ground bombardment missiles. She therefore sought to impress upon the United States on the urgent need of being supplied with rockets and missiles to enable her to deter a possible attack by the UAR.

Kennedy's Middle East Policy

President John F. Kennedy,[37] who recognized that peace in the Middle East was ultimately dependent on a balance of military power, realized the threat that the new development posed for Israel. He strongly "believed in America's moral commitment to Israeli security" and hence he agreed in September 1962, to allow Israel to purchase a number of short-range ground-to-air 'Hawk' missiles in order to enable her to counter the UAR air threat and to match the Soviet SAM II—surface-to-air missiles possessed by Egypt. This move was intensely resented in the UAR and throughout the Arab world where aid to Israel was invariably equated with hostility to the entire Arab world. But while Kennedy took steps to strengthen Israel's ability to resist aggression, he also wanted to "preserve an *entrée* to Nasser in order both to restrain Egyptian policy toward Israel and to try to work more

---

Israeli government demanded that West Germany bar its nationals from working on armaments in Egypt. Since this was not possible legally under the Constitution of the Federal Republic, the West German government sought to persuade some of its nationals to quit the UAR by offering them jobs at home.

[37] John F. Kennedy was elected President of the United States in 1960. He was assassinated in Dallas, Texas, in November 1963.

Period of Trial and Hope

closely with the modernizing forces in the Arab world".[38] Consequently he decided on granting the UAR substantial assistance mainly in the shape of "foodstuffs".[39] But this move was resented in some quarters. Thus in a letter to President Kennedy, Senator Ernest Gruening of Alaska stated that Nasser was left free to exchange his cotton for Russia's missiles largely because the United States was supplying a vital part of the food needs of the Egyptian people under P.L. 480. It was as if American dollars were being used directly to pay for the arms purchased. Senator Gruening felt that unless the U.S. policy of building up Nasser was reversed, it was going to result in a "bloody war in the Middle East" for which the United States would bear a certain responsibility.[40] Echoing a similar point of view, Senator Jacob Javits of New York stated in August 1963 that the UAR's expression of complete hostility against Israel pointed to the necessity for safeguards to prevent the misuse of economic assistance provided by the United States. The situation, according to him, called for a sharp change in USA's policy toward the UAR whose actions demonstrated that it was pursuing policies which were in direct contravention to the objectives of U.S. foreign aid program. He felt that U.S. assistance was making it possible for the UAR to indulge in aggressive acts.[41] A request to the U.S. government to "give aid and help" to her friends and not to her enemies was made by Representative Milton W. Glenn of New Jersey. He argued that since Israel was known to be "pro-American and

---

[38] Arthur M. Schlesinger, Jr., *A Thousand Days: John F. Kennedy in the White House*, New York, 1967, p. 522.

[39] President John F. Kennedy, Press Conference, 7 June 1962, *Public Papers of the President of the United States, John F. Kennedy*, 1962, Washington, D.C., 1963, p. 461.

[40] *Congressional Record*, 35n., p. 8292.

[41] *Ibid.*, p. 14821.

anti-Communist", she had a better claim to generous U.S. assistance than the UAR.⁴²

The official policy of the U.S. government was, however, defended by Assistant Secretary of State Frederick G. Dutton who pointed out that "free world interests in the Near East were at their greatest peril in the mid and late fifties when the United States had no aid program to the UAR". This dangerous situation had been gradually reversed by the policy followed by the Kennedy Administration in the early sixties, and the capacity of the United States to exert a constructive influence on a wide variety of issues pertaining to the Middle East, while still limited, was far greater in 1963 than at any time in the past.⁴³ This, to a large extent, was due to President Kennedy's ability in penetrating to the heart of the complex problem of Israeli-Arab affairs and in adopting a basically correct attitude to this problem—that of real understanding and sympathy for both the Jewish and Arab national liberation movements, without in any way placing one against the other or accepting one of these movements' case at the expense of the other. Kennedy understood the explosive potential of the Arab-Israeli claims regarding Palestine and the difficulties involved in solving it by direct confrontation. He therefore maintained an attitude of strict impartiality in respect to it

Kennedy also showed great sensitivity to the internal problems of the Middle Eastern countries. He addressed himself not exclusively to the threat of communism, but also showed concern about the people and states involved. He understood the "necessity of dealing with the reality of other people's situation, using

---

⁴² *Ibid.*, 28n., p. 8101.

⁴³ *Ibid.*, 35n., p. 20576. U.S. officials, as a matter of fact, came to believe during the Kennedy Administration that Arab friendship was a prime requisite for American security in the Middle East, and they felt that an open display of U.S. sympathy for Arab problems, stepped up aid and similar overt acts would serve to win over the Arab states. *Ibid.*, 28n., p. 22124.

discussion, persuasion, and the search for mutual interests to keep the question open until it could be moved toward some solution".[44] He attempted to gain the trust and confidence of both the Arab and Jewish national leaders and then, on the basis of this trust and understanding, to try to break down the deep enmity between them. Although Kennedy did not succeed in his mission, his endeavours, nevertheless, went a long way in ensuring much improved relations between Washington and the Arab capitals.

The Kennedy Administration reconciled itself to the Middle East countries policy of positive neutrality. This marked a radical change in the policy followed by the previous (Eisenhower) Administration which had stressed on the creation of military blocs and regarded neutralism as tantamount to "pro-communism". Under President Kennedy, the United States no longer aspired to bring the Middle Eastern countries within its exclusive orbit, but recognized their right to choose their own paths. It no longer imposed a strict choice on the states of the region and a state was no longer considered to be unfriendly to the United States if it adopted a neutralist policy. Egypt's policy of non-alignment, for instance, was no longer regarded with hostility and suspicion.[45] As Kennedy said: "The question is not whether we should accept the neutralist tendencies of the Arabs, but how we can work with them. The question is not whether we should recognize the force of Arab nationalism, but how we can help to channel it along constructive lines".[46]

[44] John S. Badeau, *The American Approach to the Arab World*, New York, 1968, p. 136.

[45] The early sixties witnessed a diminution of the Middle East's strategical importance. During this period, there took place a general relaxation in the East-West tension following the Cuban Missile Crisis. This made it easier for the United States to change its political strategy in the Middle East region.

[46] *New Outlook,* January, 1964, p. 4.

Israel, however, had her misgivings about the Arab states which had openly announced their dedication to her destruction by force of arms. In this respect, the sale of the 'Hawk' missiles by the United States was only partially satisfactory to the Israelis who wanted ground-to-ground missiles like those Nasser was acquiring. To allay Israeli fears, President Kennedy pledged that the United States would "act promptly and decisively against any nation in the Middle East which attacks its neighbor," and he called for "an international effort to halt the arms race in the Middle East.[47] He warned that if this was not accomplished, the United States would not permit an imbalance to exist which might threaten the right of any country to self defense.

Since this gave rise to some misgivings among the Arab states, Kennedy dispatched a letter to each of the principal Arab heads of state in the first half of 1961, in which he assured them that the United States had really never wavered in its determination to assist the Arab peoples in their struggle for self realization. Even more important was his further assurance that the American government fully supported the right of those Arab refugees who were peacefully inclined to return to their homes in Israel.[48] This went a long way in creating an improved climate for exchanges between the U.S. and the Arab states. But Kennedy's pledge to "act promptly" in the event of an attack failed to satisfy the Israeli government which argued that a lightning attack by the Egyptian air force could destroy most of Israel's big cities in a matter of hours. Israel, therefore, desired a mutual

---

[47] On 11 August 1963, President Nasser declared that there could be no disarmament in the Middle East until the rights of the Palestinian people had been restored in Israel. The armed forces, he said, must stand as a "national shield" against Israel. *New York Times,* 12 August 1963.

[48] In August 1961, Nasser sent a lengthy reply to Kennedy's letter. After this, a correspondence sprang up between the two Presidents which went on intermittently through the Kennedy years and served as a substitute for a face to face encounter. Schlesinger, 38n., p. 522.

Period of Trial and Hope

defense pact with the United States with a view to deterring Nasser from indulging in a rash policy toward her. The United States, however, considered the possibility of an irrational air attack from Cairo to be too slight to warrant a policy shift in the shape of a defense pact with Israel that would undercut American interests in the Arab world.

American policy in the Middle East during the Kennedy Administration was, as a matter of fact, marked by its "pro-Nasserism". Nasser represented a force which Kennedy sought to win. He regarded Nasser's regime as a stable one and the UAR leader himself as a non-communist who was not inclined to tie himself hands and feet to the Soviet Union. For instance, while accepting Soviet aid, Nasser refused to accept even implied political commitment to the Soviet Union. He supported the Soviet diplomatic position when it happened to coincide with his own interests, as on the Congo issue. But at the conference of the neutral nations held in Belgrade in September 1961, he spoke out strongly against the Soviet resumption of nuclear testing; his delegation was openly in league with the Chinese against the Russians at the Afro-Asian conference in Moshi, Tanganyika, in February 1962; and he repeatedly persecuted local communist elements despite protests from Moscow. Nasser made it clear that although his views on certain international questions happened to coincide with those of the Soviet Union, his affiliation was with the neutral and not the Soviet camp. Nasser had, moreover, adopted a surprisingly moderate attitude when the United States had its showdown with the Soviet Union over the Cuban missile bases in October 1962, even though Nasser had been a big booster of the Cuban Premier Fidel Castro in the past.[49] All these factors convinced Kennedy of the desirability of fostering friendly relations with Nasser. This, as I have pointed out earlier, was sought to be achieved partly through the grant of assistance to the UAR, main-

[49] *Washington Post*, 11 January 1963.

ly in the shape of "foodstuffs". In 1960, the food supplied by the United States to the UAR totalled only $125 million. This amount increased in 1961-62 to $236 million. During the two subsequent years, the total value of foodstuffs sent to the UAR was also substantially higher than the 1960 figure; $198 million in 1962-63, and $220 million in 1963-64. In contrast, U.S. aid to Israel totalled only $82 million in 1962-63, and $78 million in 1963-64.[50]

In April 1962, Chester Bowles and Edward Mason as representatives of the Kennedy Administration visited the UAR to examine the economic situation there and to consolidate the economic ties still further. They presented an encouraging report, and the UAR reported that the United States had agreed to supply food products of the total value of $500 million over the following three years.[51] But the UAR-US relations suffered a setback when the U.S. Senate passed a resolution in 1963, that the Administration halt aid to any recipient in the Middle East if it should be proved that it was being used for the preparation of aggression against another recipient (Israel) of the U.S. assistance. Toward the end of the same year (1963) President Kennedy was assassinated and his death came as a deep shock to all the Arabs who felt that they had lost the first American statesman with some sympathy for their point of view. They were not reassured when President Lyndon B. Johnson, who succeeded Kennedy, made a pledge to continue Kennedy's policies, and to

---

[50] The modest U.S. aid to Israel was justified on the ground of Israel's better economic position. The United States, however, overlooked the fact that because of her tremendous immigration and development burden, Israel's requirement of aid, despite her favourable economic condition, was far greater than what she received from the United States. At the same time, it might be noted that Israel received substantial contribution from private sources in the United States such as the United Jewish Appeal as well as from the sale of Israeli bonds in the United States. *Congressional Record*, 27n., p. 11040.

[51] *New Outlook*, January, 1964, pp. 17-18.

search for a "permanent settlement . . . dealing with the basic causes of conflict". As a matter of fact, President Johnson soon gave evidence of being sensitive to the pressure of the American Jewish vote and maintained only a "limited friendship" with the UAR till about the middle of 1966. But by the end of 1966 U.S. attitude had become "cold", and by 1967 UAR was convinced that the goal of U.S. policy was "to overthrow the [Nasser] regime in Egypt".[52]

SHARING OF THE JORDAN RIVER WATERS

It would not be out of place at this point to mention about the efforts made by the United States to promote the well-being of both Israel and her Arab neighbours through the regional development of the Jordan Valley waterpower and irrigation resources. This project was of considerable importance to both Israel and her neighbouring Arab states since a crisis had arisen over the sharing of the waters of the Jordan River due to Israel's need to bring water to its barren Negev southland where most of the immigrant settlement was taking place. Israel contended that the water was needed to enable her to absorb another two million immigrants. The Arab states, which regarded any growth of population in Israel as a threat to their security, opposed this project and publicised a number of their own schemes to divert the head-waters of the river before they reached Israeli territory. The Arab states of Lebanon, Syria and Jordan, in particular, expressed fear that the diversion of the Jordan River by Israel would deprive them of their rightful share of water and, moreover, would increase the salinity of the river south of the Sea of Galilee.

[52] Statement made by David G. Nes, Charge d'Affairs of the U.S. Embassy in Cairo from March till May 1967. He resigned from the State Department early in 1968. *New York Times*, 9 February 1968.

In an effort to resolve the conflicting claims, President Eisenhower sent Eric Johnston, Chairman of the International Advisory Board of the TCA, in 1953, as his personal agent to the Middle East. In four trips to the area, extending to 1955, Mr. Johnston hammered out a compromise plan which won the approval of both the Arab and Israeli engineers. This plan sought to allocate to Lebanon, Syria and Jordan a total of 60 per cent of Jordan River waters and 40 per cent to Israel. Neither side, however, wholly accepted the implementation of the plan. The Lebanese and the Syrian governments, moreover, threatened to divert their sources of the Jordan River to prevent Israel from carrying out its diversion plans. The Soviet government declared that the Israeli plan to divert the Jordan waters into the Negev desert was tantamount to "robbing the Arab world of its own water", and supported the envisaged effort on the part of the Arabs to divert the Jordan waters.[53]

The Arab governments, however, feared that Israel might be prepared to go to war on the Jordan water issue to assert her claim to at least the amount of water allocated to her under the Johnston Plan.[54] The Arab governments, therefore, decided at a summit meeting held in January 1964, to establish a joint military command to meet any possible threat from Israel. The Arab-Israeli dispute over the Jordan waters thus had the effect of bringing the Arab governments close together. Shortly after the Arab summit conference, the official Soviet news organ *Izvestia* alleging that the Israeli plan had the backing of the Western powers,

[53] *Mizan*, vol. 9, no. 3, May-June, 1967, p. 99.

[54] As a matter of fact, from early 1964, Israel started diverting the Jordan waters from the Sea of Galilee which was well within the Israeli jurisdiction. Since the diversion took place entirely within Israeli territory and since only the amount allocated under the Johnston Plan was taken, Israel felt perfectly justified in resorting to it. G. Smith, "Diversion of the Jordan Waters", *The World Today*, vol. 22, November, 1966, pp. 493-94.

declared: "One can understand the position adopted by the Arab states in the face of the aggressive policy of the Israeli extremists".[55] The Soviet Union thus clearly expressed its partisanship for the Arab cause.

The United States has consistently held the view that a solution to the dispute might be found if the Arabs and the Israelis could be made to work together on projects that would benefit both economically. In this connection, the striking advances made in the field of nuclear energy production and its application to the art of desalting saline water that can be used for intensive agriculture assumes particular significance in view of its possible use in the Sinai-Negev area.[56] American interest in this matter became evident within a few days after the end of the June 1967 Arab-Israeli war, when Admiral Lewis L. Strauss, a former Chairman of the Atomic Energy Commission, submitted a memorandum calling for the establishment of three large nuclear power and desalting plants in Israel and Jordan.

Following this development, Senator Howard H. Baker of Tennessee introduced a resolution in the Senate in October 1967, calling upon the President to pursue the objective of promptly making available American technology and resources for the "design, construction and operation of nuclear desalting plants that will provide large quantities of fresh water to both Arab and Israeli territories". He expected the desalting plants to "produce a quantity of fresh water greater than the combined flow of the major tributaries of the Jordan River".[57] It was believed that the abundant supply of fresh water would make it possible to

[55] *Izvestia*, 26 January 1964.
[56] *Times of India*, Delhi, 25 May 1968, p. 6.
[57] U.S. Senate, Congress 90, Session 1, Committee on Foreign Relations, Hearings on S. Res. 155, *Construction of Nuclear Desalting Plants in the Middle East*, Washington, D.C., 1967, p. 3. For the text of Senate Resolution 155, see Appendix IX.

irrigate vast desert regions and thus help to bring into bloom a new area in the Middle East, large enough to resettle all the Arab refugees. It was also hoped that the living standards of the people in that region would also, generally speaking, rise along with the development of industry stimulated by cheap atomic power.

But the United States now appears to believe that economic cooperation between Israel and the Arab nations would have to be founded on political understanding, and in its absence it would be premature for her to press for regional cooperation on them. The United States would probably wish to get the Soviet Union involved in any project for desalination in the Middle East involving the use of atomic energy. The ground has already been prepared for fruitful collaboration between the two superpowers in this respect. In November 1964, the United States and the Soviet Union had signed an agreement for cooperation in the area of desalination including the application of atomic energy. It is hoped that both the superpowers would take an initiative in this matter jointly in which event it would be difficult either for the Arabs or the Israelis to brush it aside. The aim should be to change the atmosphere in the Middle East, to turn the focus of thoughts from the hatred and feuds of the past to the opportunities of the future.

SOVIET MIDDLE EAST POLICY SINCE KHRUSHCHEV

Soviet Middle East policy under Nikita Khrushchev underwent a radical change particularly with the rise of Nasser in Egypt. Arab nationalism had become the most vital revolutionary force in the Middle East in the fifties, and the Soviet Union, feeling constricted by the extension of the NATO into the Middle East with Turkey's adherence and by the subsequent agreement leading toward the Baghdad Pact, came to see Arab nationalism as their logical ally. "The Arab world . . . emerged in Soviet eyes as the great progressive force in the Middle East",[58] and Soviet interests in the Middle East by 1955 coincided with the policies of a number of Arab countries in that region.

However, Soviet Union's relations with Egypt did not always run smoothly despite the aid given by her and the rapidly expanding trade between the two countries.[59] While welcoming Soviet arms and Soviet aid, Nasser had his misgivings about communist activities in certain countries in the Middle East and, in 1959, he took steps to curb the propaganda activities of the Soviet mission in Cairo. At the same time he invigorated his drive to extirpate local communist influence within he UAR. He lashed out in particular against the Syrian communists and also ordered wide scale arrests of communists throughout the UAR. The anticommunist nature of UAR's internal policy led Khrushchev to remark that Nasser was making a great mistake in trying to suppress "progressive and democratic forces". He termed Nasser's manifestations of anti-communism "a reactionary affair",[60] and warned that this policy would not bring him victory. Nasser retorted sharply on 17 March 1959, declaring that:

> Mr. Khrushchev's defence of communists in our country is unacceptable to the Arab people. We do not interefere in the

---

[58] Laqueur, *USSR and Middle East,* 4n., p. 156.

[59] Egyptian trade with the USSR increased four-fold between 1954 and 1958, and, combined with the trade with Eastern Europe, it amounted to about 35 per cent of Egypt's total foreign trade. Leo Tansky, *U.S. and U.S.S.R. Aid to Developing Countries: A Comparative Study of India, Turkey and the UAR,* New York, 1967, p. 150.

[60] Khrushchev, however, made it clear that although there were ideological differences with the UAR, "in questions connected with the struggle against imperialism", their views coincided. *Mizan,* vol. 10, no. 6, November-December, 1968, p. 220.

internal affairs of the Soviet Union and we do not support any section of the people there against another.[61]

Following the meeting of the eighty-one communist parties in Moscow in November 1960, Soviet attitude towards the UAR somewhat stiffened. Resolutions adopted there stipulated that full communist support should be given only when the country concerned carried out a consistent, anti-Western line on foreign policy, pursued "progressive" internal reforms and gave local communists complete freedom of action. The UAR government was criticized for its anti-communist measures, especially the harsh treatment meted out to the Egyptian and Syrian communists.[62] The UAR had gone to the extent of banning the local communist party. But her dependence upon the Soviet Union for economic and military aid compelled her to modify her stand and strive for a closer understanding with the USSR. After the November 1960 meeting of the eighty-one communist parties, the UAR gradually modified its internal policy under Soviet pressure and adopted "socialist" measures.

The visit of Premier Khrushchev to the UAR in May 1964,[63] on the occasion of the completion of the first stage of the Aswan Dam marked a turning point in the Soviet-UAR relations. The occasion was marked by a reaffirmation of the ties between the two countries which Khrushchev hoped would grow stronger and more profound. At the conclusion of Khrushchev's visit it was announced that Russia had agreed to give the UAR a long-term

[61] *Mansfield*, 26n., p. 92.

[62] *Mizan*, vol. 1, no. 4, April 1959, Appendix, pp. 3-4.

[63] One of the principal aims of Khrushchev's visit to the UAR in May 1964, was to seek President Nasser's support for the recognition of Russia as an Afro-Asian power and of her claim to be invited to the Second Bandung Conference—which was eventually held in Algiers. Khrushchev was seeking Afro-Asian support against China while Nasser was attempting to enlist Soviet support against the British in Yemen and South Arabia as well as against Israel. *Amrita Bazar Patrika*, Calcutta, 15 May 1964.

Period of Trial and Hope

loan of 252 million roubles and that she had also agreed to set up a steel plant in the UAR with an annual capacity of a million tons as well as to furnish aid for the building of a thermal electric power station.[64] As a matter of fact, during Khrushchev's regime extensive economic and military assistance programs had been initiated and these had become the principal Soviet instrumentalities for establishing a Soviet presence in the Middle East and for pursuing other political objectives in the area. Soviet aid commitments had been directed towards such multiple economic activities as technical assistance, agricultural development, industrial development and the building of large scale national enterprises. The Soviet aid programs made a political impact on the Middle East and enabled the Russians to establish their presence in the area. However, Soviet efforts in economic development had been marked by both success and failure. Their military program had been, on the whole, more effective. As the primary vehicle for Soviet offensive in the Middle East, it enabled the Soviet Union to achieve a position of influence in some areas very important to the United States' and Western interests.[65]

After Khrushchev's fall from power in October 1964, the new leadership under Leonid Brezhnev, First Secretary of the Communist Party of the Soviet Union, and Alexei Kosygin, Chairman of the Council of Ministers, made no substantial changes in the Soviet approach to the Middle East. The political line of the Soviet Union, however, seems to have been aimed after Khrushchev's downfall more at the promotion of "common interests" than at the mere granting of unconditional aid to some of the countries of the Middle East. The new leadership also undertook a reassessment of Soviet aid commitments and early in 1965, aid was cut back. Internal economic problems and an awareness of

---

[64] *Ibid.*, 26 May 1964.
[65] For an evaluation of the effect of Soviet foreign aid programmes, see 34n., pp. 968-73.

the contradiction in the means and ends of Soviet foreign aid were cited as reasons for the cutback.[66] The Soviets thereafter appeared to place greater stress on "common interests" as a criterion for aid and sought to establish firmer control over regimes which, like Nasser's, had by that time appeared to have gone beyond the point of retreat in their conflict with the West. For example, the new Soviet arms shipment to Egypt clearly served a common interest: it enabled Nasser to continue his war in Yemen, while simultaneously enabling the Soviets to maintain their influence in Yemen with the opportunities it offered for penetrating East Africa and the Persian Gulf region.[67]

The danger of Chinese competition in the Middle East also made it seem advisable to the Soviet Union to replace the merely voluntary engagement of the "neutralist" countries of the region with more solid ties. The Chinese were, in fact, competing with the Russians for influence and friends among the Arabs.[68] China pressed her case by supporting liberation wars, particularly those to which the Soviet Union seemed to hesitate to commit herself, such as the Palestine Liberation Movement.[69] To befriend the Arabs, China also offered prospects of gainful trade and em-

[66] Marshall I. Goldman, *Soviet Foreign Aid,* New York, 1967, p. 197.

[67] Arnold Hottinger, "Moscow's influence in the Arab World", *Swiss Review of World Affairs,* vol. 15, April, 1965, pp. 11-12. According to a press report from Cairo in May 1966, the Soviets had about 1,000 technicians and medical personnel in republican Yemen and strongly backed the Egyptian military presence there. *Christian Science Monitor,* 12 May 1966, p. 1.

[68] The Arabs on their part appeared to be anxious to preserve contacts with China since they apprehended that as a result of the Sino-Soviet conflict, the Russians might be compelled to take the side of the West publicly. *Al Akhbar,* Cairo, 4 September 1963, cited in *International Studies* 15n., p. 366.

[69] The Chinese leaders have long used the Palestine issue to turn the Arabs against the West and the Soviet Union, thus enlisting them as a 'special force' in the latent basic struggles which centre on the Taiwan

Period of Trial and Hope

phasized cultural links between the Arabs and Chinese Muslims. The Chinese Premier Chou en-lai, for instance, during a visit to the UAR in 1964, emphasized "the unity of the ancient civilization of China embodied by the Great Wall and the Egyptian civilization symbolized by the Pyramids".[70] China's support for the Arabs was also manifested in her condemnation of "American support" and "aid" to Israel and of "criminal acts committed by Israel." It should be noted, however, that China's interest in the Middle East were not identical with those of the Soviet Union.[71] Unlike the latter China did not have global security worries, and any fundamental change in the Middle East was unlikely to have much impact on her. On the other hand, the Soviet Union, as also the United States, were directly involved in this area. The lack of global commitments together with freedom for diplomatic manoeuvre gave China an advantage over the Soviet Union. Chinese support for the Arabs, for instance, was total and therefore embarrassing to the Russians who were more cautious in their approach.

Realizing Russia's handicaps, Brezhnev and Kosygin adopted a flexible and less doctrinaire approach in dealing with the Middle East. Criticism of Arab socialism, a marked characteristic of the latter period of Khrushchev's regime, was muted and distinctions between "scientific" socialism and their variants in the underdeveloped areas were blurred. Stress was now given to the re-

Straits and the long frontiers in Central Asia. See W.A.C. Adie, "China's Middle East Strategy", *The World Today*, August 1967, p. 318.

[70] *Summary of World Broadcasts*, Pt. 1, 12 May 1964.

[71] The basic difference in approach between China and the Soviet Union lay in the Soviet desire for peaceful co-existence, detente with the West and peaceful settlement in areas of tension so as to prevent local wars from escalating into a general one, and the Chinese stress on the fight against imperialism and armed struggle as a means of achieving their aims. A further difference was the Chinese refusal to compromise with the "imperialists" in national liberation wars.

volutionary substance of Nasser's "Arab socialism",[72] for example; but distinctions were still made between this variant and the undiluted Soviet type.[73] The "new look" in the Soviet attitude was designed essentially to link the "bourgeois" revolutionary leaders of the underdeveloped areas to Soviet political and ideological interests. In practical terms, for the Middle East this meant a close alliance with Arab nationalism and all its constituent parts. The immediate goal was to inject Soviet political influence and to use it as a lever for rolling back Western power and influence. The long term goal was to transform the regimes into socialist and ultimately communist models whose interests would presumably be symmetrical with those of the Soviet Union.[74] Peaceful coexistence was the principle applied in achieving these goals. It established the framework for policy formulation and prescribed the instrumentalities for policy execution. War in the thermonuclear age was considered rationally unacceptable; but this did not imply the denial of communism's historic commitment to revolutionary action. Accordingly, Soviet policy in the Middle East was based on the assumption that a direct military confrontation with the United States was to be avoided and that Soviet goals, particularly in the Arab states, were to be pursued at a lower threshold of danger, mainly through programs of extensive military and

---

[72] Kremlin's desire to foster closer relations with the UAR led to a visit by Nasser to the Soviet Union in August 1965. In a joint communique issued on that occasion, the Soviet leaders noted with satisfaction the efforts of the UAR government in building and improving the economic structure of the UAR and creating a democratic socialist state.

[73] Philip E. Mosely, "Communist Policy in the Third World", *Review of Politics*, vol. 28, April 1966, p. 215.

[74] For discussions of this change in Soviet theory, see Richard Lowenthal, "Russia, the One Party System, and the Third World", *Soviet Survey*, January 1966, pp. 43-58; and Jaan Pennar "Moscow and Socialism in Egypt", *Problems of Communism*, vol. 15, September-October, 1966, pp. 41-47.

economic aid.⁷⁵ In pursuance of these objectives, the Soviet Union (a) continued efforts to reduce the Western power position and undermine capitalism in the area, using the instrumentalities of economic aid; (b) made efforts to strengthen Soviet influence by supporting Arab aspirations, opposing the goals of Israel, and by expanding military and economic assistance to the Arab world; and (c) expressed its opposition to open hostilities in the area and its desire to avoid any military confrontation with the United States.⁷⁶

Under the new Soviet leadership, the tendency towards improving relations with the Arab states appeared to continue. Generally speaking, the Soviet Union pursued a policy of lowering political pressures everywhere in the Middle East with the exception of the Persian Gulf states which were criticized as pawns of British strategy and of the Western oil monopolies. The Kremlin directed particular attention to strengthening and improving its ties with the UAR. With this end in view, Premier Kosygin paid an eight day visit to the UAR in May 1966. The visit gave the Soviet leader an opportunity to tighten the Cairo-Moscow relationship with promises of economic aid and by Soviet support for Egyptian foreign policy objectives. It also gave the Soviet Union the chance to demonstrate her influence in the Third World,⁷⁷ and served as a reminder to the West that the Russians

---

[75] It might be noted that while the emphasis in Soviet Union's relations with Turkey and Iran was mainly on economic collaboration, Soviet political and military help together with economic assistance was the great attraction for the Arab states.

[76] Institute for Strategic Studies, London, "Sources of Conflict in the Middle East", *Adelphi Papers,* No. 26, March, 1966, pp. 6-7.

[77] For the Soviet leaders their success in the Middle East was particularly important because of their concern to demonstrate to the Communist World that their moderate policies vis-a-vis Chinese intransigence had paid off. The fact that the UAR and other "progressive" regimes were gradually shifting from non-alignment toward open support of the Soviet

had established a paramount position in what was widely regarded as the most influential country in the Arab world.[78]

RENEWED SOVIET INTEREST IN IRAN AND TURKEY

Among the non-Arab states along the Northern Tier—Iran and Turkey—the Soviet Union pursued a policy of accommodation. The establishment of military bases by the West in both the countries in the fifties made the Soviet "southern belly" somewhat vulnerable. The Soviet Union therefore had a vital interest in neutralizing the strategical advantages of the West on her southern flank and hence she started cultivating friendly relations with both Iran and Turkey. In these two countries, the relaxation in bipolar confrontation in the sixties gave rise to a conviction that the military danger from the North had passed away and that the Soviet Union had given up its old annexationist aims.[79]

The Soviet Union moved to improve her relations with Iran after she had received assurances in September 1962, about Iran's intention not to permit rocket bases on her territory, by concluding agreements on trade, frontiers, transit traffic, and economic cooperation.[80] The Shah of Iran visited the USSR in 1965. This

camp was a tremendous feather in the Russian cap, sorely needed in view of Chinese inroads into the liberation movement of the Far East. David Kimche, "Soviet Aims in the Middle East", *Midstream*, August-September, 1967, p. 58.

[78] *Current Digest of the Soviet Press*, 8 June 1966, pp. 3-6.

[79] Suspicion on the part of Turkey and Iran of their powerful neighbour in the North did not, however, fade away completely. It emerged again with the appearance of the Soviet fleet in the Mediterranean and Soviet intervention in Czechoslovakia in 1968.

[80] In October 1962, the Soviet Union concluded a transit agreement with Iran that resorted for the first time in more than two decades Iran's right to send goods to Europe through the Soviet Union; and in 1963, the Soviet Union granted Iran a credit of 35 million roubles to enable her to meet her share of the cost of a joint barrage on the frontier river Araxes.

was followed by the signing of a technical aid agreement in January 1966, and aid was promised for a number of projects such as iron and steel works, a gas pipe line etc. In February 1966, a $110 million arms agreement was signed and the USSR provided a $100 million credit to be repaid in eight years at $2\frac{1}{2}$ per cent interest. Under a new long-term trade agreement signed in March 1967, Iran and the Soviet Union agreed to exchange some $540 million worth of goods by 1972. Soviet credits extended to Iran already total $500 million.[81] In January 1967, Iran obtained from the Soviet Union trucks, anti-aircraft guns and other equipment worth $90 million[82] in exchange for her natural gas. Though this deal was more symbolic than strategic, yet it was considered a slap in the face of the United States which had poured more than $1 billion worth of arms aid into Iran since 1950.[83]

The Soviet deal demonstrated the extent to which the Soviet Union had undermined the U.S. backed Central Treaty Organization (CENTO), with which the former Secretary of State John Foster Dulles had hoped to forge an anti-Soviet alliance along Russia's southern flank. Besides Soviet desire to cultivate close relations with Iran with a view to making her less dependent on the West, two other factors tended to bring the

G. G. Stevens, ed., *The United States and the Middle East*, New Jersey, 1964, p. 104; *Times of India*, Delhi, 30 January 1965.

[81] *Foreign Affairs*, vol. 47, January, 1969, p. 301.

[82] President Nasser was believed to have been shocked by the Soviet-Iran arms agreement. For years vigorous rivalry existed between the Shah and Nasser, and the latter presumably looked upon the agreement as a measure designed to constrict his pretentions of political leadership in the Middle East. *New York Times*, 19 February 1967, p. E4.

[83] Some observers believed that Iran's purchase of (non-sensitive) weapons from Russia was designed as much to persuade the United States to sell her (Iran) sophisticated items like Phantom jets, as to open new channels for contingency procurement if the United States were to withhold future exports for whatever reasons.

two countries together. First was the Shah's growing desire in recent years to demonstrate that, despite the massive outpouring of American aid, he was not a catspaw of the West. The second element was Teheran's growing dissatisfaction with the terms of U.S. military aid. As Iran grew more prosperous, the United States began phasing out direct grants of military equipment. It agreed to continue selling arms to the Shah, but at prices and interest rates on credit that the Iranians considered too high. These factors, *inter alia,* prompted Iran to normalize her relations with the Soviet Union.

Soviet relations with Turkey manifested the same tendency toward accomodation as in the case of Iran. The so-called Turkish revolution of May 1960, had signalled a serious Soviet attempt to improve relations. Socialist trends in Turkey came to be looked upon in terms similar to that of Arab socialism; un-Marxian but still deserving of Soviet support because it opposed capitalism. Moreover, the withdrawal of U.S. missiles from the Turkish soil in 1964 was looked upon with satisfaction by the Soviet Union and it made a dramatic move in the early part of 1965 to befriend Turkey by endorsing the latter's stand in favour of a federal solution in Cyprus.[84] The primary Soviet interest concerning Cyprus was to see that the island did not turn into a Western military base aligned to NATO. On her part, Turkey, though still loyal to NATO and to its American connection, had become increasingly restive and was seeking a more independent policy and hence welcomed the Soviet friendly gesture. By contrast, the lack of U.S. support for Turkey's aspirations in respect of Cyprus resulted in considerable disappointment in Ankara and, perhaps, played a part in bringing about its rapprochement with Moscow.

[84] This constituted a basic departure from Khrushchev's earlier support to President Makarios and the Greek Cypriots in their fighting against the Turkish Cypriots. *Times of India* (Delhi), 30 January 1965.

Period of Trial and Hope

Soviet relations with Turkey appeared to reach a new high with the Soviet Premier's visit to Turkey in December 1966. This was followed by the conclusion of a significant economic aid agreement with Turkey on 25 March 1967. In September 1967, the Turkish Premier visited the Soviet Union[85] and soon thereafter several aid projects were inaugurated, including an oil refinery near Izmir and an iron and steel complex. There had also taken place a marked increase in the value of trade between the two countries from seven million roubles in 1961 to 45 million roubles in 1966.[86] As a matter of fact, the Soviet Union having recognized and reversed the mistakes of Stalin's time, has been striving actively since the early sixties to demonstrate a friendly attitude toward Turkey and Iran and to impress upon the two countries the great benefit that would accrue to both of them from closer economic relations with her. Moscow has, at the same time, encouraged them to adopt a less committed position which would make them less dependent on American support and, therefore, on American policy.[87] It has to be remembered that Turkey and Iran lie adjacent to the southern border of the Soviet Union and that

---

[85] After his return from the Soviet Union, the Turkish Premier declared that the visit had eliminated "the last traces of hostility" from Soviet-Turkish relations. "I think we have entered a new era in our dealings with the Russians", he declared in an interview. "As you know", the Turkish Premier said, "there has been great strain between our countries over the years, and in the period after World War II, we had no relations at all." He went on to say:"Now that gap has been bridged. I am not suggesting that all the doubt's are gone, but I think the hostility is gone". *New York Times,* 13 October 1967, p. 9.

[86] Geoffrey Wheeler, "Soviet Interests in Iran, Iraq and Turkey", *The World Today,* May, 1968, p. 200.

[87] Soviet thrust into the "Northern Tier" region of the Middle East coupled with increased Soviet involvement in the triangular area embracing the Red Sea Basin, North Africa, and Northeastern Africa, led some American officials to predict that this important strategic area might be the

both the countries have been used as forward military bases by the United States and the West. It is, therefore, in Soviet interest to maintain friendly relations with them and, if possible, to win them over.[88]

scene of the next Soviet-American confrontation. *Washington Post*, 9 April 1967, p. A1.

[88] The bitter Soviet relations with China and, particularly, her controversy with the latter over her eastern boundaries also led the USSR to desire for peace along her south-western frontier bordering Turkey and Iran.

CHAPTER THREE

The Third Arab-Israeli War: Prelude and Aftermath

Eruption of Border Conflicts between Israel and the Arab States

The sudden eruption of the Middle East crisis in May-June, 1967, had its genesis in the Syrian-Israeli border conflicts. For nine years after the cataclysm of Suez, Israel lived in relative peace. The calm ended on the nights of January 3 and January 7, 1965, when two water installations were dynamited inside the Israeli border by Arab irregulars known as Fedayeens[1] belonging to a terrorist organization called Al Fatah[2] which had

---

[1] The word 'Fedayeen' comes from the Arabic root 'sacrifice', i.e., those who sacrifice themselves or assume a suicidal mission. See Institute for Strategic Studies, London, *Adelphi Papers*, No. 53, December, 1968, p. 1.

[2] Al Fatah was founded around 1955 by a Palestinian named Yasir Arafat who had become disillusioned with the official Arab leadership for the liberation of Palestine. During the early years however, the group was small and had no substantial financial support and was in no way prepared to engage in military action. From January 1965, the Al Fatah received some assistance from the Syrian intelligence. But with the advent to power of a new Syrian government in February 1966, a decision was taken to support the Al Fatah in a much bigger way than before, and from July 1966, the organization came entirely under Syrian control.

been formed by the Palestinians to liberate their homeland from Israel. The organization received active support from Syria which trained its men and furnished arms and equipments. The Fedayeen raids created a sense of insecurity in Israel and compelled the Israeli government to retaliate every now and then by attacking Fedayeen bases as well as public property in Arab villages and towns across the border. Till July 1966, these retaliatory raids were carried out against Jordan and Lebanon which were held responsible for Al Fatah activities from their soil. In July 1966, however, Israeli airforce bombed and strafed across the Syrian border and on 15 August 1966, both sides fought a major battle with planes, artillery and patrol boats in the Lake Tiberias area. The Israeli-Syrian situation became increasingly critical, and in October 1966, Israel requested an urgent meeting of the U.N. Security Council complaining that armed groups operating from Syria had been committing acts of aggression against Israeli citizens and property and that high Syrian officials had been making open threats against Israel's territorial integrity and political independence. Syria denied responsibility for the activities of Al Fatah and at the same time refused to halt its infiltration operations into Israel.[3]

During the Security Council debates the United States along with other Western powers pressed Syria to recognize her "responsibilities" to prevent raids from being mounted from her soil.[4] The Soviet Union, on the other hand, expressed concern over Israeli "threats of aggression" against Syria. A six-power

---

Al Asifa, the military branch of Al Fatah, was set up in 1965. Its members received specialized military training and they were given explosives and arms by Syria for their raids into Israel. Walter Laqueur, *The Road to War*, Baltimore, 1969, pp. 68-69. Hereafter cited as Laqueur, *Road to War*.

[3] *New York Times*, 15 October 1966.
[4] U.N. Doc. S/7568.

The Third Arab-Israeli War

proposal[5] calling upon the Security Council to "deplore" the incidents was vetoed by the Soviet Union on the ground that the proposal wrongly implied that Syria was to blame for the Al Fatah incursions. Israel, however, felt the large support for the six-power proposals represented a rebuke to Syria and a political and moral victory for her.[6]

In November 1966, Syria and Egypt[7] signed a defense pact which provided that if one of the parties became the victim of aggression, the other would immediately use all means at its disposal, including armed forces, to repulse the aggressor. Although this was clearly intended to deter Israel from aggressive actions, Nasser was not in favour of a military showdown with her at least until the Arab world was adequately prepared for war. The Soviet Union too, anxious to avoid a major upheaval in the Middle East, urged Syrian leaders to restrict the scale of Arab guerrilla operations against Israel.[8]

Tension between Syria and Israel had hardly subsided somewhat before a grave crisis developed unexpectedly between Israel and Jordan. On November 13, 1966, Israel launched her biggest offensive since Suez against Jordan. A reprisal raid on a Jordanian frontier village, which had harboured Syrian terrorists, escalated into a major conflict. Israel contended that her retaliatory assault was meant to be a warning of her determination not to allow attacks against her citizens to proceed unchecked. She also claimed that an attacked state had a right to defend itself so long as the Security Council did not adopt

---

[5] *Ibid.*, S/7575.
[6] *New York Times*, 29 December 1966.
[7] Egypt and Syria had united together in 1958 to form the United Arab Republic with Abdel Gamal Nasser as President. This union was terminated on 28 September 1961, by the Syrians who had never been entirely happy under Nasser's leadership. U.S. in *World Affairs*, 1961, p. 182.
[8] *New York Times*, 23 December 1966.

effective measures to stop the aggressor.[9] The Security Council met soon after the Israeli action and censured her.[10] The U.S. government not only supported this move, but also airlifted several million dollars worth of defensive weapons and equipment to Jordan in order to bolster the internal position of King Hussein who was threatened with deposition by the militant groups within Jordan. It was also intended to preclude the need for Jordan to turn to the Soviet Union for arms. It might be noted here that through West Germany, the United States had also supplied Israel substantial quantity of arms in 1965, and in February 1966, she had shipped directly to Israel 200 Patton tanks.[11]

Despite Israel's "warning" action against Jordan and her efforts to seal her frontiers against Al Fatah raids, by the middle of January 1967, border incidents and infiltrations by Arab commandos began to occur again with increasing frequency and the Syrian-Israeli frontier once again became the scene of a series of incidents. On April 7, 1967, one of the most serious military clashes took place on the Syria-Israel border as a dispute over ploughing rights in the demilitarized zone. Tanks, mortars and artillery were involved and seven of Syria's most modern Russian MIG fighters were shot down by Israeli planes. Egypt, despite her defence pact with Syria, made no move. The

[9] *Ibid.*, 16 November 1966.
[10] U.N. Doc. S/7598.
[11] In 1965, the United States permitted the transfer of some American manufactured military hardware, tanks in particular, by the West German government to Israel. Shortly afterwards, the Bonn government felt compelled to cut off military aid to Israel in order to forestall the official recognition of Communist East Germany by the UAR. Under the circumstances, Israel appealed to the United States for direct military assistance especially in view of the arms supplied by the Soviet Union to Syria, Iraq and the UAR. This situation necessitated a shift in United States' policy and she sold tanks to Israel directly in February 1966. *Summary of World Broadcasts*, Pt. 3, FE/2155/A4/1, 4 May 1966.

The Third Arab-Israeli War

April 7 incident, however, multiplied the pressures on Nasser to take a more direct and active role in supporting their Syrian ally the next time she was attacked.[12] The Soviet Union did not appear to seek an immediate change in the *status quo* of the area and seemed inclined toward caution and restraint. This was evident from Moscow's cool response to a Syrian request for Soviet support for a "war of liberation" against Israel.[13] In response to the April 7 incident, the Soviet Union sent what appeared to be a fairly routine note to Israel—well after the incident occurred—blaming Israel for the attack and warning her for following a risky policy "dangerous to the cause of peace".[14]

TRIGGERING THE CRISIS

Events in May 1967 pointed towards a confrontation. Arab commandos showed increasing daring and proficiency in attacking Israeli positions and Syrian officials made threatening statements. These were countered by warnings on 11 and 12 May, 1967, by Israeli leaders that the continuance of incidents within Israel caused by terrorists coming from Syria would be met by severe reprisals. *The New York Times* reported that Israeli leaders had decided that "the use of force against Syria of considerable strength, but of short duration and limited in area", might be the only way to curtail the increasing terrorism.[15] The Israeli view was that since the Soviet Union was unwilling

---

[12] Nasser was accused by the Saudi Arabians, Jordanians and Syrians of speaking bravely—when Israel launched her large-scale reprisal assaults against Jordan and Syria—but acting meekly. *New York Times*, 10 April 1967; Charles W. Yost, "The Arab Israeli War: How it Began", *Foreign Affairs*, January, 1968, p. 305 f.
[13] *Washington Post*, 3 February 1967, p. A 21.
[14] *Pravda*, 26 April 1967.
[15] *New York Times*, 17 May 1967.

to use its influence to curb the radical Syrian leaders who talked of a liberation war against Israel, and since the United States and the other Western powers were not in a position to do anything about it, the only deterrent lay in the use or threat of Israeli force. Syria, on her part, made it known that in the event of another Israeli attack she would invoke her defense agreement with Egypt.

On 13 May 1967, Nasser received diplomatic reports which claimed that Israel was building up her forces for a military attack on Syria on 17 May. On 14 and 15 May, the UAR began major troop movements in the Sinai region. This was followed by a formal request to the U.N. Secretary General U Thant on 18 May 1967, to withdraw the U.N. Emergency Force (UNEF) from the Gaza Strip and the Sharm-el-Sheikh area; and finally, on 21 May 1967, Nasser announced the blockade of the Gulf of Aqaba and the closure of the Strait of Tiran to Israeli ships.

According to the *London Times,* the demand for the withdrawal of the UNEF was "a calculated piece of Nasserite intransigence", and that he did not expect the demand to be met, at least, not at once. At that stage all he was aiming for was "a diplomatic furore which would effectively spike any Israeli pre-emptive action against Syria."[16] The U.N. Secretary General U Thant, however, to the amazement of the Egyptians capitulated within 24 hours. The Israeli Foreign Minister Abba Eban protested that Nasser did not have the power to order the departure of the U.N. Emergency Force.[17] This decision, accord-

---

[16] *Times* (London), 28 May 1967.

[17] Israel contended that the former U.N. Secretary General, Dag Hammarskjold, had stated in a (secret) memorandum dated 5 August 1957, that since the UNEF had been set up by bilateral agreement, there were two parties to the bargain. The consequence of such a bilateral declaration was that, "were either side to act unilaterally in refusing continued pressure or deciding on withdrawal . . . an exchange of views would be

ing to him, could be taken only by the Security Council. But U Thant held that since the U.N. Emergency Force had entered Egypt with Egyptian consent, it could not remain there if the consent were withdrawn,[18] or if the conditions under which it operated were so qualified that the force was unable to function effectively.[19]

Soon after U Thant's decision to withdraw the UNEF and Nasser's declaration of blockade of the Gulf of Aqaba, the U.S. Ambassador to the UAR, Richard H. Nolte, met the UAR Foreign Minister Mahmud Riyad and presented to him the pro-

called for towards harmonizing the position". U. Thant countered this by stating that it was not an official paper but a "purely private memorandum" in which Mr. Hammarskjold appears to have recorded his own impresisons and interpretations of his discussions with President Nasser. Therefore it had no official standing and could not affect the basis for the presence of the U.N. Emergency Force in Egypt. See Laqueur, *Road to War*, 2n., p. 104.

[18] The U.N. Secretary General, U Thant, in a report on 27 June 1967 stated that the stationing of the UNEF on Egyptian territory was subject to the latter's permission and, therefore, he was obliged to withdraw the Force when Egypt so demanded on 18 May 1967. This position was supported by the two states, Yugoslavia and India, which had contingents in the UNEF. The refusal of Israel to allow the U.N. Force to operate on its side of the ceasefire line in 1967, when the Secretary General suggested that it be moved across the line from Egypt, further indicates the need for consent of the state where such a force is stationed on the basis of a "recommendation" of the General Assembly as was the case with the UNEF. See Report of the Secretary General on the withdrawal of the U.N. Emergency Force, U.N. Doc. A/6730/Add. 3, 27 June 1967. For Excerpts from the Report see Appendix VII.

[19] It has been contended by some observers that irrespective of whether U. Thant took the correct stand, the instant withdrawal of the U.N. Emergency Force contributed to the outbreak of the June 1967 war. Even if it is true that the UAR was not really prepared for so hasty a withdrawal of the UNEF, surprise soon turned into exultation when it found it had scored an easy victory. Early success acted as "heady wine" and led to glib talks of destruction of Israel. *Indian Express*, Delhi, 20 July 1967.

posal that (i) the UNEF should remain in Gaza and Sharm el-Sheikh until a decision was taken by the General Assembly; and (ii) that no armed forces should proceed to Sharm el-Sheikh until the UAR Government issued an official statement confirming the freedom of navigation in the Straits of Tiran and the entry to the Gulf of Aqaba without any conditions.[20] The proposals were, however, rejected by the UAR Foreign Minister who accused the United States of being biased towards Israel.

Some competent observers believed that the unilateral decision of the UAR to close the Gulf of Aqaba and the Straits of Tiran before the outbreak of hostilities on 5 June 1967, was contrary to the accepted practices of international law.[21] President Nasser claimed that the Gulf was his *'mare clausum'* and that it was his sovereign right to decide who would and who would not use it for shipping.[22] But the general consensus among international experts was that if a gulf was less than six miles in width, and if it was surrounded by more than one State, then the States have to come to an agreement. In the case of the Gulf of Aqaba, apart from the UAR and Israel, Saudi Arabia and Jordan also had their coastline on it. The UAR therefore could not claim the Gulf as its *'mare clausum'*. Moreover under international law and the Convention of 1958 on the territorial sea, international straits—such as the Straits of Tiran—connecting parts of the high seas or portions between the high seas and the territorial sea of a foreign state, are open to innocent passage by vessels of all states.[23] The Western

[20] *Summary of World Broadcasts,* Pt. 4, ME/2476/A/6, 26 May 1967.

[21] If the closure of the Straits of Tiran was to be taken as a precedent, it might lead to dangerous consequences. For instance, Spain might then close the Straits of Gibralter and Panama might choose to close the Panama Canal.

[22] *Summary of World Broadcasts,* Pt. 4, ME/2477/A/1, 28 May 1967.

[23] *American Journal of International Law,* vol. 52, 1958, p. 834.

Powers therefore warned that any obstruction of free passage in the Straits of Tiran or the Gulf of Aqaba was contrary to international law "entailing a possible resort to the measures authorized by Article 51 of the U.N. Charter", namely, measures that may be undertaken in exercise of the right of self-defence.[24] The freedom of the Straits of Tiran and the Gulf of Aqaba was assumed after the hostilities in 1956, particularly by the United States,[25] and the withdrawal of Israel from the Sinai area was to some extent contingent on this assumption. UAR's unilateral closure of the Straits in May 1967, was therefore a violation of the rights of Israel as well as of other states.[26] This act provided Israel with what the United States considered to be a legitimate *casus belli*. The problem was essentially one of free passage of shipping through the Straits. This was the *casus belli,* and on this question the Americans were directly involved owing to guarantees given by previous American governments which they could not ignore.

UAR's action was, however, openly supported by the Soviet Union which sought to exploit this opportunity to demonstrate to the world its support for the "Arab cause" by dramatically

---

[24] Walter Laqueur, *The Israel Arab Reader: A Documentary History of the Middle East Conflict* (New York, 1969), p. 220. Hereafter cited as Laqueur, *Documentary History.*

[25] Secretary of State Dulles declared in an aide memoire to the Israeli Ambassador on 11 February 1957 that: "The United States believes that the the Gulf of Aqaba comprehends international waters and that no nation has the right to prevent free and innocent passage in the Gulf and through the Straits giving access thereto" *Department of State Bulletin,* vol. 36, 11 March 1957, p. 387.

[26] Nasser, however, held that Israel had no lawful navigational rights in the Gulf of Aqaba, and that Israel's presence in the port of Eilat had come into existence after the 1956 armistice agreements. It was therefore within UAR's rights to ban navigation in the Straits of Tiran which she considered to be part of her territorial waters. *Al Ahram* (Cairo), 24 May 1967.

dispatching her naval vessels through the Dardanelles.[27] A warning was also given that an attempt to "unleash aggression in the Near East" by any power would be met not only with the united strength of the Arab countries, but also with strong opposition from the Soviet Union.[28] However, while in public the Russians used militant language, in private they urged restraint on both sides for they feared that an Arab-Israeli war might bring about a military confrontation between them and the Americans, and this they wanted to avoid at almost all costs. It is unlikely therefore, that while supporting Nasser, the Soviets had bargained for a war situation such as evolved on 5 June 1967. At the same time, it has been contended by some observers that Soviet support for Nasser had been a crucial factor in bringing the turbulent Middle East beyond the boiling point.

Nasser's dismissal of the U.N. Emergency Force and the blockade of the Straits of Tiran were based on intelligence information of a purported Israeli mobilization intended to overthrow the leftist regime in Syria—a lead, which informed observers believed, was supplied by Russia. Nasser himself stated after the June 1967 war that the Soviet Union had told a UAR Parliamentary Delegation which was visiting Moscow in the first half of May 1967, that there was "a calculated intention on the part of Israel to invade Syria".[29] Randolph Churchill

---

[27] Some ten Soviet naval ships moved into the Mediterranean through the Dardanelles in the last week of May 1967. The Soviet ships did not appreciably change the military balance in the region, but the seeming show of Soviet support emboldened Nasser to maintain his position on the blockade.

[28] *New York Times*, 24 May 1967, p. 17.

[29] On this point Walter Laqueur has raised a pertinent question: "An Israeli invasion of Syria with the aim of overthrowing the Damascus regime was certainly no small matter; would the Soviet Union have chosen an Egyptian parliamentary delegation visiting Russia to convey to Cairo

writing in the *Washington Post* of 3 July 1967, contended that the Soviet Government had passed on to Cairo, in early May, the report of a large concentration of Israeli troops along the Syrian border when, in fact, there were no more than a company of 120 Israeli soldiers in that particular area at that time. Even the U.N. observers along the Israeli-Syrian borders confirmed toward the end of May that they had no evidence of the alleged troop movements. According to Churchill, the Russians were probably alarmed by the possibility of a punitive Israeli raid on Syria and wanted Nasser to commit his forces "to deter the Israelis from attacking".[30] The U.S. Ambassador to the UAR at that time, Richard H. Nolte, subsequently expressed the same view that the Soviet Union "had connived in triggering" Nasser's initial move that led to the war.[31] A similar point of view was also expressed by the *Christian Science Monitor* which believed that the Soviet Union had "played a major role in the events leading to the six-day Arab Israeli war (in

information of such vital and urgent importance? There are other channels of information in such cases. Why then was the attempt made to cover up the origins of the warning?" Laqueur, *Road to War*, 2n., p. 86.

[30] *Washington Post*, 3 July 1967, p. B1.

[31] Mr. Nolte believed that after the Israeli reprisal raids against Jordan and Syria, particularly the shooting down of the seven Syrian MIG fighters on 8 April 1967, by the Israeli Air Force, the Russians quite possibly decided that this could not be allowed to go on further and that there had to be some resolute action by Nasser to stop the Israelis and to protect the Syrians and thereby recapture the "hero image". Nasser's frustration in Yemen and elsewhere in the Arab world perhaps prompted him to make a big show of reinforcing the UAR troops in the Sinai and call for the removal of the U.N. Emergency Force. Mr. Nolte also believed that the Russians encouraged Nasser to think that they were better prepared militarily than was actually the case. He suggested that Moscow was willing to help Nasser in his efforts to bolster his declining prestige, but it was not clear whether they initiated the entire manoeuver, i.e., the closing of the Strait of Tiran. But if they did, events quickly got out of their control. *New York Times*, 12 September 1967, p. 6.

June 1967)," and that the conflict might never have come about if the Soviet Union had not warned the UAR of Israel's supposed intentions to attack Syria.[32]

However, in justification of Nasser's action, it might be said that in view of his defense treaty with Syria, he had no alternative but to come to the latter's aid after the alleged Soviet warning of Israel's purported invasion. In order to act he had to overcome the presence of the U.N. Emergency Force and hence he asked for its removal. U Thant's early compliance with his request automatically returned the Strait of Tiran and the Sharm el-Sheikh area to Egyptian control. Having found that he had scored a victory over Israel in the Strait of Tiran without firing even a single shot, Nasser could not help taking the next step, that is, to declare a blockade of the Gulf of Aqaba. Politico-military moves have a tendency of developing their own momentum, and once the Strait of Tiran was reoccupied, the blockade of the Gulf, so to say, had to be declared. Nasser himself confirmed this when in answer to a question by Noel Hudson of the British Reuter's he said: "When Eshkol threatened to occupy Syria, it became our duty to come forward and help our Arab brothers. Thus we had to ask for the withdrawal of the UNEF, and since the UNEF withdrew it was inevitable for us to go to the Gulf of Aqaba and restore the pre-1956 conditions there".[33]

As expected, Nasser's action provoked strong Israeli reaction. Expressing the sentiments of the people, the Israeli newspaper *Ma'ariv* warned that the "closure of the Strait of Tiran" was "tantamount to a declaration of war".[34] But Nasser paid no heed to such warnings and moves to break the blockade by Israel and the West were encountered by the signing of a mutual

[32] *Christian Science Monitor*, 16 November 1967.
[33] *Summary of World Broadcasts*, Pt. 4, ME/2478/A/5. 28 May 1967.
[34] *Ibid.*, Pt. 4, ME/2474/A/19, 23 May 1967, Broadcast by the Israeli Home Service.

defense pact between the UAR and Jordan and by the formation of a joint Arab command. This completed the encirclement of Israel and the latter decided to strike before the Arabs had time to temper the steel ring. Israel's last hope was that the Western maritime nations would provide some kind of support for free passage through the Strait of Tiran. But after it became clear that any resolution on their part would not include the necessary use of force, Israel decided not to wait any longer and proceeded to take action on her own.

SOVIET MOTIVES

As regards Soviet Union's role during the several weeks preceding the outbreak of the Arab-Israeli conflict on 5 June 1967, the object probably was to raise tension under her control with the aim of producing a demonstration of Arab military power, stopping short of war but redounding to the credit of the Russians as the Arabs' protector.[35] Some observers also believed that one of the purposes behind the Soviet behaviour in the Middle East crisis was to pressure the United States into de-escalating the war in Vietnam and create a diversion by raising the specter of possible American military involvement somewhere else in the world. Nasser's ambition to reclaim his role as Arab leader was a convenient tool, it was said, and the Soviets "deliberately set out to use it".[36] But at this point it was generally believed that the Soviet Union did not want the crisis to escalate into a war that might involve her in a clash with the United States. In a word, she wished to reap

[35] While not desiring an Arab-Israeli war because it would force upon Moscow the difficult choice of risking a clash with the United States by intervention, or risking Arab resentment by abstention, the Soviet Union had always sensed profit in Arab-Israeli tension short of war, *New York Times*, Weekly Review, 18 June 1967, p. 1.

[36] *Washington Post*, 28 May 1967, p. C7.

political gains, but not at the risk of war, and in doing so she kept open all her options.[37] The Soviet Union believed that success in this power play could have a positive effect on her position in the Middle East; it could also strike a blow at American prestige internationally. Presumably these, among other possible potential political gains, were for the Soviet Union worth the risk. To pursue such an ambivalent, risk-taking course called for considerable diplomatic agility. As an ally of the Arabs, the Russians rejected proposals for any Four-Power action to prevent the outbreak of war; they preferred to deal with the problem independently, not wishing to be identified with the West. In the United Nations, they vigorously championed Arab interests[38] and toward the end of May 1967, sharpened their propaganda attacks on the United States, Israel and the West. The basic interest of the Soviet Union was to establish herself firmly in the Middle East, and to minimize and eventually exclude U.S. influence in that area.

However, the negative steps taken by the Soviet Union were of no great consequence since they did not deal with the central issues in the crisis; they were essentially on the periphery. But she was cautious when it came to dealing with the central issues. Thus she avoided taking any public stand on Nasser's claim of sovereignty over the Strait of Tiran since a principle was involved here that bore directly on a Soviet

[37] *Christian Science Monitor,* 25 May 1967, p. 6.

[38] The apparent Soviet support for the Arab cause was assumed by the Arabs as an indication of the Soviet commitment against Israel. The Soviet propaganda that it was their nuclear threat which had halted the 1956 Suez War also helped in creating an image in the Arab mind that in the event of a military confrontation with Israel and the Arabs, they could depend upon the armed might of the Soviet Union. According to some observers, this encouraged them to think in terms of an eventual violent and "final solution" of the Israeli problem rather than of some kind of peaceful accommodation. See K. R. Singh, "The Soviet-UAR Relations", *India Quarterly,* April-June, 1969, p. 147.

vital interest, i.e., use of the Turkish Straits. Furthermore, when on 26 May 1967, Nasser announced that Egypt's main objective, if war came, was "the destruction of Israel", the Soviet Union immediately urged moderation and restraint. The Soviet envoy in Cairo woke up Nasser at 3 a.m. on 26 May 1967, to request him not to start a war with Israel at any cost.[39] The fact that the call was made at 3 a.m. suggests that the Soviet Union had its own fears that President Nasser was about to launch an action against Israel within hours. The Soviet request presumably carried the implied warning that if Nasser started a war he would have to fight on his own.[40]

At a press conference, a few days before the outbreak of hostilities with Israel, Nasser in reply to a question whether Egypt would ask Russia for help if the United States intervened, said: "We will leave this to the friendly nations themselves". This meant, in effect, that he had been unable to get any firm undertaking from Russia. The next day, however, in an atmosphere of rising war hysteria, Nasser quoted a message from the Soviet Premier Kosygin as saying that the Soviet Union "stands with us in this battle".[41] While much of the world saw this as a pledge of Soviet military support, the Soviet press made no mention of Kosygin's supposed message, thus casting a doubt about the alleged promise by the Soviet Premier. The suggestion of

[39] Curiously, the Israeli Prime Minister, Levi Eshkol, was also awakened by the Soviet Ambassador in Israel at 2.40 a.m. on 27 May 1967, and handed over an urgent note accusing Israel of "collusion with imperialist powers" and of "aggressive designs" against Syria and Egypt. It warned Israel against any attack. *Jerusalem Post,* 4 June 1967.

[40] On the other hand, it has also been argued that Nasser's willingness to comply with the Soviet request (not to fire the first shot), despite his show of force in closing the Gulf of Aqaba and successfully demanding the withdrawal of the U.N. Emergency Force, indicated the extent to which Nasser relied upon Soviet support and expected help in the event of a confrontation with Israel. Singh, 38n.

[41] *Times of India* (Delhi), 21 June 1967.

Russian support to Egypt in the crisis came from President Nasser himself and not from the usual publicity media of the Soviet Union. It is true that the Soviet Union had pumped a lot of arms and equipment into the Arab countries, particularly in Egypt and Syria, before 5 June 1967[42] and had encouraged Egypt in its mobilization against Israel till the blockade of the Gulf of Aqaba. But the Russians did not endorse the blockade of the Gulf, probably because they knew that it would touch a raw Israeli nerve, and when matters reached a crisis point, urged Nasser not to provoke a conflict against Israel.[43] When the worst fears of the Russians turned out to be true and the Israeli army poured across the Sinai, they deserted the Arabs altogether by endorsing a United Nations call for a cease-fire. However, it should be noted, as mentioned earlier, that the alleged false Soviet warning of an impending Israeli attack on Syria helped to precipitate the six-day war in June 1967; and once hostilities broke out, the Soviet Union thereafter could do little to control the forces which she had helped to unleash.

U.S. Position

The blockade of the Gulf of Aqaba had resulted in tremendous pressures being applied on the U.S. government by pro-Israeli

[42] These included, according to authoritative accounts, 2,500 tanks (about 1,400 of them going to Egypt), 250 assault guns, 130 field guns, 950 mortars and howitzers, 2,000 armoured and unarmoured personnel carriers, 200 bombers and 700 fighters. A large volume of this aid went to Egypt and Syria.

[43] However, it has been contended by some observers that the Soviet Union was "almost certain that the United States would prevail over Israel to accept the blockade". For the Russians, "it was inconceivable that the United States, deeply involved in Vietnam, would plunge into a second far-away foreign war and, because of the proximity to the Soviet Union, risk an atomic conflagration. Benjamin Shwadran, "Soviet Posture in the Middle East", *Current History*, vol. 53, December, 1967, p. 332.

groups, individuals and politicians within the United States to open up the Straits of Tiran by force, if necessary, and to intervene militarily if Israel was attacked by the Arabs. The U.S. government was also pressed by the Israeli government and the press. Thus the Israeli newspaper *Hatsofeh* called for a "firm and clear stand" by the United States against the naval blockade especially in view of "Soviet Union's unequivocal support for Nasser against Israel".[44] In response, the U.S. government increased and alerted its military forces in the Eastern Mediterranean, and on 23 May 1967 President Johnson declared that Egypt had no right to interfere with the shipping of any nation in the Gulf of Aqaba. At the same time he assured Israel that the United States was "firmly committed to the support of the political independence and territorial integrity of all the nations" in the Middle East and would "strongly" oppose "aggression by anyone in the area".[45] Moreover, in an interview with the Israeli Foreign Minister Abba Eban on 26 May 1967, Johnson reaffirmed that he would honour the undertakings given by his predecessors to keep the Strait of Tiran open.[46]

American officials were, however, seriously concerned that a major Arab-Israeli conflict might escalate into a world war. Hence they urged restraint upon Israel until they had a chance

[44] *Summary of World Broadcasts*, Pt. 4, ME/2476/A/11, 25 May 1967.

[45] According to a Cairo Radio Broadcast, the former British Prime Minister Douglas-Home had stated on 24 May 1967, that a secret military agreement had been concluded between the United States and Israel in 1964 (when he was the Prime Minister) which stipulated among other things that the United States should militarily intervene if Egyptian strength grows and threatens Israel. *Summary of World Broadcasts*, Pt. 4, ME/2476/A/1, 25 May 1967.

[46] At the same time President Johnson also made it clear that, constitutionally, he was not a free agent and that he needed the full support of the Congress. Moreover, he wanted to see first whether action could be taken by the Security Council. Laqueur, *Road to War*, 2n., p. 156.

to deal with the problem through diplomatic channels. But Israel had made it clear that she would act militarily if the Gulf was not opened quickly to her shipping.[47] The United States therefore sought to act hurriedly and pressed for action through the U.N. On 31 May 1967, she introduced an "interim" draft resolution which called upon the parties concerned, as a first step, to comply with the U.N. Secretary-General's appeal to "exercise special restraint, to forego belligerence and to avoid all other actions which could increase tension" in order to provide an essential "breathing spell". The resolution also encouraged the immediate pursuit of diplomacy in the interests of pacifying the situation and seeking reasonable, peaceful, and just solutions to all major Arab-Israeli problems. The United States interpreted the resolution to mean that Egypt would have to reopen the Gulf of Aqaba to Israel, at least for the time being.[48] This was opposed by the Arabs who accused the United States of acting on behalf of Israel. The American draft resolution was, however, supported by most of the Security Council members; but the Soviet Union, to show her solidarity with the Arabs, rejected it. Once the United States realized that she could not obtain the approval of the Security Council for any resolution acceptable either to the West or to Israel, she resorted to diplomatic efforts outside the U.N., urging both the Arab and Israeli leaders to do everything possible to avoid war. But because by this time all Arabs considered the United States to be acting as a partisan of the Israelis, the American

---

[47] On 27 May 1967, the Israeli Prime Minister Levi Eshkol received a cable from President Johnson urging him not to take military action in view of the likely catastrophic consequences. On the same day, the Israeli Foreign Minister Abba Eban stated that "the United States has assured him of its support to Israeli measures to open the Gulf of Aqaba." *Ibid.,* p. 163.

[48] U.N. Doc. S/PV 1345, 31 May 1967.

government found that it was less able than ever to exert influence on Arab countries.⁴⁹

In contrast, American relations with Israel were good, and the United States was in a position to apply pressures on her. However, pro-Israeli sentiment was so strong in Washington and throughout the United States that Israel was encouraged to refuse to make any concessions and to use force. Nonetheless, American officials pressed Israel at least not to make an immediate test of the blockade and to give them a little time in which to seek a peaceful solution acceptable to her.⁵⁰ The vast U.S. oil holdings in Arab lands made it inadvisable for Washington to appear to act on behalf of Israel and against the Arabs, especially in view of the fact that on the question of Israel all Arabs united. Yet, for domestic political reasons as well as past commitments, Washington could not ignore Israel.

In general, the tasks facing American diplomacy were: (a) to hold a rein on Israel; (b) to find some face-saving formula for Nasser; (c) to seek Soviet aid in containing the crisis and preventing the outbreak of an open conflict; and (d) to uphold international maritime rights in the Gulf of Aqaba. The United States was hopeful that peace would be maintained despite the gravity of the situation.⁵¹ American thinking, in part, was based upon the expectation that the contestants would be gradually worn to the point where they would be more receptive to reasonable compromise. What gave this point of view some credibility was the high cost both to Egypt and Israel of keeping their armed forces and reserves in a prolonged state of

---

⁴⁹ *New York Times,* 5 June 1967.

⁵⁰ The Pentagon was totally opposed to military intervention for forcing Nasser to lift the blockade of the Gulf of Aqaba. It did not wish to have "a second Vietnam in the Middle East", and according to it, the United States was not prepared for such a contingency. Laqueur, *Road to War,* 2n., p. 155.

⁵¹ *Washington Post,* 30 May 1967, p. A1.

alert.⁵² But while the United States sought a compromise as a way out of the crisis, the Soviet Union in general supported Nasser and appeared to be satisfied with a solution that would avoid war, but still preserve Nasser's (and her) political gains. Having gained popularity among the Arabs, the Russians wanted to reap what political yield was possible, but with minimal risk.⁵³ Accordingly, the Russians gave no concrete evidence that they were actually seeking to impose restraints on Egypt, short of war, in the highly explosive issue of Aqaba, although in private they were stated to have urged restraint.⁵⁴ At least on the surface, they treated Aqaba as a minor issue, asserting that the real issue was the repudiation of "imperialist aggression" against the Arab countries on behalf of the "oil monopolies and reaction".⁵⁵

The United States made an effort to obtain an agreement among the major Western maritime nations for creating an international naval task force to test the blockade of the Gulf of Aqaba. But none of the Western maritime powers, barring Netherlands, were enthusiastic about this plan which was fraught with the risk of a clash with the Arabs, and could result in an eventual involvement with the Soviet Union. Although this unencouraging response appeared to have left the United States in a lurch, even President Johnson was reported to have felt uneasy about a situation that was fraught with the possibilities of a Soviet-American confrontation. According to Max Frankel, the diplomatic correspondent of the *New York Times,* "His [President Johnson's] overriding concern was to avoid a conflagration in which the United States and the Soviet Union might become involved".⁵⁶ The United States, as a matter of

⁵² *New York Times,* 29 May 1967, p. 6.
⁵³ *Washington Post,* 1 June 1967, p. A17.
⁵⁴ *New York Times,* 2 June 1967, p. 1.
⁵⁵ *Ibid.,* p. 18.
⁵⁶ *Ibid.*

The Third Arab-Israeli War

fact, was anxious to avoid any new involvement in the Middle East specially in view of her preoccupation with Vietnam. But according to some informed observers, she failed to recognize how much her own military actions in Vietnam had promoted militancy in the Middle East.[57] In addition, U.S. action in discontinuing—a few months before the outbreak of the June 1967 conflict—the sale of surplus wheat to Egypt which she needed desperately, resulted in a marked deterioration in American-Egyptian relations and impelled Nasser to take a stronger anti-Western and anti-Israeli stand,[58] thereby aggravating an already tense situation in the Middle East.

THE SIX DAY WAR

The Israelis saw in the blockade of the Gulf of Aqaba and the closing of the Straits of Tiran an act of war, and dared alone in the face of Soviet threats[59] to enter into open hostilities

---

[57] The former French President, Charles de Gaulle, was one of those who believed that the war in Vietnam had been a contributory factor in the Arab-Israeli war. As he said: "How can you expect well-armed small powers to refrain from being tempted to settle their affairs by force of arms if the entire world remains indifferent year after year to the spectacle of a huge country bombing a small one to smithereens?" *New York Times*, Weekly Review, 2 July 1967, p. 4.

[58] *Summary of World Broadcasts*, Pt. 4, ME/2476/A/1, 25 May 1967.

[59] In a note handed to the Israeli Ambassador in Moscow after the outbreak of war, Russia warned that "unless Israel immediately halts its military actions, the Soviet Union will adopt sanctions against Israel, with all the consequences flowing therefrom." These threats caused considerable apprehensions in Israel. Some sort of Soviet action against Israel was half expected. But in contrast to the aftermath of the Suez Crisis of 1956, when Soviet threats had been largely instrumental in obtaining an Israeli withdrawal, this time Israel decided to ignore them. And the Russian threats proved to be hollow. For they had no means of carrying them out without risking confrontation with the United States. And this

with their Arab enemies on 5 June 1967, by launching devastating air attacks in which they destroyed hundreds of airplanes supplied by the Soviet Union valued at half a billion dollars.[60] Shortly thereafter, they achieved very impressive victories in the territories of the Arabs till the war came to an end on 10 June 1967, with the conclusion of a cease-fire agreement.[61] Nasser attempted desperately to force the Soviet Union to come to his aid when he found defeat staring him in the face. Part of this was Nasser's charge of U.S. and British air intervention in support of Israel.[62] But the Russians knew that the charge was false because their ships were shadowing U.S. and

they were not prepared to do. David Kimche & Dan Bawly, *The Sandstorm*, London, 1968, pp. 284-85.

[60] The extent of losses to the Arabs in the air war can be realized from the following partial list of destroyed planes—mostly Soviet built—announced by Israel on 7 June 1967: 31 TU-16s Heavy Bombers; 299 Ilyushin-28 Medium Bombers; 14 new Sukhoi-7 Fighter Bombers; 145 MIG-21 fast Fighter interceptors; 105 MIG-17's; 27 MIG-19's; 28 British made Hunter interceptor planes used by Jordan; 8 Antonovs, huge troop carriers; 31 Ilyushin-14 troop transport planes; 16 Soviet MI-6 & MI-4 helicopters, plus a number of planes of other types. *U.S. News and World Report*, 19 June 1967, p. 38.

[61] After the war, Nasser accused the United States of playing a political trick on him by calling for self restraint, by telling the UAR that any action taken by her would expose the entire region to dangers, by sending the U.S. Vice-President to confer with him and by agreeing to receive the Vice-President of the UAR on 6 June 1967, to confer on the subject and to reach a solution. Nasser contended that it was only natural in the light of these activities to expect that "the explosion would not occur soon", and he was caught off his guard when Israel attacked the UAR on 5 June 1967. He asserted that all these had been planned in advance and he had been the subject of a "political deception" by the United States. Nasser's speech delivered on the occasion of the 15th anniversary of the Egyptian Revolution on 23 July 1967. Laqueur, *Documentary History*, 24n., pp. 201-202.

[62] *Washington Post*, 7 June 1967, p. A22.

The Third Arab-Israeli War

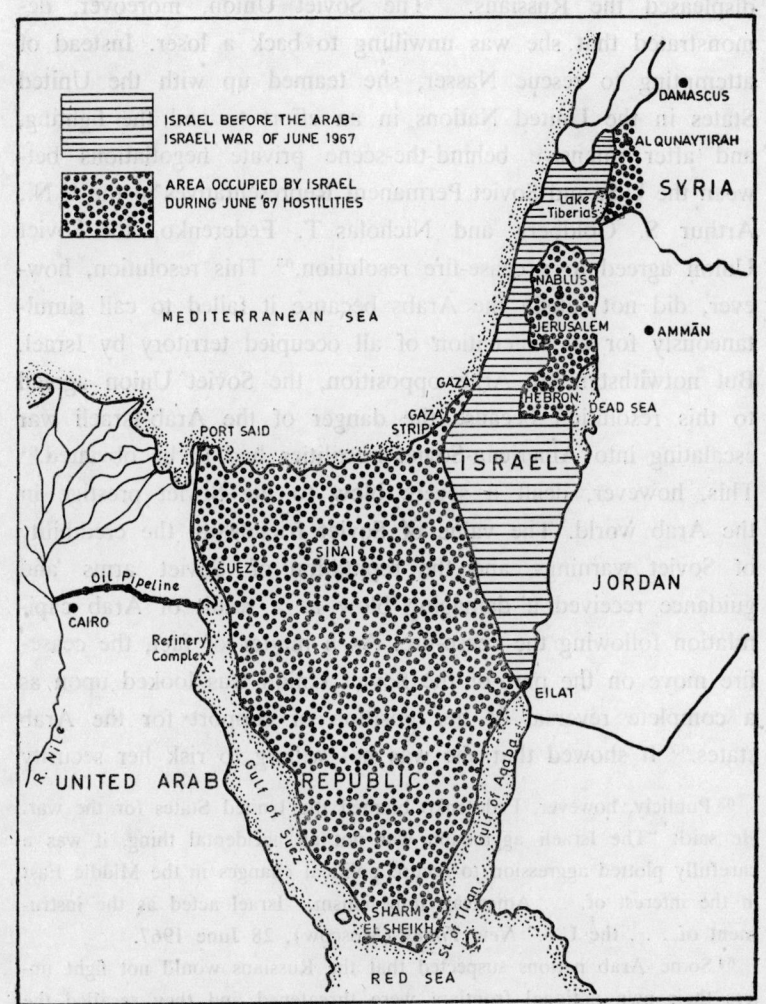

TERRITORY OCCUPIED BY ISRAEL AFTER THE JUNE 1967
HOSTILITIES WITH THE ARABS

British aircraft carriers. This attempt, through false charge of American and British participation, to drag them into war displeased the Russians. The Soviet Union, moreover, demonstrated that she was unwilling to back a loser. Instead of attempting to rescue Nasser, she teamed up with the United States in the United Nations in an effort to end the fighting, and after intensive behind-the-scene private negotiations between the U.S. and Soviet Permanent Representatives in the U.N., Arthur S. Goldberg and Nicholas T. Federenko, the Soviet Union agreed to a cease-fire resolution.[63] This resolution, however, did not satisfy the Arabs because it failed to call simultaneously for an evacuation of all occupied territory by Israel. But notwithstanding Arab opposition, the Soviet Union agreed to this resolution because the danger of the Arab-Israeli war escalating into American-Soviet hostilities had to be obviated.[64] This, however, dealt a severe blow to the Soviet prestige in the Arab world. The value of Soviet friendship, the credibility of Soviet warnings, and the reputation of Soviet arms and guidance received a damaging blow as a result of Arab capitulation following the cease-fire. As a matter of fact, the cease-fire move on the part of the Soviet Union was looked upon as a complete reversal of her position of support for the Arab states.[65] It showed that she was not willing to risk her security

[63] Publicly, however, Federenko blamed the United States for the war. He said: "The Israeli aggression was not an accidental thing, it was a carefully plotted aggression to secure political changes in the Middle East in the interest of. . . American imperialism. Israel acted as the instrument of . . . the U.S." *New Times* (Moscow), 28 June 1967.

[64] Some Arab nations suspected that the Russians would not fight unless their own national frontiers were threatened and they recalled the way in which the Soviet Union had backed out during the Cuban missile crisis. *Indian Express* (Delhi), 11 July 1967.

[65] Soviet failure to come to the assistance of the Arabs following the outbreak of hostilities led to an intense anti-Soviet feeling in Cairo which became all the more pronounced because it became known that China, in the middle of 1966, had offered fullest military collaboration with the UAR, including sharing of nuclear secrets, if Nasser agreed to denounce

on behalf of her Arab friends.[66] It was obviously embarrassing for Moscow to appear to be letting down the Arabs after years of support in the name of anti-imperialism. Yet Moscow preferred not to be embroiled in the Arab-Israeli conflict.[67]

In retrospect, it appears that the Soviet Union wanted to keep the Arab-Israeli relations in a state of sustained aggravation; but she did not want a spreading crisis that would involve her in a confrontation with the United States. The Soviets sided with the Arabs for their own selfish reasons, and this did not include the destruction of Israel.[68] The Arab leaders were mistaken in assuming that the Soviet Union would accept for their sake risks which they had not accepted for Berlin, Cuba or Viet-Nam.

Before Nasser's action in blockading the Gulf of Aqaba, when the crisis was essentially localized, the Soviets appeared to give unqualified support to the Arabs. But immediately after the blockade, when the crisis became internationalized, a note of caution and equivocation was evident in Russian pronouncements. The Soviet Union was willing to support Nasser on the

Moscow in the ideological war which he refused. *Statesman* (Calcutta), 11 June 1967.

[66] This brought forth scathing comments from Communist China which accused the Soviet Union of "collusion" with U.S. and British "imperialism" to betray the Arab people. *New York Times,* Weekly Review, 2 July 1967, p. 1.

[67] An important lesson of the June 1967 Arab-Israeli conflict has been that a country has to be prepared on its own—irrespective of the cost involved—to defend itself. The manner in which the Soviet Union refused to come to the aid of the Arabs during the conflict might serve as a lesson to India not to seek or to rely upon any kind of foreign military support in the hour of need.

[68] Since the creation of Israel in 1948 till the present day, the Soviet Union has never supported the Arab demand for the "liquidation" of Israel. Even when the Arab-Israeli dispute had already reached its "limit", Khrushchev had not condemned Israel but only its links with the West. *New Times* (Moscow), 10 June 1964, p. 36.

Aqaba issue, hoping apparently to secure political gains for both herself and Egypt, but at the same time she was careful not to take a public stand on Nasser's claim of sovereignty over the Straits of Tiran. In a word, the Soviets sought maximum gains from a highly critical situation so long as they could avoid a confrontation with the United States. They supported the Arabs upto the time it became imperative to part company with them in the interest of avoiding a conflict with the United States.[69]

The Soviet Union had hoped that the United States, having been isolated by the unwillingness of the Western maritime powers to risk war by a test of blockade, would reach a settlement on terms reasonably favourable to Nasser. A settlement on such a basis could redound to Soviet credit; it could have a positive effect on her position in the Middle East; it could also strike a blow at American prestige internationally. But this acute situation was quickly changed by Israel's attack on the Arabs and her seizure of the Sinai. And after the outbreak of Arab-Israeli war, when the risk of a Soviet-American confrontation loomed large,[70] the Russians backed off and opted

---

[69] In avoiding an entanglement with the Arabs and a collusion with the United States, the Soviet leadership has been faithful to tradition. During the centuries of expansion by which the principality of Muscovy grew into the great Russian Empire and the Greater Soviet Union, two principles were almost always respected: to advance by land into adjoining regions to which troops and settlers could easily be moved, and to avoid a clash with a superior or even an equal power.

[70] Both the Soviet Union and the United States were so fearful of finding themselves, through some miscalculations, at war, that they quickly made use of the "hot-line" link between Moscow and Washington to assure each other that they would make every effort to end the fighting in the Middle East and to avoid precipitate actions which might cause an escalation of the Arab-Israeli confrontation. *New York Times,* 9 June 1967, p. 18; "The Night the Hot Line Went Up", *Look Magazine,* 12 December 1967, p. 31.

for a policy of caution. The Russians, in other words, were willing to play Nasser's game upto a point where political gains seemed possible; but when the risks became too high and with the Arab defeat undeniable,[71] they cut their losses and tried to make the best of a bad situation.

Aftermath of Ceasefire

After the cease-fire, the Russians were faced with the awkward task of recovering on the diplomatic front what Nasser had lost on the battlefield. Though Nasser had failed to drag the Soviet Union militarily into the conflict, he succeeded in creating the impression that the whole Arab world had been let down by the men in the Kremlin.[72] Since this was damaging to the Soviet interest in the Arab world, the Soviet Premier Kosygin tried desperately to remove that impression, after fighting had stopped, through a series of diplomatic moves.[73] In the U.N. Security Council, Russia concentrated her efforts on bringing about a condemnation of Israel and a withdrawal of her forces to behind the armistice lines. But she failed to secure the approval of the Security Council to her resolution. After this, she intensified her efforts on behalf of the Arabs both inside as well as outside the U.N. in order to offset the growing Arab discontent which stemmed from what the Arabs consi-

---

[71] The Egyptian Army and Airforce, in spite of receiving Soviet equipment and training on a massive scale for 10 years, demonstrated to Russia's dismay that they were no better able to fight the Israelis than they had been in 1956.

[72] The Arab defeat was more a blow to Soviet prestige than a lethal strike at their position in the Middle East. For the Russians, Nasser's defeat was no loss of a vital interest; their position was damaged, but not irreparably, and what was lost could be quickly recouped. *The World Today,* vol. 23, July, 1967, p. 272.

[73] *New York Times,* Weekly Review, 25 June 1967, p. 1.

dered to be inadequate Russian military and political backing during the war crisis, and also to exploit to the maximum the bitter anti-American feelings which had developed in the wake of the Arab defeat. The desperate economic, military, and political situation of the Arab states, following their disastrous defeat at the hands of Israel, and the refusal of the United States to help most of them in any way gave the Soviet Union an opportunity to impress upon the Arabs that she was their only powerful friend and supporter. Because the Arabs were so enraged with the West, and because they quickly discovered that only the Russians were willing and able to provide the considerable political, military, and economic aid which they desperately needed, the Soviet Union did not find it difficult to restore and even to extend her influence in the Arab world.[74]

As a matter of fact, by its total military defeat the UAR, and to a lesser extent, the other Arab states were reduced to greater dependency on the Soviet Union.[75] Although Soviet behaviour during the crisis had disappointed the expectations of the Arab states, Arab losses were so great, and post-war Arab bargaining position was so weak, that their dependence on the Soviet Union after their defeat became heavier than ever before. Nasser, on his part, realized that his leadership position in the Middle East rested largely on Soviet power, and he could hope to retrieve sufficient prestige and reassert his political authority over the Arab world only by continuing his connections with the Soviet Union. This realization coupled with the quick replenishment of arms by the Kremlin led Nasser and the other Arab leaders to cast aside their initial bitterness and

[74] For many radical Arab groups, the conflict with Israel is the central reason for close ties with the Soviet Union which is looked upon as the principal source of weapons and the guarantor against Western intervention. Samuel Merlin, ed., *The Big Powers and the Present Crisis in the Middle East*, Madison, 1968, p. 58.

[75] *New York Times*, Weekly Review, 2 July 1967, p. 1.

declare toward the end of June 1967, their "heartfelt gratitude to the Soviet Union".[76]

Nasser's dependency on Moscow[77] has given the Russians substantial political leverage in dealing with him, and they have applied it apparently with good results in setting down new and stricter conditions on their military aid, such as the stationing of Soviet military advisers with Arab troops and vesting them with increased guidance over the direction of Arab military affairs, and the purging of anti-revolutionary elements from the Egyptian armed forces. This in turn has permitted deeper Soviet penetration into Egypt and has increased the opportunities for its control over the UAR political apparatus.

As soon as hostilities had ended, Russia began to rush military and economic aid to the Arabs. She supplied new MIG's and airlifted other badly needed military equipment to the UAR and other Arab states.[78] The Soviet Union thereby not merely sought to recoup some of her lost prestige, but also to bolster the existing governments in Egypt and Syria, and to make the Arabs more dependent upon her and thus to increase her power in the area.[79] It was also intended to restore

---

[76] *Hindustan Times* (New Delhi), 30 June 1967.

[77] It seemed that despite their failure against Israel, the Russians had won a considerable political success against the United States which found itself being ignominiously evicted from most Arab countries.

[78] The Soviet Union rearmed Egypt at an estimated cost of $500 million.

[79] Taking advantage of the friendly feelings generated by the quick replenishment of military equipment and the verbal support for the Arabs, the Russians have swiftly built up their naval forces in the Mediterranean. At the time of the June 1967 Arab-Israeli War, the Russians had only a small fleet in the Mediterranean without the support or fire power of a self-contained striking force, and in addition, depended upon Turkey's goodwill in the Dardanelles. In order to improve its position vis-a-vis the U.S. Sixth Fleet, the Russians began a massive build-up of their naval forces in the Mediterranean soon after the June War, and by 1968, they had become a force to be reckoned with, with an estimated forty-five

some of the military balance of power between the Arab countries and Israel, and to strengthen the political bargaining position of the Arabs in case efforts were made to force upon them a political settlement with Israel.[80] In an effort to provide further evidence of Russia's determination to help the Arabs, the Soviet Premier Kosygin personally attended the Emergency Special Session of the U.N. General Assembly which was convened on 17 June 1967, at Russia's request,[81] and called for a vigorous condemnation of Israel's "aggressive activities", immediate and unconditional withdrawal of Israeli forces from the occupied areas, and payment by the Israeli government of full reparations. But this resolution also failed to secure the approval of the General Assembly since most of the delegates felt that it was too one sided. Russia was undoubtedly aware from the beginning that her proposal would not muster the required two-thirds vote, but she must have felt that it would demonstrate her staunch support of the Arabs' cause.

vessels in the area and with crews numbering close to 25,000. As a matter of fact, the Soviet Mediterranean Fleet has now acquired a tremendous position of power at both ends of the Mediterranean Sea where they have Arab harbours that they can visit. These include Alexandria and Port Said in Egypt, Latakia in Syria, and Mers-el-Kebir in Algeria, which is only 260 miles from the Straits of Gibralter.

[80] The Russians do not want to see another Arab-Israeli war occur which could create pressure for their intervention on behalf of the Arabs. Consequently, at least until 1968, the Soviet Union provided the Arabs with only enough arms to enable them to deter further Israeli efforts at expansion and to strengthen their bargaining position, but not enough for them to consider an early renewal of hostilities. The June 1967 war revealed to the Soviets the danger of their deepening commitment to the Arab states without corresponding gains in political control. The Soviet problem has been how to exercise control without alienating the Arab 'client' states jealous of their independence.

[81] The Soviet purpose in calling the Emergency Session of the General Assembly soon after the end of the Arab-Israeli fighting in June 1967, was to assure its Arab friends that notwithstanding its inability to offer

The Third Arab-Israeli War

The pro-Arab policy of the Soviet Union was severely denounced by Israel which accused the Russians of aiding and abetting the Arabs in their endeavours to destroy her.[82] Had it not been for Soviet weapons and political support, the Arabs could not, Israel claimed, have threatened to make war on her and they would have been more willing to come to the peace table. The Israelis wondered whether the Soviet Union would have been so anxious for the cease-fire and withdrawal resolutions if the Arabs had emerged victorious. They insisted that Russia would have them move "backward to belligerency" rather than "forward to peace", and that they could not be expected to withdraw their forces until the Arabs were ready to insure Israel's peace and security—and this could be done only through a peace settlement achieved by direct negotiations.[83] The Israeli Foreign Minister Abba Eban declared that it would be "very difficult" to make a lasting peace in the Middle East unless the Soviet Union abandoned its pro-Arab stand for a more "balanced position".[84]

On the other hand, the Arabs accused the United States of being anti-Arab and pro-Israel, of working and voting in the Security Council to defeat any resolution opposed by Israel, and of disregarding her "obligations" under the U.N. Charter to condemn aggression[85] and to insist, as she had done in them the type of active support during the fighting they expected, Moscow was still their best friend.

[82] Soviet policy vis-a-vis Israel does not apparently aim at the destruction of the state, but through threats and political pressure to make it give up its gains and to isolate it politically. Although the Kremlin does not advertise the fact, it clearly wants recognition of a permanent state of Israel, for without Israel's implicit threat to the Arabs, Russia could never hope to retain their favour. *New York Times,* Weekly Review, 9 February 1969, p. 6; *Foreign Affairs,* vol. 47, January, 1969, p. 305.

[83] *Israel Digest,* 16 June 1967, p. 7, 30 June 1967, p. 3.

[84] *International Herald Tribune,* 26 June 1967, p. 2.

[85] According to the Soviet commentator Y. Bochkaryov, Israel would not

1956, that an aggressor should not be allowed to enjoy the "fruits" of his "illegal" actions. They also questioned why the United States was not making any effort to fulfill the pledge given before the outbreak of the June 1967 war that she was committed to safeguard the political independence and territorial integrity of "all" countries in the Middle East? They further asked whether the United States would have been so reluctant to carry out her commitments had Israel been the vanquished party and the Arabs the victors?[86]

UNITED STATES FEELS CONCERNED

The United States, rightly or wrongly, gave the impression of identifying American interests with that of Israel and thereby embittered the Arabs and forced them to turn more and more to the Soviet Union for material help and political support. The latter proclaimed itself as the patron and the chief supporter of the Arab cause in the dispute with Israel and labelled the United States as the protector of Israel. For a while after the June 1967 conflict, some American officials had apparently hoped that if Israel's forces remained in the conquered areas

have dared to refuse to pay heed to the Security Council Resolution of 6 June 1967, calling upon her to cease-fire and to withdraw her troops, if it had not felt that "it had the support of the United States, which both during and after the Security Council discussion of the issue in no way condemned the aggression." Y. Bochkaryov, "The Forces Behind the Aggressor", *New Times,* Moscow, 21 June 1967, p. 2.

[86] According to the *London Economist,* "it has always been obvious that, had the Arabs done well, the United States could not have allowed Israel to go under altogether". The American government realized that once the fighting started between the Arabs and the Israelis, "it could only be spared the necessity of intervening", which it certainly did not want to have to do, "if the Israelis did well enough not to need rescuing". There was, therefore, "a feeling of relief" when it became apparent that the Israelis could, once again, take care of themselves. *The Economist,* London, 10 June 1967, p. 1096.

and the United States refused to aid any of the Arab states, the deteriorating economic and political situation would compel the Arab masses to apply pressures for a settlement with Israel in order to bring about her withdrawal from the occupied territories and reopen the Suez Canal. At the same time, it was hoped that the more extremist Arab leaders would be held responsible for the Arab calamity and would be overthrown and replaced by more moderate Arab leaders. But within a short while it became evident that these expectations would not materialize. In fact, the rigid stand assumed by Israel on the one hand, and the military, political and economic assistance given by the Soviet Union to the Arabs on the other hand, enabled even the most militant Arab regimes to survive and paved the way for the extension of Soviet influence within the Arab world.

The United States became concerned about the extensive inroads Russia was making in the Arab world and about the hardening attitude of Israel. While leaving the initiative largely to the Arab governments, American officials, by the latter part of 1967, indicated a desire to restore normal relations with most Arab states, as well as a willingness to resume economic aid and the sale of military equipment to some of the more pro-Western Arab countries.[87] In the meanwhile, the Arab leaders met at a Summit Conference at Khartoum on 29 August 1967, after having witnessed the failure of the Soviet Union to bring about a withdrawal of Israeli forces from the occupied areas.[88] The Khartoum Conference was designed to prod the

[87] Thus the United States made good Jordan's losses after the June 1967 war.

[88] At the Khartoum Conference Nasser obtained from Saudi Arabia, Libya and Kuwait a commitment to pay him a subsidy of $266 million annually to compensate for the revenues lost because of the closure of the Suez Canal. In return, Nasser agreed to evacuate his troops from Yemen and not to oppose the resumption of oil shipments to the United States and

United States into putting pressure on Israel to withdraw to the pre-June 1967 demarcation lines, for it was felt that America alone was capable of doing this. As *quid pro quo* the Arabs were willing to tone down their propaganda campaign against the United States and the West.

While the United States was keen on bringing about a settlement in the Middle East, at the same time she wanted to ensure that the situation that prevailed before 5 June 1967, would never return. She was therefore unwilling to press Israel to pull back its armies until the Arabs joined Israel in a peace effort. The United States, in fact, strove for a durable and just peace settlement in the Middle East[89] instead of mere armistice arrangements which had proved inadequate to keep the peace. An effort in this direction was made by President Johnson on 19 June 1967,[90] when he announced certain principles as guidelines for a peace settlement. These were later embodied in a draft resolution in the U.N. General Assembly by the U.S. Permanent Representative in the U.N., Arthur Goldberg. The resolution called for "the withdrawal of armed forces from occupied territories; termination of claims or states of belligerence, and mutual recognition of and respect for the right of every state in the area to sovereign existence, territorial integrity, political independence, secure and recognized boundaries, and freedom from the threat or use of force". It further affirmed the necessity "for guaranteeing freedom of navigation

Great Britain. Nadav Safran, *From War to War: The Arab Israeli Confrontation*, 1948-67, New York, 1969, p. 387.

[89] The United States has sought to promote peace and stability in the Middle East both because the preservation of the *status quo* has been more favourable to its interests than any conceivable alternative and because it has seen that an intensified conflict within the Arab-Israel zone only serves to multiply the intraregional demand for intervention by outside powers, in particular by the Soviet Union.

[90] *Department of State Bulletin,* vol. 57, 10 July 1967, p. 31.

through international waterways in the area; for achieving a just settlement of the refugee problem; for guaranteeing the territorial inviolability and political independence of every state in the area; and for achieving a limitation of the wasteful and destructive arms race".[91] But the American draft resolution, like the Soviet draft resolution (which had condemned Israeli aggression and called for indemnities) failed to gain acceptance in the U.N. General Assembly. There appeared to be some possibility of a Soviet American adjustment calling for troop withdrawal, acknowledging the right of every member of the United Nations to maintain an independent national state of its own and renouncing all claims and acts inconsistent with this principle. But this was unacceptabe to the Arab states. The Emergency Session of the U.N. General Assembly, therefore, had to adjourn without further action.

After the failure to obtain a solution to the Middle East crisis through the United Nations, the Soviet Premier, Alexei Kosygin, and the U.S. President, Lyndon Johnson, met at Glassboro (near New York) on 23-24 June 1967, in an effort to search for a solution that would establish peace in the Middle East. At Glassboro, Kosygin's sole interest was to obtain the withdrawal of Israeli forces to older positions. President Johnson was not opposed to this scheme but he was insistent that it should be coupled with other measures. The basic difference was that Premier Kosygin feared another military eruption if the Israelis stayed too long in the occupied territory. President Johnson, on his part, feared the same eventuality if the Arabs were allowed to return to close the Gulf of Aqaba, to occupy the heights of Syria (from which they used to bombard Israeli villages before the June 1967 war), and to positions surrounding Israel, menacing its existence.[92]

[91] *Ibid.,* 18 December 1967, p. 835.
[92] At the Glassboro meeting Kosygin reportedly told Johnson that if

The Superpowers and the Middle East

Political and Economic Considerations

In terms of geographic location, economic resources and influence upon the world balance of power, the Arab states are considered more important in the eyes of the United States than Israel even though the strategic value of the Middle East region as a whole for the United States has diminished in importance since the mid-sixties. This has been due to certain technological developments and changes in nuclear strategy which has taken place in recent years. The technology of nuclear warfare has made fixed land bases less desirable than mobile marine vessels like nuclear powered submarines equipped with polaris missiles. More significantly, the development of long range delivery systems like the ICBM's have made the need for bases near the Soviet Union less important now than in the fifties and early sixties.[93] Further, the importance of the Middle East as a source of oil has also diminished in recent years since large sources have been discovered in other areas.[94] which have made the rest of the world

Israel completely and unconditionally withdrew from Arab territory, Moscow would influence the UAR and other Arab states to secure for Israel freedom of shipping and recognition of its right to exist. *Hindustan Standard*, Calcutta, 9 August 1967.

[93] The Soviet Union is likely to continue to attach importance to political developments in the Middle East even if the concern of the United States declines somewhat. This is because the Middle East is much closer to the Soviet Union than it is to the United States. The Middle East is, in geopolitical terms, Russia's back garden and the Soviet leaders seem to believe that an area so close to their borders should become their sphere of influence even though at present the Middle East neither constitutes a military threat to the Soviet Union nor does the latter have any economic stake in the region. Walter Laqueur, *The Struggle for the Middle East: The Soviet Union and the Middle East,* 1958-68, London, 1969, pp. 188-9. Hereafter cited as Laqueur, *Struggle for the Middle East.*

[94] For instance, the Soviet Union has lately discovered enough oil within its territory to be able not only to meet its requirement but also to export

The Third Arab-Israeli War

less dependent upon Middle Eastern oil.[95] Although Western Europe still has most of its oil supplied from the Middle East, North African and Western Hemisphere sources have become substantially more important now than they were at the time of the 1956 Suez crisis; and the U.S. needs are mostly met from Latin America with only small quantities coming from the Eastern Hemisphere. In other words, Middle Eastern oil is no longer considered to be of crucial importance for Western security. In spite of this fact, however the United States still has a vital stake in maintaining access to oil supplies in the Middle East. This is because U.S. oil companies have heavy investments in Middle Eastern petroleum development, and U.S. income from oil investments approximates one-fourth of her income from all overseas investments. Since this income affects her balance of payments position, she is naturally concerned about shielding the investments of the U.S. oil companies.[96] The United States is, moreover, vitally concerned about the preservation of the Middle East region from communist control, since conversion of that area into "an exclusive Soviet sphere of interest" would result

oil. She is, therefore, not dependent upon Middle Eastern oil and most likely will not become involved in a war to get that oil. The United States, consequently, no longer needs to seek "desperate means" for denying the Soviet access to petroleum which they do not need.

[95] The Shah of Iran, however, seems to think that the West would not be able to survive for very long if it were to lose the Middle Eastern oil. According to him, Europe would consume 340 million tons of oil by 1975 —which is approximately the total U.S. production. The United States has to meet her own internal requirements, and besides, she could not sustain such a rate of production indefinitely. The Shah estimated that if Venezuela continued to produce at the present rate, her oil reserves would be finished in 20 years. Transcript of interview with His Imperial Majesty, the Shah of Iran, Kennedy Library Oral History Project, Kennedy Papers, John F. Kennedy Library, Waltham, Massachusetts, U.S.A.

[96] *Congressional Record,* Congress 88, Session 2, vol. 110, 1964, p. 11041.

in a decisive shift in the balance of power and this, in turn, would have far-reaching repercussions not only on the area concerned but in other parts of the world as well.

The United States is, therefore, faced with a dilemma: while on the one hand, it seeks to protect the Arab states against Israel's superior military power by either preventing its use altogether or, if that proves impossible, by preventing its decisive use; on the other hand, it has the responsibility of underwriting the continuing existence of Israel as an independent state and giving it the support necessary to hold its own against the Arab states.[97] The United States, in fact, has been attempting to pursue a 'balance of power' policy, seeking a position between the extreme claims of Israel and the Arab states and a means of preventing the erosion of her influence among the Arabs. She has sought to support both sides upto a point with a view to maintaining the existing distribution of power and preserving the *status quo*. However, the United States' apparent acceptance of the Israeli view that no Arab territory need be given up except as part of a comprehensive settlement, is looked upon by the Arabs as a convincing evidence of U.S. partiality towards Israel.[98] As a matter of fact, internal political considerations—the existence of powerful Zionist pressure groups[99] and strong pro-

[97] The United States has not, however, entered into any security arrangement with Israel with a view to avoiding antagonizing the Arab states.

[98] Basically, there are three things that Israel wants from Washington: First, to deter the Russians, as in June 1967, from direct military intervention against her. Second, to refrain from imposing, alone or with others, a solution which Israel judges contrary to her interests. Third, to ensure that Israel's armaments do not fall dangerously below the level of the Arab states.

[99] The powerful Zionist pressure groups in the United States dangle the Jewish vote before American politicians, claiming that that they can deliver or withhold it on the basis of a candidate's policy toward Israel. They exercise great control over newspapers, magazines, radio, television

Israeli sentiments among large segments of the American population, and the need for not antagonizing the Jewish voters, especially before an election,[100] has placed limitations on the U.S. government's capability to apply pressures on Israel.[101] As an instance, it may be mentioned that after the June 1967 war, the U.S. government agreed to supply Israel with modern—especially supersonic—jets without seriously trying to use them as levers to persuade her to abide by the Security Council resolution of 22 November 1967.[102] In January 1968, the late Israeli Premier Levi Eshkol pleaded with President Johnson for permission to buy 50 supersonic Phantom F-4 jet fighters. President Johnson agreed to keep "Israel's military defense capability under active and sympathetic examination and review in the light of the shipment of military equipment by others to the area", and finally on 27 December 1968, the U.S. government announced its decision to sell 50 Phantom F-4 jet fighter planes to Israel.[103]

and other media of mass communication. *Middle East Forum*, vol. 40, May, 1964, p. 16.

[100] 1968 was a Presidential election year in the United States.

[101] The support of American jews for Israel is extended to a blanket belief in general American support for that country by the Arabs who contend that American support for Israel will continue because no American politician will risk losing the jewish vote by altering it. *Amrita Bazar Patrika*, Calcutta, 2 August 1968, p. 6.

[102] As long as influential groups in the United States sponsoring the Israeli cause remain active and official American rebukes remain only verbal in nature, Israel most probably would not feel the need to change her attitude or to abide by the U.N. resolutions.

[103] *Statesman*, Calcutta, 29 December 1968, p. 11. Delivery of the Phantom jets was to begin before the end of 1969 and continue through 1970. The total cost of the purchase was estimated at $200 million. The sale of the Phantoms was looked upon by the UAR as a serious development since, according to her, it was likely to encourage Israel to continue its "aggression" and undermine hopes of a peaceful solution of the Middle East crisis.

Nasser looked upon this decision as a clear indication of U.S. support for Israel. As he said: "giving of arms to Israel while she is still occupying Arab territories means that the U.S. supports Israeli occupation of these territories. And supplying Israel with aircraft means that the U.S. fully backs and supports Israel". The Soviet Union endorsed this point of view and further warned that the acquisition of the Phantoms would intensify "Israel's expansionist aspirations".[104] The *New York Times* commented that whenever the U.S. government officials referred to the necessity to "preserve a balance of power" between Israel and the Arabs, they have always meant "enough arms for Israel to enable her to defend herself against all Arab challengers without the need for direct United States intervention in any war."[105] In other words, the balance has to be kept heavily in Israel's favour, for this was the only way to insure that American involvement would never be required.

However, Israel's subsequent request for 25 more Phantom F-4 jet fighters and 80 Skyhawk fighters was kept in abeyance by President Richard M. Nixon early in 1970, in an effort to "cutback on the flow of arms to the area", and maintain "a balance between the forces in that area which will contribute to peace". Nixon's decision was based on the consideration that Israel enjoyed "aerial superiority over its Arab enemies".[106] Moreover, it

[104] *Current Digest of the Soviet Press*, 12 February 1969, p. 9.
[105] *New York Times,* 11 June 1967.
[106] Israel acknowledges her superiority in the air at the moment which, according to her, is the result of technical decisions taken years ago. But this superiority could be endangered over the long haul and Israel is looking ahead to 1971 and beyond. According to her, "Egypt has hundreds of pilots training in the Soviet Union who are coming back this year (1970) and next." By then the ratio of superiority will have changed, unless Israel is able to get more planes for her pilots to fly. Israel is also concerned about the impending arrival in Libya of 110 Mirage Jets from France. The arrival of the planes could coincide with the completion of

The Third Arab-Israeli War

was felt that the United States would find it awkward to fill the request at a time when it was diplomatically trying to help defuse the worsening Middle East crisis, and also improve her relations with the Arab states in order to counter the increasing Soviet influence among them.

President Nixon, however, uttered the warning that "if the USSR, by its military assistance programs to Israel's neighbors, does essentially change the balance, then the United States would take action to deal with that situation".[107] The situation appeared to have changed rather seriously when on 29 April 1970, Israel announced that "Soviet pilots were flying operational missions over Egypt" from bases in the country under their control.[108] Informed observers believed that the presence of Soviet pilots in Egypt following close upon the supply of SAM-3, surface-to-air missiles,[109] to her by the Soviet Union, upset the precarious balance of power in the Middle East that President Nixon has

training courses for the pilots. Although the Mirages are officially destined for Libya, Israeli officials operate on the theory that they must be taken into consideration in evaluating Arab strength on the Egyptian front against Israel. Israel is bent on retaining her air superiority in the years ahead with a view to deterring the Arabs and it was on this basis that she made her request for more American jet planes.

[107] *Boston Evening Globe,* 22 March 1970, p. 18.

[108] *Ibid.*, 29 April 1970, p. 1. It has been reported that there are three squadrons or more of Russian flyers in Egypt. Besides many of the Egyptian radars and much of the ground control apparatus are now manned by Russian troops. The Russians, in fact, appear to have taken over the main air defense of Egypt, leaving the Egyptian airforce to defend only a narrow strip along the Suez Canal itself.

[109] The SAM-3, surface-to-air missile is reported to be extremely accurate and especially designed to deal with low flying aircraft. The success of Israel's air campaigns against Egypt has been largely due to the ability of Israeli pilots to sneak under the radar of the older Egyptian missile defense, and this is likely to be threatened with the Soviet installation of SAM-3 in Egypt.

tried to maintain. They also believed that the new assertion of Soviet power was based on the calculation that the United States, in view of her involvement in Cambodia, would not be able to adopt a strong posture in the Middle East. Soviet pilots were reported to be providing umbrella cover deep inside Egypt, leaving Egyptian aircraft free to mount raids against Israeli held territory, thereby encouraging Nasser to renew his 'war of attrition' against Israel.

In view of the changed situation which resulted in a substantial alteration of the military balance in the Middle East, Israel pressed the United States once again for the supply of the jet fighters (which had been requested earlier) so that her qualitative strength may not be jeopardized. Israel moreover contended that the supply of the planes would firmly indicate that the United States would not allow the Arabs and the Soviets to dominate the area by default.[110] President Nixon has been deeply concerned about the new development in the Middle East, and although he is committed not to permit the balance of power to be changed between Israel and the Arab states, he has withheld a decision on the Israeli request pending a review of the Middle East situation by the U.S. Department of State.[111]

SEARCH FOR A FORMULA

In essence, American policy appears to have been aimed at sustaining two parallel sets of power-relationships: continued

[110] On 23 May 1970, seven U.S. Senators—Alan Cranston of California, Harold E. Huges of Iowa, George McGovern of South Dakota, Charles Goodell of New York, Stephen Young of Ohio, Philip A. Hart of Michigan and Thomas F. Eagleton of Missouri—urged President Nixon to permit the sale of new warplanes to Israel in view of the open use of Soviet pilots and Soviet troops in Egypt which they considered to be "an unprecedented assertion of Soviet power" that threatened "not only Israel, but also world peace." *Boston Evening Globe,* 24 May 1970, p. 17.

[111] *Ibid.,* 22 May 1970, p. 13.

The Third Arab-Israeli War

Israeli superiority over the Arabs, and continued U.S. superiority over the Soviet presence in the Middle East. But Soviet moves have thwarted the United States from achieving the latter objective. In fact, neither the United States nor the Soviet Union are willing to permit each other to dominate the Middle East. In view of this, the advantages of an agreement between them seems to be obvious; and since early 1969, when it became evident that Dr. Gunnar Jarring, the U.N. Secretary General's special envoy in the Middle East,[112] had failed to find a way out of the Arab-Israeli impasse, the United States and the Soviet Union along with France and Great Britain have been searching for a formula under which the warring parties could negotiate a peace settlement. In January 1969, France made a proposal that the permanent representatives of the Big Four Powers in the Security Council should meet to discuss the means of establishing a "just and lasting peace in the Middle East."[113] Although the Soviet Union was not opposed to this proposal, she preferred bilateral conversations with the United States on the framework of a settlement.

As regards the aims of the two superpowers, whereas the

[112] Dr. Gunnar Jarring, the Swedish Ambassador in Moscow was appointed by the U.N. Secretary General, U. Thant, soon after the adoption of the Security Council Resolution of November 22, 1967, as a U.N. peace envoy to seek to bring about agreements between Israel and the Arab states on implementing steps. He has shuttled between Israel and the Arab states for over two years trying to promote a settlement, but without any success. His efforts have been continuously frustrated by the intransigence of both sides. Arab governments informed Mr. Jarring that the unconditional withdrawal by Israel from occupied territories was a precondition for any political settlement, while Israel has insisted upon "direct negotiations" as the only way of achieving peace. The stalemate eventually prompted the Big Four Powers to undertake a series of talks in search for ways to bring support and eventual success to the Jarring Mission. But even these have not yielded any results.

[113] *New York Times*, Weekly Review, 26 January 1969, p. 3.

United States has been searching for a formula which would remove from the Middle East the state of perpetual tension, hostility and belligerency which had existed before 5 June 1967; the Soviet Union, on the other hand, appears to be striving for a settlement which would bring an Israeli withdrawal from the occupied territories with minimal Arab concessions, in order that the pre-June 1967 state of tension between the Arabs and the Jews could be perpetuated. The Russians seem to have come to the conclusion that their continued presence in the Arab world largely depends on this factor. Thus it is evident that the settlement desired by the two superpowers is not exactly of the same nature, and the real problem is one of finding an acceptable formula that would satisfy both of them as well as the Arab states and Israel.

Despite this formidable hurdle, both the superpowers have made efforts to break the Middle East impasse, and in the latter part of 1969, they reportedly reached "substantial agreement" on a plan comprising of four points: (i) the Israelis would lay down a specific timetable for their withdrawal from occupied territory; (ii) the Arabs would agree to the signing of a peace treaty with Israel; (iii) a peace-keeping force would be positioned in various sensitive buffer zones; and (iv) the details of this plan would have to be worked out by the Arabs and the Israelis in direct or indirect negotiations.[114] Again in March 1970, it was announced that the Big Powers were working on a plan, the first part of which called for Israeli withdrawal linked with a pledge by the Arab nations to maintain peace, and the second

---

[114] *Statesman,* Calcutta, 15 November 1969, p. 6. However, the peace plan did not appear to state anything about the two crucial issues: the future of the dispossessed Palestinian people and the future of Jerusalem. Further, it also overlooked the fact that the military effort by the Fedayeen commands groups to regain their lost homeland can no longer be controlled by any Arab government.

part dealt with the Palestinian refugee problem and with setting up recognized frontiers.[115] No final agreement has been reached with regard to any plan, but it is realized by both the superpowers that they are not in a position to impose a *diktat* in the Middle East. They can only hope to apply pressure on their 'client' states, and as yet, neither of them have shown any inclination to do this.[116]

The Soviet Union has, however, sought to persuade the Arabs to accept a policy of realism towards Israel and to concentrate their energies on social and economic improvement with Soviet help. Also, she has tried to convince the Arabs that as a result of the difficulties of occupation, Israel will find herself in increasing political isolation; that generally speaking, time works for the Arabs and that they should avoid becoming involved in rash adventures. The Soviet Union has made it clear that she does not share the sentiments of the Arab extremists—belonging to the Al Fatah and the Palestine Liberation Movement—who talk of continuing the fight till the destruction of Israel, for Moscow maintains that Israel exists and will continue to exist. Moscow considers the Arab extremists to be a major threat to the peace of the entire region in view of their uncompromising attitude, and *Pravda* has accused them of "hurting their own cause with hysterical appeals for an early war of revenge". It has pointed out that such threats made it less likely that Israel would agree

[115] *Boston Evening Globe*, 9 March 1970, p. 1.

[116] In the case of the Soviet Union, there are limitations in her applying pressure even though the Arabs are heavily dependent upon her for arms and assistance. If, for instance, the Soviet Union withheld arms supplies as a means of pressuring the Arabs, it could do her irreparable harm in her struggle with China for, the latter can, in part at least, replace the arms, enough to keep the Arabs in the fight anyway. The Soviet Union cannot run the risk of the Arabs making a pro-Chinese switch.

to withdraw to its prewar boundaries, and has urged the Arabs to adopt a more realistic attitude.[117]

The Soviet leaders, according to the Israelis, are very anxious to see the Suez Canal opened up again. Soviet interest in maintaining a viable fleet in the oil rich Arabian Gulf area, especially with the impending departure of the British from that area in 1971, and with it the removal of Western military power from that area, depends on easy access through the connecting waterway. The opening of the canal would also enable the Soviets to avoid the unnecessary expense involved in detouring their supplies for Hanoi by other routes.[118]

ARAB POSITION

The Arab leaders are finding themselves under renewed pressure to start a war once again against Israel. There has been a mounting fear in Cairo that the passage of time has been lending a degree of permanence to the Israeli occupation of the Sinai Peninsula and their presence on the east bank of the Canal. Moreover, it is also felt that if the Arabs are seen to accept the *status quo,* the international community will lose interest and the ceasefire lines will solidify over the years into borders as was the case after the Arab-Israeli conflict of 1948. This anxiety prompted the Egyptians to start shelling across the Suez Canal, especially after the middle of 1968, when they observed that the Israelis were digging in on the eastern bank of the Canal in preparation of what looked like a long stay.[119] At the same time Cairo started

---

[117] *Mizan,* vol. 9 (5), September-October, 1967, p. 215.

[118] *New York Times,* Weekly Review, 14 July 1968, p. 3.

[119] Israel started entrenching herself along the Suez Canal when with the passage of time, she found that the Arabs were unwilling to agree to peace on her terms. Therefore, to force the Arabs to come to the conference table, she tried to make the interim peace as painful and costly as possible by denying Egypt the use of the Suez Canal.

issuing bellicose statements threatening another round of fighting with Israel. Israel, on her part, has warned that as long as the Arabs continue with their "war of attrition", she will continue to carry out measures to reduce her casualties and show them that "their war of attrition works against them",[120] and as a matter of fact, by her successful reprisals and pre-emptive strikes,[121] Israel has to a large extent succeeded in proving her point.

The UAR, however, has carefully kept open the possibility that a peaceful settlement might be attained and it has not given up hopes of regaining the Sinai and other occupied areas as part of a settlement imposed by the superpowers that would force Israel out of the occupied territories. In fact, if the superpowers succeed in bringing about a settlement—which however appears to be improbable at the moment—President Nasser can blame them for any uncomfortable concessions that he might have to make to the Israelis. This has become particularly important now since the Fedayeens—who reject any peaceful settlement—have caught the imagination of the Arab world. They are the new heroes of the Arab youth and the idols of grown-up Arabs. They create unrealistic hopes with their promises of eventual victory and, in doing so, reduce the already slight prospects for meaningful negotiations to end the stalemate.

It has been pointed out that the Arab demand for Israeli withdrawal from all occupied territories which were under Arab control prior to 5 June 1967, has been supported by the U.N.

---

[120] *Record American*, Boston, 14 February 1970, p. 4.

[121] Israelis have been hitting at targets in the UAR almost at will with little opposition, and early in 1970, Egypt lost two radar installations and a battle over an island in the Red Sea. All these have demonstrated that militarily, the Arabs are still no match for the Israelis. Israeli action, including the shelling across the Suez Canal, led the Soviet Union to accuse her of "intimidating the UAR". *Current Digest of the Soviet Press*, 26 March 1969, p. 24.

Security Council resolution of 22 November 1967, which cannot be said to be an "Arab formula for peace". It requires them to give up positions which for twenty years they have held tenaciously as a matter of principle: (a) refusal to accept the existence of the state of Israel and to end the state of belligerency with her; and (b) refusal to grant to Israeli shipping the right to use the Suez Canal. The giving up of those positions, as seen by the Arabs, is an immense concession. Reluctantly, after three wars they have concluded that they must agree that Israel is a reality of geography in the Middle East and is not going to disappear. The Egyptian Foreign Minister Mahmoud Riad acknowledged this when he declared: "Now we accept realities, and one of those is Israel".[122] The Arabs, as a matter of fact, seem to be willing to put an end to the conflict provided Israel withdraws from the territories she has occupied since June 1967. The Arab states, particularly the governments of Jordan and the UAR, recognize that the Fedayeens belonging to the Al Fatah and the Palestine Liberation Organization are an influential force in opposing such a political settlement.[123] However, they argue that if a "just" peace plan is implemented with total Israeli withdrawal from conquered territories and proper satisfaction of the Arab refugee claims, the Fedayeen commando groups will eventually accept the settlement as the best attainable solution,[124]

[122] *New York Times,* Weekly Review, 14 July 1968, p. 3.

[123] The Fedayeen commando groups refuse to acknowledge any settlement to which they are not a party and insist on setting forth their own demands. They pose a threat to Israel and also contribute toward maintaining an atmosphere of tension. In this situation, Israel finds it easier to play the role of the injured party—the victim of Arab intransigence.

[124] While it is realized that the Arab states should establish control over commando groups operating from their territories, no progress is likely to be achieved toward such control until the Arab governments and their peoples have reason to believe that there are real prospects for a fair and just settlement and the cease-fire lines of June 1967, are not being frozen

as will, they believe, the more irreconcilable elements in all Arab states.

But the Israelis are skeptical about this and they believe that so long as the Fedayeen commandos continue to grow in power and influence, no settlement is likely to be forthcoming unless the Arab governments are able to take care of them. The Arabs, on the other hand, contend that the chief barrier to a political settlement is the refusal of the Israelis to end their military occupation of the Arab lands and to withdraw from the conquered territories. They believe that only external pressure from the Big Powers will ever persuade Israel to withdraw. They therefore welcome the talks among the Big Four Powers on the Middle East. The U.N. Secretary General U. Thant has also called upon the Big Powers to take strong measures to prevent "a new catastrophe in the Middle East" in view of the fact that the ceasefire proclaimed at the end of June 1967 Arab-Israeli war now appears to be "totally ineffective."[125]

ISRAELI VIEW

Israel sees little hope of a peace settlement since the Arab states are neither prepared to sign a peace treaty nor have direct talks with her which she insists upon.[126] The Israeli Foreign Minister Abba Eban made it clear soon after the June 1967 war that:

into permanent boundaries. Competent observers, however, believe that Arab governments would find it increasingly difficult to come to any settlement with Israel as long as the Fedayeen commandos continue their fight against the Israelis and die, and are looked upon as heroes by the entire Arab public.

[125] *Boston Evening Globe,* 18 February 1970, p. 10

[126] Israel believes that no agreement reached with either President Nasser of the UAR or any other Arab leader will have any meaning if they are unwilling or unable to agree to a direct peace treaty. *New York Times,* Weekly Review, 14 July 1968, p. 3.

"There can be no substitute for a directly negotiated peace settlement.... We will reject any form of armistice designed to provide our neighbours with an escape route from the necessity of formal, interstate relations".[127] Israel, moreover, believes that any solution to be effective will have to envisage the elimination of resistance movement led by the Fedayeen commando groups. Until the Arabs are prepared to come and sit down for direct negotiations—and the Israelis recognize that this is unlikely to happen for a long time[128]—Israel seems to be prepared to hold all of the conquered territories and to believe that an indefinite prolongation of the present stalemate would serve her long term interests. By letting things "settle", Israel hopes that the Arabs (and the world) would get accustomed to the new *fait accompli*, and that with time they would learn to live with it. Israel also feels that the holding of the occupied territories is essential to her security until a comprehensive peace can be negotiated with the Arab states. Israel's strategy is to emphasize strength and security for she believes that the most effective way of preventing a full-scale conflagration in the Middle East is to prove to the Arabs that they cannot win a war against her.

Officially Israel has never declared her long range intentions toward the occupied areas. But Israeli spokesmen have repeatedly stated that Israel (a) will never give up the newly absorbed Arab sector of Jerusalem; (b) will never withdraw from the Golan Heights; (c) will never again accept the boundaries north of Jerusalem which gave the country a "pinched waist" in the center; (d) will not withdraw from Sharm el-Sheik at the southern tip of Sinai, and (e) will absorb the Gaza Strip.[129] The

---

[127] *Ibid.*, 20 August 1967, p. 5.

[128] There was a deep rooted hope among the Israelis that they would be able to exchange the territory they had occupied for recognition and peace. That hope, the Israelis feel, has turned into a disillusion.

[129] *Statesman*, Calcutta, 7 October 1968, p. 6.

Israelis, as a matter of fact, see no point in surrendering the fruits of a brilliantly successful campaign in return for a mere hypothesis that the Arabs thereafter just possibly might consent to talk in realistic terms. Israel does not regard the 22 November 1967 Security Council Resolution[130] as providing a correct formula for peace. She believes that the implementation of its provisions on withdrawal from occupied territories would entail an unacceptable threat to Israel's security from the Arab states which have not abandoned their long proclaimed dream of 'driving Israel into the sea'. Israel further considers the Big Four Powers efforts to promote a settlement as futile and likely to lead only to greater intransigence on the part of the Arabs, and the Israeli Prime Minister, Golda Meir, has made it known that her government is unalterably opposed to Big Power intervention in the quest of peace in the Middle East. Even U.S.-Soviet consultations were considered harmful for while they lasted there was very little hope of any Arab leader making any effort toward direct negotiations. The Israelis moreover contend that even if a settlement with the help of the Big Powers is agreed upon, it would not be fairly enforced. The events of May 1967, when Nasser evicted the U.N. Emergency Forces, has stiffened Israel's resolve never to accept such a force, even with Big Power guarantees, as a substitute for a peace treaty.[131] Premier Golda Meir has made it clear that Israel will not agree to withdraw from occupied Arab territories on the basis of Big Power guarantees as she had done after the 1956 Suez Crisis. "We have learnt to stand up to any attempt to force

---

[130] This resolution called in effect for (i) the withdrawal of Israeli occupation forces; (ii) freedom of navigation through international waterways in the Middle East; (iii) solution of the Arab refugee problem; and (iv) in general, for a burying of hatchets in the area. For the text of the resolution, see Appendix VIII.

[131] *New York Times,* Weekly Review, 14 July 1968, p. 3.

on us a medicine that would not cure the illness but aggravate it", she said.[132] In other words, the Israeli government is in no mood to trust again guarantees given by the Big Powers, and does not believe that peace is really possible now or for several years.[133]

Israel refuses to acknowledge any major responsibility for the Arab refugee problem. She puts the entire blame upon the Arab governments, both for the original flight of the refugees and for more than twenty years of their impoverished exile, since it was the Arab armies that started the conflict by attacking Israel on the very day the state was proclaimed. Informed observers, however, contend that psychologically and politically the Arabs cannot reach any real settlement with the Israelis until the latter accept a major share of the responsibility for the Arab refugee problem and take positive steps to provide restitution and compensation for Arab losses.[134] It is also believed that the growing bitter attitude of the refugees, whose number now approximates two million,[135] constitutes the greatest threat to Israel. The refugees claim the right to return to their land and they vow that "they

[132] *Statesman,* Calcutta, 20 April 1969, p. 1.

[133] The hanging of nine Jews in Baghdad in January 1969, on doubtful "espionage" charges exacerbated Israeli feelings. This incident drove home the feeling of futility about negotiating with the Arabs, and the Israelis seemed to be saying: "Whom are we going to deal with? With those who turn a mock trial and public hanging into a carnival?" *New York Times,* Weekly Review, 9 February 1969, p. 7.

[134] While Israel is prepared to discuss the question of compensation, she is opposed to repatriation of the refugees who, in view of their intense hatred and desire to secure the extinction of Israel, are considered as a security risk. Israel, moreover, contends that she has already contributed to a solution of the refugee problem by receiving several hundred thousand Jewish refugees from Arab lands among its immigrants. Laqueur, *Documentary History,* 24n, p. 162.

[135] In 1948 there were about 700,000 refugees. By the time of the Six Day War in June 1967, there were 1.3 million refugees. Since then 700,000 more have fled from Israeli occupied territory.

will return even if it takes them 1000 years". The antagonism of the Arabs toward the Israelis, in fact, goes on increasing steadily as the occupation continues. "Without a settlement of the issues [including the refugee problem] that caused the [June 1967] conflict", commented the *New York Times,* "Israel will have gained only another breathing spell and the Middle East will remain an area of ferment and danger".[136]

PERILS OF CONTINUING CONFRONTATION

It appears that the present Israeli policy of prolonging indefinitely the military occupation of Arab territories and of disclaiming all responsibility for the plight of Arab refugees, plus the repeated statements made by Israeli leaders that some, if not all, of the lands taken over since 5 June 1967, are now permanently Israeli—all these have made the negotiation of an Arab-Israeli settlement extremely difficult. A realistic appraisal of Arab politics and of Arab popular emotions clearly indicates that Arab governments could not yet consent to deal directly with Israel and

[136] *New York Times,* Weekly Review, 11 June 1967, p. 6. It is a pity that the Arabs should be engaged in a conflict with Israel when cooperation with her offers far greater rewards to them. In relation to population and land area, Israel is today one of the world's treasure troves of trained human resources. The managerial, technical, scientific and medical wealth of Israel are precisely the elements that are most scarce in the Arab nations. And with these, Israel can make a real contribution to the economic advancement of the Middle East, if the political situation permits this kind of cooperation. There can hardly be any more fruitful combination than the union of the Arab nations' resources—including their enormous wealth of oil and their huge population—with the skills and knowledge of Israel. Then with international assistance, which most probably would not be lacking, the deserts of Arabia could be made to bloom and the lot of the ordinary Arab peasant could be quickly lifted to heights that would be otherwise difficult for them to achieve in the foreseeable future.

agree to an unfavourable peace settlement in the face of violent popular opposition.[137] Any Arab leader who might do so, might find himself in "serious political and personal peril". To the Arabs, Israel's quest for "secure frontiers" in an effort to obtain "absolute security" is frightening, for after every clash with them Israel has come forward with a fresh definition of what she regards as "secure frontiers".

Such a stance might be ultimately self-defeating for Israel and might result in another Arab-Israeli war with unforeseeable consequences. In the long run, as Arab societies modernize and as competent leaders increasingly succeed in guiding them into greater effectiveness in technology, industry and science, the prospects for a small state like Israel which had not won the goodwill of its immediately encircling neighbours would not appear to be very encouraging. No matter how many more great military victories the Israelis may win, the sea of Arab peoples ringing them cannot be eliminated from the picture, and as they become modernized—even if it takes a long time—they would be in a position to wage war effectively. Yasir Arafat, the Al Fatah leader, stated in an interview with the *Time* correspondent Gavin Scott that: "As Napoleon and Hitler were drowned in the snows of Russia, the sands of our deserts will swallow the Israelis. Our people can put up with many invasions".[138]

Israel, in other words, will have to realize that she will not

---

[137] It is possible that Israel had deliberately set conditions so unacceptable that the Arabs could not possibly agree to them in order that she could both justify her retention of the occupied areas and place full responsibility on the Arabs for the failure to achieve any peace treaty. As Joseph Alsop wrote in the *Evening Bulletin*: "Since the overwhelming majority of Israelis wish to retain the territorial conquests, but wish to avoid the blame for doing so, having the Arabs refuse to negotiate is intensely convenient to Israel." *The Evening Bulletin* (Philadelphia), (14 November 1967).

[138] *Time*, U.S. Edition, 30 March 1970, p. 32.

always be able to depend upon her superior military strength, and that her long term prospects of survival will depend not on her power alone but upon her accommodation and cooperation with her Arab neighbours—in her becoming an integrated and accepted member of the Middle Eastern community. The Arabs, on their part, will have to realize that the activities of the Fedayeen commando groups are not likely to have any decisive effect militarily and politically; and, on the other hand, could lead them to further disasters. There have been indications that Israel might soon have her own nuclear weapons which she might be tempted to use in a final act of desperation if the country were threatened by destruction.[139] The Arab leaders should therefore realize that if faced with annihilation, the Israelis would undoubtedly ruin the Arab states as well. To survive, both the Arabs and the Israelis will have to make mutual concessions, and might even have to give up "many of their cherished beliefs" as well as undergo changes in their "basic political orientation".

INTERESTS OF THE SUPERPOWERS

A question that has been engaging the attention of both the United States and the Soviet Union is the emergence of a relative power-vacuum in the Middle East. The United States is naturally concerned lest the Soviet Union should step into the vacuum. However, although the influence of the Soviet Union in the Middle East has increased considerably since the June 1967 war, it is unlikely that any Arab country will surrender to the Russians its own power of decision. So far the radical Arab states have exploited Soviet influence and resources for their own advantage. But the Russians have had the satisfaction of knowing that their influence have been growing while that of the United States has been retreating.

[139] *Boston Evening Globe*, 8 February 1970, p. 41.

The Superpowers and the Middle East

In view of the Soviet movement toward a *status quo* position in the world, its growing concern for international stability[140] accompanied by an erosion of its revolution-promoting ideology,[141] one would expect the Soviet Union to favour the restoration of peace and stability in the turbulent Middle East region. However, from the present indications it appears that while the Soviet Union is keen on avoiding another war in the Middle East that could bring her into a clash with the United States, at the same time, she is unwilling to witness the return of American influence in that region. As such she seems to welcome limited strife and instability that would keep the 'pot boiling', but will not result in a general war. The Soviet Union appears to think that her continued presence in the Arab countries depends largely on the perpetuation of the Arab-Israeli conflict, a continuation of the pre-June 1967 state of tension between the Arabs and the Jews.[142] Without this, the Arabs most probably would have little

---

[140] The Soviet Union shares a common concern with the United States in several important respects which has led to agreements between them on matters of mutual interest. These include agreements to limit the use of space for nuclear warfare and to use it only for peaceful purposes; to limit the spread of nuclear weapons by signing the nuclear non-proliferation treaty; and to reduce the contamination of the atmosphere through nuclear testing by signing the nuclear test-ban treaty in July 1963.

[141] Soviet Union's appeal as "the home of communism" scarcely extends beyond her own borders. She has become essentially, a "conservative society" with a superstructure of revolutionary ideological phraseology. See Laqueur, *Struggle for the Middle East*, 93n, p. 187.

[142] The Russians have high stakes in the Middle East. A Russian oriented Middle East would be the fulfilment of age long Russian aspirations. The Middle East could serve as a window looking out towards the Indian Ocean on the one side and the African continent on the other. The possibility of using the Arab countries as forward bases could open up new vistas for Soviet moves in the cold war. Moreover, Russian entrenchment in this vital area—including the southernmost tip in Yemen—is looked upon with great significance especially in view of the immi-

The Third Arab-Israeli War

need for the Soviet Union, and the greater potential of the United States to provide economic aid might eject her from the present position of influence in the Arab world. Hence Moscow seems to favour the perpetuation of the conflict, but it does not want the conflict to explode once more into an open war that could escalate into a Soviet-American confrontation.

Despite a warning by President Nixon that the United States "would view any effort by the Soviet Union to seek predominance in the Middle East as a matter of grave concern",[143] the Soviet Union appears to be willing to take some calculated risks perhaps for fear of losing influence in the Third World or of being out-manoeuvred by China. It is possible, however, that the increasing unrest in Eastern Europe,[144] the growing threat of China and

nent departure of the British from the Persian Gulf region in 1971. The former U.S. Secretary of Defense Robert McNamara realized this when he warned about the danger of communist threat in the direction of "the Horn at the approaches to the Red Sea." The Soviet Union, in other words, has every interest in deepening her penetration in the Middle East, and the continuation of the Arab-Israeli conflict is considered to be the most vital factor for her success in this respect. See U.S. House of Representatives, Congress 90, Session 1, Committee on Armed Services, *Report of Secretary of Defense on 1968 Defense Program and Defense Budget*, Washington, 1967, p. 22, for McNamara's statement.

[143] *Boston Evening Globe,* 18 February 1970, p. 18.

[144] The Middle East crisis in June 1967 revealed the deterioration of discipline within the Communist bloc. After the end of the Arab-Israeli war, the Soviet bloc countries, with the exception of Rumania, broke off diplomatic relations with Israel. Guided by its national interest, Rumania decided to adopt an "attitude of neutrality". In Czechoslovakia, although the government toed the Soviet policy of supporting the Arabs, the intelligentsia as well as the public opinion sympathised with the Israelis. They tended to identify Israel threatened with annihilation by an Arab world ten times superior in both men and military potential, with pre-war Czechoslovakia threatened and invaded by Nazi Germany. It is significant that the Czechoslovak Writer's Congress of June 1967, which unleashed the forces leading to Novotny's fall and the political uprising in

the probable struggle for power within the Soviet leadership[145] may, at some stage, deflect the Soviet Union from its preoccupation with the Middle East. But for the time being, she is seeking to keep open as many alternatives as possible. As long as events do not compel the Soviet leaders to make radical policy choices, they will probably continue to pursue a flexible strategy that would enable them to cope with the "complexities" and "contradictions" of the Middle East.

Prospects of Peace

Insofar as the prospects of peace in the Middle East in the discernible future are concerned it, to a large degree, depends on the extent to which the superpowers can bring about a reduction in the level of violence in the area—so that another probable war can be averted; and define and support, more decisively than they have done uptil now, a comprehensive political settlement. A general peace settlement in the Middle East would probably depend on how far the United States and the Soviet Union are prepared to risk their future influence and interests in that area by urging and, if necessary, by applying pressures on both sides to make the concessions which would be needed. The basic issue

---

April 1968, was dominated by two themes: protest against the anti-Israeli campaign, and protest against censorship. *Problems of Communism*, vol. 17, November-December, 1968, pp. 34-5.

[145] Informed observers of the Soviet scene appear to believe that there have been severe differences of opinion inside the Kremlin over the Soviet Middle Eastern policy. Red Army commanders backed by the more dogmatic elements in the Soviet Communist Party led by Alexander Shelepin, have demanded a much tougher line against Israel and the West than the political leadership under Brezhnev, Podgorny and Kosygin, have been willing to take. The political leadership, on the other hand, consider the strategy of a "tough policy" to be secondary to the prime Soviet aim of maintaining their policy of peaceful co-existence with the West and preventing a Soviet-American confrontation.

as seen from an impartial observer's stand-point is whether the Soviet Union can persuade President Nasser of the UAR to go any further toward meeting the Israeli demand than the *de facto* recognition of Israel that has been given by acknowledging its existence as a reality,[146] and whether the United States can persuade Israel to relax its insistence on formal recognition? But from the Arab standpoint, the basic issue seems to be whether the two superpowers can get the Israelis to pull out of the Sinai without demanding of Nasser concessions that the Arabs regard as too humiliating to accept?

The Arabs consider it unthinkable to negotiate freely a peace with a neighbour which not only continues to occupy portions of their territories, but also talks about territorial issues in such terms as to lend credence to the belief about her having territorial ambitions. It has to be realized, however, that Arab paranoia over the prospects of unlimited Israeli territorial expansion is matched by a Jewish paranoia toward the prospects of unceasing Arab determination to destroy Israel and slaughter all Jews. The Fedayeen attacks on Israel as well as the declarations and calls by Arab leaders for a "Holy War" seem to support Israeli charge that the Arabs will not accept the existence of Israel in any form. It is evident that the emotionally overcharged atmosphere in the Middle East must be cleared, the mutal fears and hatreds must somehow be abated, and the beginnings of mutual credibility must be established if the first steps toward a settlement are ever going to be taken.

The United States and the Soviet Union can make a contribution in this direction by coming to an understanding between themselves on the essentials of a fair settlement. Although an imposed solution is ruled out since it would not be acceptable to either the Arabs or the Israelis, nevertheless, if the superpowers

---

[146] Statement made by the UAR Foreign Minister, Mahmoud Riad, *New York Times*, Weekly Review, 14 July 1968, p. 3.

can jointly sponsor an equitable, fool-proof formula and present it to the Arabs and Israelis in the right way, it will be difficult for both the antagonists to turn it down. The withdrawal of Israel from the occupied territories, a disavowal on her part of any future expansionist aims, a willingness to settle the refugee problem with international help, and an agreement on international supervision of Jerusalem may be linked to the complete termination of the state of belligerency and an acceptance by the Arab states of the existence of Israel, her recognition and her right of access to both the Gulf of Aqaba and the Suez, to the demilitarization of the Sinai and the West Bank of Jordan, and the stationing of U.N. peace keeping forces on Egyptian soil. At the same time the superpowers might commit formally to guarantee the security of Israel and the Arab states if, and when, a final peace settlement is reached. Such a guarantee might encourage both sides to make substantial concessions without the fear that they would be endangering their security. The superpowers will also have to refrain from encouraging the arms race by stopping to compete with one another in supplying arms to the region in a struggle for influence.[147] This latter aspect is particularly important since the persistence of Soviet-American political rivalry in the Middle East is fraught with dangerous potentialities even though both sides are determined not to permit the Arab-Israeli rivalry to flare up to the point where it might be transferred into a fight between themselves. The danger exists because neither the United States nor the Soviet Union can control the actions of the Israelis or the Arabs. The Soviet Union may be friendly towards

---

[147] Due to the extent to which the United States and the Soviet Union, and to a lesser degree, France and Great Britain, had supplied arms to the Middle East rivals during the decade following the Suez Crisis of 1956, the Big Powers in a real sense made it possible for the crisis of 1967 to occur. Once the Arabs and the Israelis received arms, it was they who determined how and when to use them.

the Arabs, hostile towards Israel, and thus be able to exert more influence over the Arabs; but this does not mean that she can prevent the Arabs from taking action on their own, let alone dictating to them.[148] Similarly, American support may be essential to Israel's survival, but the United States cannot prevent Israel from acting in any way she likes. And so long as the United States has a special sponsor relationship with Israel, and the Soviet Union has a special sponsor role towards some of the Arab states, continued conflict between Israel and the Arab states poses the possibility of the superpowers becoming involved in it.[149] Despite the common interest of both the superpowers in avoiding such an eventuality, tactical considerations and mutual suspicion have led them to line up with their respective "proteges", and to engage with each other in a "contest by proxy" which has tended to draw them further apart than they needed to be.

But in their own interest, the superpowers must strive to remove the Middle East as an arena in which they compete politically and seek, instead, to bring about a settlement of the outstanding issues between the Arabs and the Israelis since they have a vital stake in not allowing hostile relations between the two antagonists to continue indefinitely lest another round of fighting should drag them into it. In this connection it may be mentioned that Israel and the UAR agreed to a ceasefire on 8 August

---

[148] In view of the stalemating "balance of terror" which has prevented the superpowers from using all of their influence for fear of one another, the Arab states have not considered it necessary to join any bloc to win favors.

[149] The provocations for a new conflict are not lacking and it is possible for the Arabs and the Israelis to stumble into another war. With Israel likely to have her nuclear weapons soon, there would be a heightened risk this time that they might be introduced into the conflict, though possibly, only in the last resort. This gloomy prospect underscores the urgency of a negotiated settlement. *Boston Evening Globe*, 8 February 1970, p. 41.

1970,[150] following the acceptance by both sides of a U.S. proposal for a 90-day "standstill ceasefire" as embodied in the "Rogers Plan" put forward by the U.S. Secretary of State William Rogers.[151] The Big Powers agreed to place their full weight behind the new peace drive in the Middle East.[152] Informed observers believed that this unity was dictated by the fear shared by both the United States and the Soviet Union that their respective client could not be allowed to further raise the tempo of the war without endangering their own security.[153] However, within a week after the ceasefire came into effect, Israel charged on 14 August

---

[150] The Palestinian commando organizations, however, refused to observe the ceasefire and they made guerrilla rocket raids upon Israel from Jordan soon after the announcement of the ceasefire. Israel warned that she would hold Jordan responsible for any "acts of aggression" committed from its territory and would hit back at any breach of the ceasefire. *Statesman*, Calcutta, 9 August 1970, p. 1.

[151] Some observers believe that the United States acted under the compulsions of a fast deteriorating situation in the Middle East when it came out with the "Rogers Plan". So long as Israel had a field day on the battle front, the United States seemed to subscribe to the Israeli theory that Tel-Aviv could alone take care of the situation; and that left to themselves the Arabs and the Israelis would finally settle their disputes. A change in this situation occurred after the installation of surface-to-air SAM-3 Soviet missiles in the UAR and the flying of operational missions by Soviet pilots over Egypt from the end of April 1970. This resulted in an increased momentum of the war on the Suez front, and heightened the possibility of the superpowers becoming involved in a clash with one another. The "Rogers Plan", which was in essence a reassertion of the Security Council resolution of 22 November 1967, was the American response to the above challenge.

[152] Following the ceasefire agreement in the Middle East, the U. N. Secretary General U. Thant reactivated the Jarring Mission immediately thereafter to begin spadework for peace in the Middle East on the basis of the "Rogers Plan" and the Security Council resolution of 22 November 1967. *Statesman*, Calcutta, 9 August 1970, p. 1.

[153] As a result of the ceasefire, the United States is expected to keep

1970, that the UAR had installed Soviet SAM-2 and SAM-3 missiles within 19 kilometres of the west bank of the Suez Canal which constituted a violation of the 90-day ceasefire that took effect on 8 August 1970, and called upon the United States to intervene in the matter.[154] The Israeli Defence Minister General Moshe Dayan stated that both Egypt and Israel had agreed to a military standstill in an area 50 kilometres on either side of the Suez Canal during the limited ceasefire. He said that this central clause of the ceasefire agreement had been broken when missile pads were moved up on the Egyptian side of the canal. The Israeli Foreign Minister Abba Eban said that Israel would give Washington "a certain amount of time" to make the UAR end its "violation of the ceasefire", and hoped that the United States would make the "UAR batteries return to where they were before the ceasefire". If this did not happen, Eban said, there would be a "new situation". He also said that the UAR would be to blame if the Jarring mission failed. He referred to a press conference by Hassanein Heykal, the UAR National Orientation Minister and the editor of *Al Ahram,* who said that there would be no negotiations and no peace treaty. Mr. Eban said: "I say in reply that in that case we will not budge a metre from the lines we occupy today".[155]

Israel in line with its peace plan while the Soviet Union exercises restraint over Cairo. The major problem now facing the superpowers is maintaining the ceasefire under mutually acceptable terms. The ceasefire under the "Rogers Plan" is also expected to be a military standstill. A mutual suspicion on this point has been sought to be set at rest by allowing each side to police the other's performance. Israel, however, still believes that the UAR may use the ceasefire for a further build-up of missile bases, preparatory to a later attack. The Egyptians similarly believe that the Israelis will use it to fit sophisticated jamming devices for the missiles, and may also resume deep aerial penetration later.

[154] *Statesman,* Calcutta, 15 August 1970, p. 13.
[155] *Ibid.*

From 8 August 1970, when the ceasefire agreement came into effect, uptil 19 August 1970, the U.S. State Department refused to confirm the Israeli allegation about the installation of SAM-2 and SAM-3 missiles by the UAR on the Suez Canal bank because it was reluctant to open up a crisis situation that might wreck the peace move that it had itself initiated.[156] But in the first week of September, 1970, the U.S. government was compelled, mainly on account of domestic pressure, to acknowledge the violation of the ceasefire by the UAR.[157] In view of the danger inherent in the new situation,[158] Washington has been prodding Moscow and Cairo for "rectification" of the situation in the Suez Canal zone. In the meanwhile, Israel announced on 6 September 1970, that she was pulling out of the U.S. initiated peace talks with the UAR until the situation on the Suez Canal "ceasefire line" was "restored to its previous form" before the shooting halt took effect.

This development has dealt a serious blow to the prospects of an early settlement of the long standing Arab-Israeli conflict

[156] President Nasser took grave political risks in accepting the "Rogers Plan" which split the Arab world and earned him the displeasure of the Palestine resistance movement. Having done that, and having for once succeeded in forcing Israel into a difficult position, it was believed that Nasser would not throw all this into jeopardy for the sake of a certain number of missiles being moved forward in the Suez Canal zone. This was one of the principal reasons why the United States refused to give credence to the early Israeli accusations. According to some observers, one explanation for Nasser's action is that perhaps, the presence of the missiles in the Suez Canal zone is of such paramount military importance to Egypt that he was prepared to incur the odium of pretending to accept the "Rogers Plan" in order to obtain the military respite necessary for the missiles forward deployment.

[157] *Statesman*, Calcutta, 6 September 1970, p. 1.

[158] If words and diplomatic pressure fail to bring about the removal of the missiles by the UAR from the Suez Canal zone, Israel will have its hands free to strike at the missile sites and the United States, most probably, will no longer be in a position to advise restraint.

and, it appears, that a lasting peace in the Middle East is not likely to be achieved without a fundamental understanding between the two superpowers—an understanding that would (a) ban the supply of armaments to both the contestants; (b) remove the area from the grip of the cold war, for as long as the conflict remains enmeshed in cold war politics, the prospects of peace appear to be poor indeed; and (c) finally, impress upon both the Arabs and the Israelis that some mutual concessions must be made and risks taken to open the way for some early progress towards resolving the most pressing issues in the dispute. Otherwise the situation is likely to deteriorate and both the parties are likely to become involved in greater sacrifices and risks in the future.

Appendixes

APPENDIX I

THE TRUMAN DOCTRINE: MESSAGE OF THE PRESIDENT OF THE UNITED STATES TO THE U.S. CONGRESS, MARCH 12, 1947*

MR. PRESIDENT, MR. SPEAKER, MEMBERS OF THE CONGRESS OF THE UNITED STATES:

The gravity of the situation which confronts the world today necessitates my appearance before a joint session of the Congress.

The foreign policy and the national security of this country are involved.

One aspect of the present situation, which I wish to present to you at this time for your consideration and decision, concerns Greece and Turkey.

The United States has received from the Greek Government an urgent appeal for financial and economic assistance. Preliminary reports from the American Economic Mission now in Greece and reports from the American Ambassador in Greece corroborate the statement of the Greek Government that assistance is imperative if Greece is to survive as a free nation.

I do not believe that the American people and the Congress wish to turn a deaf ear to the appeal of the Greek Government.

Greece is not a rich country. Lack of sufficient natural resources has always forced the Greek people to work hard to make both ends meet.

---

* *Department of State Bulletin,* Vol. 16, Supplement, 4 May 1947, pp. 829-832.

Appendixes

Since 1940 this industrious and peace-loving country has suffered invasion, four years of cruel enemy occupation, and bitter internal strife.

When forces of liberation entered Greece they found that the retreating Germans had destroyed virtually all the railways, roads, port facilities, communications, and merchant marine. More than a thousand villages had been burned. Eighty-five per cent of the children were tubercular. Livestock, poultry, and draft animals had almost disappeared. Inflation had wiped out practically all savings.

As a result of these tragic conditions, a militant minority, exploiting human want and misery, was able to create political chaos which, until now, has made economic recovery impossible.

Greece is today without funds to finance the importation of those goods which are essential to bare subsistence. Under these circumstances the people of Greece cannot make progress in solving their problems of reconstruction. Greece is in desperate need of financial and economic assistance to enable it to resume purchases of food, clothing, fuel, and seeds. These are indispensable for the subsistence of its people and are obtainable only from abroad. Greece must have help to import the goods necessary to restore internal order and security so essential for economic and political recovery.

The Greek Government has also asked for the assistance of experienced American administrators, economists, and technicians to insure that the financial and other aid given to Greece shall be used effectively in creating a stable and self-sustaining economy and in improving its public administration.

The very existence of the Greek state is today threatened by the terrorist activities of several thousand armed men, led by Communists, who defy the Government's authority at a number of points, particularly along the northern boundaries. A commission appointed by the United Nations Security Council is at present investigating disturbed conditions in northern Greece and alleged border violations along the frontier between Greece on the one hand and Albania, Bulgaria, and Yugoslavia on the other.

Meanwhile, the Greek Government is unable to cope with the situation. The Greek army is small and poorly equipped. It needs supplies and equipment if it is to restore authority to the Government throughout Greek territory.

Greece must have assistance if it is to become a self-supporting and self-respecting democracy.

The United States must supply that assistance. We have already extended to Greece certain types of relief and economic aid, but these are inadequate.

There is no other country to which democratic Greece can turn.

No other nation is willing and able to provide the necessary support for a democratic Greek Government.

The British Government, which has been helping Greece, can give no further financial or economic aid after March 31. Great Britain finds itself under the necessity of reducing or liquidating its commitments in several parts of the world, including Greece.

We have considered how the United Nations might assist in this crisis. But the situation is an urgent one requiring immediate action, and the United Nations and its related organizations are not in a position to extend help of the kind that is required.

It is important to note that the Greek Government has asked for our aid in utilizing effectively the financial and other assistance we may give to Greece, and in improving its public administration. It is of the utmost importance that we supervise the use of any funds made available to Greece, in such a manner that each dollar spent will count toward making Greece self-supporting, and will help to build an economy in which a healthy democracy can flourish.

No government is perfect. One of the chief virtues of democracy, however, is that its defects are always visible and under democratic processes can be pointed out and corrected. The Government of Greece is not perfect. Nevertheless it represents 85 per cent of the members of the Greek Parliament who were chosen in an election last year. Foreign observers, including 692 Americans, considered this election to be a fair expression of the views of the Greek people.

The Greek Government has been operating in an atmosphere of chaos and extremism. It has made mistakes. The extension of aid by this country does not mean that the United States condones everything that the Greek Government has done or will do. We have condemned in the past, and we condemn now, extremist measures of the right or the left. We have in the past advised tolerance, and we advise tolerance now.

Greece's neighbour, Turkey, also deserves our attention.

The future of Turkey as an independent and economically sound state is clearly no less important to the freedom-loving peoples of the world than the future of Greece. The circumstances in which Turkey finds itself today are considerably different from those of Greece. Turkey has been spared the disasters that have beset Greece. And during the war the United States and Great Britain furnished Turkey with material aid.

Nevertheless, Turkey now needs our support.

Since the war Turkey has sought additional financial assistance from Great Britain and the United States for the purpose of effecting that modernization necessary for the maintenance of its national integrity.

That integrity is essential to the preservation of orders in the Middle East.

The British Government has informed us that, owing to its own difficulties, it can no longer extend financial or economic aid to Turkey. As in the case of Greece, if Turkey is to have the assistance it needs, the United States must supply it. We are the only country able to provide that help.

I am fully aware of the broad implications involved if the United States extends assistance to Greece and Turkey, and I shall discuss these implications with you at this time.

One of the primary objectives of the foreign policy of the United States is the creation of conditions in which we and other nations will be able to work out a way of life free from coercion. This was a fundamental issue in the war with Germany and Japan. Our victory was won over countries which sought to impose their will, and their way of life, upon other nations.

To insure the peaceful development of nations, free from coercion, the United States has taken a leading part in establishing the United Nations. The United Nations is designed to make possible lasting freedom and independence for all its members. We shall not realize our objectives, however, unless we are willing to help free peoples to maintain their free institutions and their national integrity against aggressive movements that seek to impose upon them totalitarian regimes. This is no more than a frank recognition that totalitarian regimes imposed upon free peoples, by direct or indirect aggression, undermine the foundations of international peace and hence the security of the United States.

The peoples of a number of countries of the world have recently had totalitarian regimes forced upon them against their will. The Government of the United States has made frequent protests against coercion and intimidation, in violation of the Yalta agreement, in Poland,

Rumania, and Bulgaria. I must also state that in a number of other countries there have been similar developments.

At the present moment in world history nearly every nation must choose between alternative ways of life. The choice is too often not a free one.

One way of life is based upon the will of the majority, and is distinguished by free institutions, representative government, free elections, guaranties, of individual liberty, freedom of speech and religion, and freedom from political oppression.

The second way of life is based upon the will of a minority forcibly imposed upon the majority. It relies upon terror and oppression, a controlled press and radio, fixed elections, and the supression of personal freedoms.

I believe that it must be the policy of the United States to support free peoples who are resisting attempted subjugation by armed minorities or by outside pressures.

I believe that we must assist free peoples to work out their own destinies in their own way.

I believe that our help should be primarily through economic and financial aid which is essential to economic stability and orderly political processes.

The world is not static, and the *status quo* is not sacred. But we cannot allow changes in the *status quo* in violation of the Charter of the United Nations by such methods as coercion, or by such subterfuges as political infiltration. In helping free and independent nations to maintain their freedom, the United States will be giving effect to the principles of the Charter of the United Nations.

It is necessary only to glance at a map to realize that the survival and integrity of the Greek nation are of grave importance in a much wider situation. If Greece should fall under the control of an armed minority, the effect upon its neighbor, Turkey, would be immediate and serious. Confusion and disorder might well spread throughout the entire Middle East.

Moreover, the disappearance of Greece as an independent state would have a profound effect upon those countries in Europe whose peoples are struggling against great difficulties to maintain their freedoms and their independence while they repair the damages of war.

It would be an unspeakable tragedy if these countries, which have so long struggled against overwhelming odds, should lose that victory for which they sacrificed so much. Collapse of free institutions and loss of independence would be disastrous not only for them but for the world. Discouragement and possibly failure would quickly be the lot of the neighboring peoples striving to maintain their freedom and independence.

Should we fail to aid Greece and Turkey in this fateful hour, the effect will be far-reaching to the West as well as to the East.

We must take immediate and resolute action.

I therefore ask the Congress to provide authority for assistance to Greece and Turkey in the amount of $400,000,000 for the period ending June 30, 1948. In requesting these funds, I have taken into consideration the maximum amount of relief assistance which would be furnished to Greece out of the $350,000,000 which I recently requested that the Congress authorize for the prevention of starvation and suffering in countries devastated by the war.

In addition to funds, I ask the Congress to authorize the detail of American civilian and military personnel to Greece and Turkey, at the request of those countries, to assist in the tasks of reconstruction, and for the purpose of supervising the use of such financial and material assistance as may be furnished. I recommend that authority also be provided for the instruction and training of selected Greek and Turkish personnel.

Finally, I ask that the Congress provide authority which will permit the speediest and most effective use, in terms of needed commodities, supplies, and equipment, of such funds as may be authorized.

If further funds, or further authority, should be needed for purposes indicated in this message, I shall not hesitate to bring the situation before the Congress. On this subject the Executive and Legislative branches of the Government must work together.

This is a serious course upon which we embark.

I would not recommend it except that the alternative is much more serious.

The United States contributed $341,000,000,000 toward winning World War II. This is an investment in world freedom and world peace.

The assistance that I am recommending for Greece and Turkey amounts to little more than one-tenth of one per cent of this investment. It is only commonsense that we should safeguard this investment and make sure that it was not in vain.

The seeds of totalitarian regimes are nurtured by misery and want. They spread and grow in the evil soil of poverty and strife. They reach their full growth when the hope of a people for a better life has died.

We must keep that hope alive.

The free peoples of the world look to us for support in maintaining their freedoms.

If we falter in our leadership, we may endanger the peace of the world—and we shall surely endanger the welfare of our own Nation.

Great responsibilities have been placed upon us by the swift movement of events.

I am confident that the Congress will face these responsibilities squarely.

APPENDIX II

TRIPARTITE DECLARATION REGARDING SECURITY IN THE MIDDLE EAST, May 25, 1950*

The Government of the United Kingdom, France, and the United States, having had occasion during the recent Foreign Ministers meeting in London to review certain questions affecting the peace and stability of the Arab states and of Israel, and particularly that of the supply of arms and war material to these states, have resolved to make the following statements:

1. The three Governments recognize that the Arab states and Israel all need to maintain a certain level of armed forces for the purposes of assuring their internal security and their legitimate self-defense and to permit them to play their part in the defense of the area as a whole. All applications for arms or war material for these countries will be considered in the light of these principles. In this connection the three Governments wish to recall and reaffirm the terms of the statements made by their representatives on the Security Council on August 4, 1949, in which they declared their opposition to the development of an arms race between the Arab states and Israel.

2. The three Governments declare that assurances have been received from all the states in question, to which they permit arms to be supplied from their countries, that the purchasing

* *Department of State Bulletin*, Vol. 22, 5 June 1950, p. 886.

Appendixes

state does not intend to undertake any act of aggression against any other state. Similar assurances will be requested from any other state in the area to which they permit arms to be supplied in the future.

3. The three Governments take this opportunity of declaring their deep interest in and their desire to promote the establishment and maintenance of peace and stability in the area and their unalterable opposition to the use of force or threat of force between any of the states in that area. The three Governments, should they find that any of these states was preparing to violate frontiers or armistice lines, would, consistently with their obligations as members of the United Nations, immediately take action, both within and outside the United Nations, to prevent such violation.

APPENDIX III

THE BAGHDAD PACT: PACT OF MUTUAL COOPERATION BETWEEN THE KINGDOM OF IRAQ, THE REPUBLIC OF TURKEY, THE UNITED KINGDOM, THE DOMINION OF PAKISTAN, AND THE KINGDOM OF IRAN, February 24, 1955*.

Whereas the friendly and brotherly relations existing between Iraq and Turkey are in constant progress, and in order to complement the contents of the Treaty of Friendship and Good Neighbourhood concluded between His Majesty the King of Iraq and his Excellency the President of the Turkish Republic signed in Ankara on March 29, 1946, which recognised the fact that peace and security between the two countries is an integral part of the peace and security of all the nations of the world and in particular the nations of the Middle East, and that it is the basis for their foreign policies;

Whereas article 11 of the Treaty of Joint Defence and Economic Cooperation between the Arab League States provides that no provision of that treaty shall in any way affect, or is designed to affect, any of the rights and obligations accruing to the Contracting Parties from the United Nations Charter;

* Department of State Publication No. 6446. *American Foreign Policy 1950-1955. Basic Documents,* Vol. I, pp. 1257-1259.

And having realised the great responsibilities borne by them in their capacity as members of the United Nations concerned with the maintenance of peace and security in the Middle East region which necessitate taking the required measures in accordance with article 51 of the United Nations Charter;

They have been fully convinced of the necessity of concluding a pact fulfilling these aims, and for that purpose have appointed as their plenipotentiaries who having communicated their full powers, found to be in good and due form, have agreed as follows:

ARTICLE 1

Consistent with article 51 of the United Nations Charter the High Contracting Parties will co-operate for their security and defence. Such measures as they agree to take to give effect to this co-operation may form the subject of special agreements with each other.

ARTICLE 2

In order to ensure the realisation and effect application of the co-operation provided for in article 1 above, the competent authorities of the High Contracting Parties will determine the measures to be taken as soon as the present pact enters into force. These measures will become operative as soon as they have been approved by the Governments of the High Contracting Parties.

ARTICLE 3

The High Contracting Parties undertake to refrain from any interference whatsoever in each other's internal affairs. They will settle any dispute between themselves in a peaceful way in accordance with the United Nations Charter.

ARTICLE 4

The High Contracting Parties declare that the dispositions of the present pact are not in contradiction with any of the international obligations contracted by either of them with any third State or States. They do not derogate from and cannot be interpreted as derogating from, the said international obligations. The High Contracting Parties undertake not to enter into any international obligation incompatible with the present pact.

ARTICLE 5

This pact shall be open for accession to any member of the Arab League or any other State actively concerned with the security and peace in this region and which is fully recognised by both of the High Contracting Parties. Accession shall come into force from the date of which the instrument of accession of the State concerned is deposited with the Ministry for Foreign Affairs of Iraq.

Any acceding State party to the present pact may conclude special Agreements, in accordance with article 1, with one or more States parties to the present pact. The competent authority of any acceding State may determine measures in accordance with article 2. These measures will become operative as soon as they have been approved by the Governments of the parties concerned.

ARTICLE 6

A Permanent Council at ministerial level will be set up to function within the framework of the purposes of this pact when at least four Powers become parties to the pact.

The Council will draw up its own rules of procedure.

ARTICLE 7

This pact remains in force for a period of five years renewable for other five-year periods. Any Contracting Party may withdraw from the pact by notifying the other parties in writing of its desire to do so six months before the expiration of any of the above-mentioned periods, in which case the pact remains valid for the other parties.

ARTICLE 8

This pact shall be ratified by the contracting parties and ratifications shall be exchanged at Ankara as soon as possible. Thereafter it shall come into force from the date of the exchange of ratifications.

In witness whereof, the said plenipotentiaries have signed the present pact in Arabic, Turkish and English, all three texts being equally authentic except in the case of doubt when the English text shall prevail.

Done in duplicate at Baghdad this second day of Rajab 1374 Hijri corresponding to the twenty-fourth day of February 1955.

APPENDIX IV

PRESS RELEASE OF 19 JULY 1956

At the request of the Government of Egypt, the United States joined in December 1955 with the United Kingdom and with the World Bank in an offer to assist Egypt in the construction of a high dam on the Nile at Aswan. This project is one of great magnitude. It would require an estimated 12 to 16 years to complete at a total cost estimated at some $1,300,000,000, of which over $900,000,000 represents local currency requirements. It involves not merely the rights and interests of Egypt but of other states whose waters are contributory, including Sudan, Ethiopia, and Uganda.

The December offer contemplated an extension by the United States and United Kingdom of grant aid to help finance certain early phases of the work, the effects of which would be confined solely to Egypt, with the understanding that accomplishment of the project as a whole would require a satisfactory resolution of the question of Nile water rights. Another important consideration bearing upon the feasibility of the undertaking, and thus the practicability of American aid, was Egyptian readiness and ability to concentrate its economic resources upon this vast construction program.

Developments within the succeeding 7 months have not been favorable to the success of the project, and the U.S. Government has concluded that it is not feasible in present circumstances to participate in the project. Agreement by the riparian states has not been achieved, and the ability of Egypt to devote adequate resources to assure the project's success has become more uncertain than at the time the offer was made.

This decision in no way reflects or involves any alteration in the friendly relations of the Government and people of the United States toward the Government and people of Egypt.

The United States remains deeply interested in the welfare of the

Appendixes

Egyptian people and in the development of the Nile. It is prepared to consider at an appropriate time and at the request of the riparian states what steps might be taken toward a more effective utilization of the water resources of the Nile for the benefit of the peoples of the region. Furthermore, the United States remains ready to assist Egypt in its effort to improve the economic conditions of its people and is prepared, through its appropriate agencies, to discuss these matters within the context of funds appropriated by the Congress.

APPENDIX V

THE EISENHOWER DOCTRINE: SPECIAL MESSAGE TO THE CONGRESS ON THE SITUATION IN THE MIDDLE EAST, JANUARY 5, 1957*

To the Congress of the United States

First may I express to you my deep appreciation of your courtesy in giving me, at some inconvenience to yourselves, this early opportunity of addressing you on a matter I deem to be of grave importance to our country.

In my forthcoming State of the Union Message, I shall review the international situation generally. There are worldwide hopes which we can reasonably entertain, and there are worldwide responsibilities which we must carry to make certain that freedom—including our own—may be secure.

There is, however, a special situation in the Middle East which I feel I should, even now, lay before you.

Before doing so it is well to remind ourselves that our basic national objective in international affairs remains peace—a world peace based on justice. Such a peace must include all areas, all peoples of the world if it is to be enduring. There is no nation, great or small, with which we would refuse to negotiate, in mutual good faith, with patience and in the determination to secure a better understanding between us. Out of such understandings must, and eventually will, grow confidence and trust, indispensable ingredients to a program of peace and to plans for lifting from us all the burdens of expensive armaments. To

---

* *Public Papers of the Presidents of the United States, Dwight D. Eisenhower,* 1957, Washington, D. C., 1958, pp. 6-16.

promote these objectives, our government works tirelessly, day by day, month by month, year by year. But until a degree of success crowns our efforts that will assure to all nations peaceful existence, we must, in the interests of peace itself, remain vigilant, alert and strong.

I

The Middle East has abruptly reached a new and critical stage in its long and important history. In past decades many of the countries in that area were not fully self-governing. Other nations exercised considerable authority in the area and the security of the region was largely built around their power. But since the First World War there has been a steady evolution toward self-government and independence. This development the United States has welcomed and has encouraged. Our country supports without reservation the full sovereignty and independence of each and every nation of the Middle East.

The evolution to independence has in the main been a peaceful process. But the area has been often troubled. Persistent crosscurrents of distrust and fear with raids back and forth across national boundaries have brought about a high degree of instability in much of the Mid East. Just recently there have been hostilities involving Western European nations that once exercised much influence in the area. Also the relatively large attack by Israel in October has intensified the basic differences between that nation and its Arab neighbors. All this instability has been heightened and, at times, manipulated by International Communism.

II

Russia's rulers have long sought to dominate the Middle East. That was true of the Czars and it is true of the Bolsheviks. The reasons are not hard to find. They do not affect Russia's security, for no one plans to use the Middle East as a base for aggression against Russia. Never for a moment has the United States entertained such a thought.

The Soviet Union has nothing whatsoever to fear from the United States in the Middle East, or anywhere else in the world, so long as its rulers do not themselves first resort to aggression.

That statement I make solemnly and emphatically.

Neither does Russia's desire to dominate the Middle East spring from its own economic interest in the area. Russia does not appreciably use or depend upon the Suez Canal. In 1955 Soviet traffic through the Canal represented only about three fourths of 1% of the total. The Soviets have no need for, and could provide no market for the petroleum resources which constitute the principal natural wealth of the area. Indeed, the Soviet Union is a substantial exporter of petroleum products.

The reason for Russia's interest in the Middle East is solely that of power politics. Considering her announced purpose of Communizing the world, it is easy to understand her hope of dominating the Middle East.

This region has always been the crossroads of the continents of the Eastern Hemisphere. The Suez Canal enables the nations of Asia and Europe to carry on the commerce that is essential if these countries are to maintain well-rounded and prosperous economies. The Middle East provides a gateway between Eurasia and Africa.

It contains about two thirds of the presently known oil deposits of the world and it normally supplies the petroleum needs of many nations of Europe, Asia and Africa. The nations of Europe are peculiarly dependent upon this supply, and this dependency relates to transportation as well as to production. This has been vividly demonstrated since the closing of the Suez Canal and some of the pipelines. Alternate ways of transportation and, indeed, alternate sources of power can, if necessary, be developed. But these cannot be considered as early prospects.

These things stress the immense importance of the Middle East. If the nations of that area should lose their independence, if they were dominated by alien forces hostile to freedom, that would be both a tragedy for the area and for many other free nations whose economic life would be subject to near strangulation. Western Europe would be endangered just as though there had been no Marshall Plan, or North Atlantic Treaty Organization. The free nations of Asia and Africa, too, would be placed in serious jeopardy. And the countries of the Middle East would lose the markets upon which their economies depend. All this would have the most adverse, if not disastrous, effect upon our own Nation's economic life and political prospects.

Then there are other factors which transcend the material. The Middle East is the birthplace of three great religions—Moslem, Christian and Hebrew. Mecca and Jerusalem are more than places on the map. They symbolize religions which teach that the spirit has supremacy over matter and that the individual has a dignity and rights of which no despotic governments can rightfully deprive him. It would be intolerable if the holy places of the Middle East should be subjected to a rule that glorifies atheistic materialism.

International Communism, of course, seeks to mask its purposes of domination by expressions of goodwill and by superficially attractive offers of political, economic and military aid. But any free nation, which is subject to Soviet enticement, ought, in elementary wisdom, to look behind the mask.

Remember Estonia, Latvia and Lithuania. In 1939 the Soviet Union entered into mutual assistance pacts with these then independent countries; and the Soviet Foreign Minister, addressing the Extraordinary Fifth Session of the Supreme Soviet in October 1939, solemnly and publicly declared that "we stand for the scrupulous and punctilious observance of the pacts on the basis of complete reciprocity, and we declare that all the nonsensical talk about the Sovietization of the Baltic countries is only to the interest of our common enemies and of all anti-Soviet provocateurs." Yet in 1940 Estonia, Latvia and Lithuania were forcibly incorporated into the Soviet Union.

Soviet control of the satellite nations of Eastern Europe has been forcibly maintained in spite of solemn promises of a contrary intent, made during World War II.

Stalin's death brought hope that this pattern would change. And we read the pledge of the Warsaw Treaty of 1955 that the Soviet Union would follow in satellite countries "the principles of mutual respect for their independence and sovereignty and non-interference in domestic affairs." But we have just seen the subjugation of Hungary by naked armed force. In the aftermath of this Hungarian tragedy, world respect for and belief in Soviet promises have sunk to a new low. International Communism needs and seeks a recognizable success.

Thus we have these simple and indisputable facts:

1. The Middle East, which has always been coveted by Russia, would today be prized more than ever by International Communism.
2. The Soviet rulers continue to show that they do not scruple to use any means to gain their ends.
3. The free nations of the Mid East need, and for the most part want, added strength to assure their continued independence.

Appendixes

III

Our thoughts naturally turn to the United Nations as a protector of small nations. Its charter gives it primary responsibility for the maintenance of international peace and security. Our country has given the United Nations its full support in relation to the hostilities in Hungary and in Egypt. The United Nations was able to bring about a ceasefire and withdrawal of hostile forces from Egypt because it was dealing with governments and peoples who had a decent respect for the opinions of mankind as reflected in the United Nations General Assembly. But in the case of Hungary, the situation was different. The Soviet Union vetoed action by the Security Council to require the withdrawal of Soviet armed forces from Hungary. And it has shown callous indifference to the recommendations, even the censure, of the General Assembly. The United Nations can always be helpful, but it cannot be a wholly dependable protector of freedom when the ambitions of the Soviet Union are involved.

IV

Under all the circumstances I have laid before you, a greater responsibility now devolves upon the United States. We have shown, so that none can doubt, our dedication to the principle that force shall not be used internationally for any aggressive purpose and that the integrity and independence of the nations of the Middle East should be inviolate. Seldom in history has a nation's dedication to principle been tested as severely as ours during recent weeks.

There is general recognition in the Middle East, as elsewhere, that the United States does not seek either political or economic domination over any other people. Our desire is a world environment of freedom, not servitude. On the other hand many, if not all, of the nations of the Middle East are aware of the danger that stems from International Communism and welcome closer cooperation with the United States to realize for themselves the United Nations' goals of independence, economic well-being and spiritual growth.

If the Middle East is to continue its geographic role of uniting rather than separating East and West, if its vast economic resources are to serve the well-being of the peoples there, as well as that of others; and if its cultures and religions and their shrines are to be preserved for the uplifting of the spirit of the peoples, then the United States must make more evident its willingness to support the independence of the freedom-loving nations of the area.

V

Under these circumstances I deem it necessary to seek the cooperation of the Congress. Only with that cooperation can we give the reassurance needed to deter aggression, to give courage and confidence to those who are dedicated to freedom and thus prevent a chain of events which would gravely endanger all of the free world.

There have been several Executive declarations made by the United States in relation to the Middle East. There is the Tripartite Declaration of 25 May 1950, followed by the Presidential assurance of 31 October 1950, to the King of Saudi Arabia. There is the Presidential declaration of 9 April 1956, that the United States will within constitutional means oppose any aggression in the area. There is our Declaration of 29 November 1956, that a threat to the territorial integrity or political independence of Iran, Iraq, Pakistan, or Turkey would be viewed by the United States with the utmost gravity.

Nevertheless, weaknesses in the present situation and the increased danger from International Communism, convince me that basic United States policy should now find expression in joint action by the Congress and the Executive. Furthermore, our joint resolve should be so couched as to make it apparent that if need be our words will be backed by action.

VI

It is nothing new for the President and the Congress to join to recognize that the national integrity of other free nations is directly related to our own security.

We have joined to create and support the security system of the United Nations. We have reinforced the collective security system of the United Nations by a series of collective defense arrangements. Today we have security treaties with 42 other nations which recognize that our peace and security are intertwined. We have joined to take decisive action in relation to Greece and Turkey and in relation to Taiwan.

Thus, the United States through the joint action of the President

Appendixes

and the Congress, or, in the case of treaties, the Senate, has manifested in many endangered areas its purpose to support free and independent governments—and peace—against external menace, notably the menace of International Communism. Thereby we have helped to maintain peace and security during a period of great danger. It is now essential that the United States should manifest through joint action of the President and the Congress our determination to assist those nations of the Mid East area, which desire that assistance.

The action which I propose would have the following features.

It would, first of all, authorize the United States to cooperate with and assist any nation or group of nations in the general area of the Middle East in the development of economic strength dedicated to the maintenance of national independence.

It would, in the second place, authorize the Executive to undertake in the same region programs of military assistance and cooperation with any nation or group of nations which desires such aid.

It would, in the third place, authorize such assistance and cooperation to include the employment of the armed forces of the United States to secure and protect the territorial integrity and political independence of such nations, requesting such aid, against overt armed aggression from any nation controlled by International Communism.

These measures would have to be consonant with the treaty obligations of the United States, including the Charter of the United Nations and with any action or recommendations of the United Nations. They would also, if armed attack occurs, be subject to the overriding authority of the United Nations Security Council in accordance with the Charter.

The present proposal would, in the fourth place, authorize the President to employ, for economic and defensive military purposes, sums available under the Mutual Security Act of 1954, as amended, without regard to existing limitations.

The legislation now requested should not include the authorization or appropriation of funds because I believe that, under the conditions I suggest, presently appropriated funds will be adequate for the balance of the present fiscal year ending June 30. I shall, however, seek in subsequent legislation the authorization of $200,000,000 to be available during each of the fiscal years 1958 and 1959 for discretionary use in the area, in addition to the other mutual security programs for the area hereafter provided for by the Congress.

The Superpowers and the Middle East
VII

This program will not solve all the problems of the Middle East. Neither does it represent the totality of our policies for the area. There are the problems of Palestine and relations between Israel and the Arab States, and the future of the Arab refugees. There is the problem of the future status of the Suez Canal. These difficulties are aggravated by International Communism, but they would exist quite apart from that threat. It is not the purpose of the legislation I propose to deal directly with these problems. The United Nations is actively concerning itself with all these matters, and we are supporting the United Nations. The United States has made clear, notably by Secretary Dulles' address of 26 August 1955, that we are willing to do much to assist the United Nations in solving the basic problems of Palestine.

The proposed legislation is primarily designed to deal with the possibility of Communist aggression, direct and indirect. There is imperative need that any lack of power in the area should be made good, not by external or alien force, but by the increased vigor and security of the independent nations of the area.

Experience shows that indirect aggression rarely if ever succeeds where there is reasonable security against direct aggression; where the government disposes of loyal security forces, and where economic conditions are such as not to make Communism seem an attractive alternative. The program I suggest deals with all three aspects of this matter and thus with the problem of indirect aggression.

It is my hope and belief that if our purpose be proclaimed, as proposed by the requested legislation, that very fact will serve to halt any contemplated aggression. We shall have heartened the patriots who are dedicated to the independence of their nations. They will not feel that they stand alone, under the menace of great power. And I should add that patriotism is, throughout this area, a powerful sentiment. It is true that fear sometimes perverts true patriotism into fanaticism and to the acceptance of dangerous enticements from without. But if that fear can be allayed, then the climate will be more favourable to the attainment of worthy national ambitions.

Let me refer again to the requested authority to employ the armed forces of the United States to assist to defend the territorial integrity and political independence of any nation in the area against Communist armed aggression. Such authority would not be exercised except at

Appendixes

the desire of the nation attacked. Beyond this it is my profound hope that this authority would never have to be exercised at all.

Nothing is more necessary to assure this than that our policy with respect to the defense of the area be promptly and clearly determined and declared. Thus the United Nations and all friendly governments, and indeed governments which are not friendly, will know where we stand.

If, contrary to my hope and expectation, a situation arose which called for the military application of the policy which I ask the Congress to join me in proclaiming, I would of course maintain hour-by-hour contact with the Congress if it were in session. And if the Congress were not in session, and if the situation had grave implications, I would, of course, at once call the Congress into special session.

In the situation now existing, the greatest risk, as is often the case, is that ambitious despots may miscalculate. If power-hungry Communists should either falsely or correctly estimate that the Middle East is inadequately defended, they might be tempted to use open measures of armed attack. If so, that would start a chain of circumstances which would almost surely involve the United States in military action. I am convinced that the best insurance against this dangerous contingency is to make clear now our readiness to cooperate fully and freely with our friends in the Middle East in ways consonant with the purposes and principles of the United Nations. I intend promptly to send a special mission to the Middle East to explain the cooperation we are prepared to give.

IX

The policy which I outline involves certain burdens and indeed risks for the United States. Those who covet the area will not like what is proposed. Already, they are grossly distorting our purpose. However, before this Americans have seen our nation's vital interests and human freedom in jeopardy, and their fortitude and resolution have been equal to the crisis, regardless of hostile distortion of our words, motives and actions.

Indeed, the sacrifices of the American people in the cause of freedom have, ever since the close of World War II, been measured in many billions of dollars and in thousands of the precious lives of our youth.

These sacrifices, by which great areas of the world have been preserved to freedom, must not be thrown away.

In those momentous periods of the past, the President and the Congress have united, without partisanship, to serve the vital interests of the United States and of the free world.

The occasion has come for us to manifest again our national unity in support of freedom and to show our deep respect for the rights and independence of every nation—however great, however small. We seek not violence, but peace. To this purpose we must now devote our energies, our determination, ourselves.

DWIGHT D. EISENHOWER

APPENDIX VI

AIDE MEMOIRE FROM SECRETARY OF STATE DULLES TO ISRAELI AMBASSADOR TO THE UNITED STATES ABBA EBAN, FEBRUARY 11, 1957*

The United Nations General Assembly has sought specifically, vigorously, and almost unanimously, the prompt withdrawal from Egypt of the armed forces of Britain, France and Israel. Britain and France have complied unconditionally. The forces of Israel have been withdrawn to a considerable extent but still hold Egyptian territory at Sharm el Shaikh at the entrance to the Gulf of Aqaba. They also occupy the Gaza Strip which is territory specified by the Armistice arrangements to be occupied by Egypt.

We understand that it is the position of Israel that (1) it will evacuate its military forces from the Gaza strip provided Israel retains the civil administration and police in some relationship to the United Nations; and (2) it will withdraw from Sharm el Shaikh if continued freedom of passage through the Straits is assured.

With respect to (1) the Gaza Strip—it is the view of the United States that the United Nations General Assembly has no authority to require of either Egypt or Israel a substantial modification of the Armistice Agreement, which, as noted, now gives Egypt the right and responsibility of occupation. Accordingly, we believe that Israeli withdrawal from Gaza should be prompt and unconditional, leaving the

---

* *Department of State Bulletin,* Vol. 36, 11 March 1957, pp. 392-393.

Appendixes

future of the Gaza Strip to be worked out through the efforts and good offices of the United Nations.

We recognize that the area has been a source of armed infiltration and reprisals back and forth contrary to the Armistice Agreement and is a source of great potential danger because of the presence there of so large a number of Arab refugees—about 200,000. Accordingly, we believe that the United Nations General Assembly and the Secretary General should seek that the United Nations Emergency Force, in the exercise of its mission, move into this area and be on the boundary between Israel and the Gaza Strip.

The United States will use its best efforts to help to assure this result, which we believe is contemplated by the Second Resolution of February 2, 1957.

With respect to (2) the Gulf of Aqaba and access thereto—the United States believes that the Gulf comprehends international waters and that no nation has the right to prevent free and innocent passage in the Gulf and through the Straits giving access thereto. We have in mind not only commercial usage, but the passage of pilgrims on religious missions which should be fully respected.

The United States recalls that on January 28, 1950, the Egyptian Ministry of Foreign Affairs informed the United States that the Egyptian occupation of the two islands of Tiran and Senafir at the entrance of the Gulf of Aqaba was only to protect the islands themselves against possible damage or violation and that "this occupation being in no way conceived in a spirit of obstructing in any way innocent passage through the stretch of water separating these two islands from the Egyptian coast of Sinai, it follows that this passage, the only practicable one, will remain free as in the past, in conformity with international practice and recognized principles of the law of nations".

In the absense of some overriding dceision to the contrary, as by the International Court of Justice, the United States, on behalf of vessels of United States registry, is prepared to exercise the right of free and innocent passage and to join with others to secure general recognition of this right.

It is of course clear that the enjoyment of a right of free and innocent passage by Israel would depend upon its prior withdrawal in accordance with the United Nations Resolutions. The United States has no reason to assume that any littoral state would under these circumstances obstruct the right of free and innocent passage.

The United States believes that the United Nations General Assembly and the Secretary-General should, as a precautionary measure, seek that the United Nations Emergency Force move into the Straits area as the Israeli forces are withdrawn. This again we believe to be within the contemplation of the Second Resolution of February 2, 1957.

(3) The United States observes that the recent resolutions of the United Nations General Assembly call not only for the prompt and unconditional withdrawal of Israel behind the Armistice lines but call for other measures.

We believe, however, that the United Nations has properly established an order of events and an order of urgency and that the first requirement is that forces of invasion and occupation should withdraw.

The United States is prepared publicly to declare that it will use its influence, in concert with other United Nations members, to the end that, following Israel's withdrawal, these other measures will be implemented.

We believe that our views and purposes in this respect are shared by many other nations and that a tranquil future for Israel is best assured by reliance upon that fact, rather than by an occupation in defiance of the overwhelming judgment of the world community.

APPENDIX VII

U. THANT, SECRETARY-GENERAL OF THE UNITED NATIONS: REPORT ON THE WITHDRAWAL OF THE UNITED NATIONS EMERGENCY FORCE, JUNE 27, 1967 (Excerpts)*

1. This report on the withdrawal of the United Nations Emergency Force UNEF is submitted because, as indicated in my statement on 20 June 1967 to the fifth emergency special session of the General Assembly (1527th plenary meeting), important questions have been raised concerning the actions taken on the withdrawal of UNEF. These questions merit careful consideration and comment. It is in the interest of the United Nations, I believe, that this report should be full and frank, in view of the questions involved and the numerous statements that have been made, both public and private, which continue to be very damaging to the United Nations and to its peace-keeping role in

---

* U. N. Doc. A/6730/Add. 3, 27 June 1967.

Appendixes

particular. Despite the explanations already given in the several reports on the subject which have been submitted to the General Assembly and to the Security Council, misunderstandings and what, I fear, are misrepresentations, persist, in official as well as unofficial circles, publicly and behind the scenes.

2. A report of this kind is not the place to try to explain why there has been so much and such persistent and grossly mistaken judgement about the withdrawal of UNEF. It suffices to say here that the shattering crisis in the Near East inevitably caused intense shock in many capitals and countries of the world, together with deep frustration over the inability to cope with it. It is, of course, not unusual in such situations to seek easy explanations and excuses. When, however, this tactic involves imputing responsibility for the unleashing of major hostilities, it is, and must be, a cause for sober concern. The objective of this report is to establish an authentic, factual record of actions and their causes.

3. It follows, therefore, that the emphasis here, will be upon facts. The report is intended to be neither a polemic nor an apologia. Its sole purpose is to present a factually accurate picture of what happened and why. It will serve well the interests of the United Nations, as well as of historic integrity, if this presentation of facts can help to dissipate some of the distortions of the record which, in some places, apparently have emanated from panic, emotion and political bias.

MAIN POINTS AT ISSUE

31. Comment is called for on some of the main points at issue even prior to the consideration of the background and basis for the stationing of UNEF on United Arab Republic territory.

THE CAUSES OF THE PRESENT CRISIS

32. It has been said rather often in one way or another that the withdrawal of UNEF is a primary cause of the present crisis in the Near East. This is, of course, a superficial and over-simplified approach. As the Secretary-General pointed out in his report of 26 May 1967 to the Security Council (S/7906), this view "ignores the fact that the underlying basis for this and other crisis situations in the Near East is the continuing Arab-Israeli conflict which has been present all along

and of which the crisis situation created by the unexpected withdrawal of UNEF is the latest expression". The Secretary-General's report to the Security Council of 19 May 1967 (S/7896) described the various elements of the increasingly dangerous situation in the Near East prior to the decision of the Government of the United Arab Republic to terminate its consent for the presence of UNEF on its territory.

33. The United Nations Emergency Force served for more than ten years as a highly valuable instrument in helping to maintain quiet along the line between Israel and the United Arab Republic. Its withdrawal revealed in all its depth and danger the undiminishing conflict between Israel and her Arab neighbours. The withdrawal also made immediately acute the problem of access for Israel to the Gulf of Aqaba through the Strait of Tiran—a problem which had been dormant for over ten years only because of the presence of UNEF. But the presence of UNEF did not touch the basic problem of the Arab-Israel conflict—it merely isolated, immobilized and covered up certain aspects of that conflict. At any time in the last ten years either of the parties could have reactivated the conflict and if they had been determined to do so UNEF's effectiveness would automatically have disappeared. When, in the context of the whole relationship of Israel with her Arab neighbours, the direct confrontation between Israel and the United Arab Republic was revived after a decade by the decision of the United Arab Republic to move its forces up to the line, UNEF at once lost all usefulness. In fact, its effectiveness as a buffer and as a presence had already vanished, as can be seen from the chronology given above, even before the request for its withdrawal had been received by the Secretary-General from the Government of the United Arab Republic. In recognizing the extreme seriousness of the situation thus created, its true cause, the continuing Arab-Israeli conflict, must also be recognized. It is entirely unrealistic to maintain that that the conflict could have been solved, or its consequences prevented, if a greater effort had been made to maintain UNEF's presence in the area against the will of the Government of the United Arab Republic.

THE DECISION ON UNEF'S WITHDRAWAL

34. The decision to withdraw UNEF has frequently been characterized in various quarters as "hasty", "precipitous", and the like, even, indeed, to the extent of suggesting that it took President Nasser by

Appendixes

surprise. The question of the withdrawal of UNEF is by no means a new one. In fact, it was the negotiations on this very question with the Government of Egypt which, after the establishment of UNEF by the General Assembly, delayed its arrival while it waited in a staging area at Capodichino airbase, Naples, Italy, for several days in November, 1956. The Government of Egypt, understandably, did not wish to give permission for the arrival on its soil of an international force, unless it was assured that its sovereignty would be respected and a request for withdrawal of the Force would be honored. Over the years, in discussions with representatives of the United Arab Republic, the subject of the continued presence of UNEF has occasionally come up, and it was invariably taken for granted by United Arab Republic representatives that if their Government officially requested the withdrawal of UNEF the request would be honored by the Secretary-General. There is no record to indicate that this assumption was ever questioned. Thus, although the request for the withdrawal of UNEF came as a surprise, there was nothing new about the question of principle nor about the procedure to be followed by the Secretary-General. It follows that the decision taken by him on 18 May 1967 to comply with the request for the withdrawal of the Force was seen by him as the only reasonable and sound action that could be taken. The actual withdrawal itself, it should be recalled, was to be carried out in an orderly, dignified, deliberate and not precipitate manner over a period of several weeks. The first troops in fact left the area only on 29 May.

THE POSSIBILITY OF DELAY

35. Opinions have been frequently expressed that the decision to withdraw UNEF should have been delayed pending consultations of various kinds, or that efforts should have been made to resist the United Arab Republic's request for UNEF's withdrawal, or to bring pressure to bear on the Government of the United Arab Republic to reconsider its decision in this matter. In fact, as the chronology given above makes clear, the effectiveness of UNEF, in the light of the movement of United Arab Republic troops up to the line and into Sharm el Sheikh, had already vanished before the request for withdrawal was received. Furthermore, the Government of the United Arab Republic had made it entirely clear to the Secretary-General that an appeal for reconsideration of the withdrawal decision would encounter a firm

rebuff and would be considered as an attempt to impose UNEF as an "army of occupation". Such a reaction, combined with the fact that UNEF positions on the line had already been effectively taken over by United Arab Republic troops in pursuit of their full right to move up to the line in their own territory, and a deep anxiety for the security of UNEF personnel should an effort be made to keep UNEF in position after its withdrawal had been requested, were powerful arguments in favour of complying with the United Arab Republic request, even supposing there had not been other overriding reasons for accepting it.

36. It has been said that the decision to withdraw UNEF precipitated other consequences such as the reinstitution of the blockade against Israel in the Strait of Tiran. As can be seen from the chronology, the UNEF position at Sharm el Sheikh on the Strait of Tiran (manned by thirty-two men in all) were in fact rendered ineffective by United Arab Republic troops before the request for withdrawal was received. It is also pertinent to note that in response to a query from the Secretary-General as to why the United Arab Republic had announced its reinstitution of the blockade in the Strait of Tiran while the Secretary-General was actually en route to Cairo on 22 May, President Nasser explained that his Government's decision to resume the blockade had been taken some time before U Thant's departure and it was considered preferable to make the announcement before rather than after the Secretary-General's visit to Cairo.

THE QUESTION OF CONSULTATIONS

37. It has been said also that there was not adequate consultation with the organs of the United Nations concerned or with the Members before the decision was taken to withdraw the Force. The Secretary-General was, and is, firmly of the opinion that the decision for withdrawal of the Force, on the request of the host Government, rested with the Secretary-General after consultation with the Advisory Committee on UNEF which is the organ established by the General Assembly for consultation regarding such matters. This was made clear by Secretary-General Hammarskjold, who took the following position on 26 February 1957 in reply to a question about the withdrawal of the Force from Sharm el Sheikh:

Appendixes

"An indicated procedure would be for the Secretary-General to inform the Advisory Committee on the United Nations Emergency Force, which would determine whether the matter should be brought to the attention of the Assembly."*

The Secretary-General consulted the Advisory Committee before replying to the letter of 18 May 1967 from the United Arab Republic requesting withdrawal. This consultation took place within a few hours after the receipt of the United Arab Republic request, and the Advisory Committee was thus quickly informed of the decision which the Secretary-General had in mind to convey in his reply to the Foreign Minister of the United Arab Republic.

As indicated in the report to the Security Council of 26 May 1967: The Committee did not move, as it was its right to do under the terms of paragraph 9 of General Assembly resolution 1001 (ES-I) to request the convening of the General Assembly on the situation which had arisen. (S/7906, para. 4).

38. Before consulting the Advisory Committee on UNEF, the Secretary-General had also consulted the Permanent Representatives of the seven countries** providing the contingents of UNEF and informed them of his intentions. This, in fact, was more than was formally required of the Secretary-General in the way of consultation.

39. Obviously, many Governments were concerned about the presence and functioning of UNEF and about the general situation in the area, but it would have been physically impossible to consult all of the interested representatives within any reasonable time. This was an emergency situation requiring urgent action. Moreover, it was perfectly clear that such consultations were sure to produce sharply divided counsel, even if they were limited to the permanent members of the Security Council. Such sharply divided advice would have complicated and exacerbated the situation, and, far from relieving the Secretary-General of

---

*Official Records of the General Assembly, Eleventh Session, annexes, agenda item 66, document A/3563, annex I, B, 2.

**The 3,400 men of the UNEF came from Brazil, Canada, Denmark, India, Norway, Sweden, and Yugoslavia. The members of the Advisory Committee were Brazil, Canada, Ceylon, India, Norway, Pakistan and Colombia.

the responsibility for the decision to be taken, would have made the decision much more difficult to take.

40. It has been said that the final decision on the withdrawal of UNEF should have been taken only after consideration by the General Assembly. This position is not only incorrect but also unrealistic. In resolution 1000 (ES-I) the General Assembly established a United Nations command for an emergency international force. On the basis of that resolution the Force was quickly recruited and its forward elements flown to the staging area at Naples. Thus, though established, it had to await the permission of the Government of Egypt to enter Egyptian territory. That permission was subsequently given by the Government of Egypt as a result of direct discussions between Secretary-General Hammarskjold and President Nasser of Egypt. There is no official United Nations document on the basis of which any case could be made that there was any limitation on the authority of the Government of Egypt to rescind that consent at its pleasure, or which would indicate that the United Arab Republic had in any way surrendered its right to ask for and obtain at any time the removal of UNEF from its territory.

41. As a practical matter, there would be little point in any case in taking such an issue to the General Assembly unless there would be reasonable certainty that that body could be expected expeditiously to reach a substantive decision. In the prevailing circumstances, the question could have been validly raised as to what decision other than the withdrawal of UNEF could have been reached by the General Assembly once United Arab Republic consent for the continued presence of UNEF was withdrawn.

42. As regards the practical possibility of the Assembly considering the request for UNEF's withdrawal, it is relevant to observe that the next regular session of the General Assembly was some four months off at the time the withdrawal request was made. The special session of the General Assembly which was meeting at the time could have considered the question, according to rule 19 of the Assembly's rules of procedure, only if two thirds of eighty-two members voted for the inclusion of the item in the agenda. It is questionable, to say the least, whether the necessary support could have been mustered for such a controversial item. There could have been no emergency special session since the issue was not then before the Security Council, and therefore the condition of lack of unanimity did not exist.

Appendixes

43. As far as consultation with or action by the Security Council was concerned, the Secretary-General reported to the Council on the situation leading up to and created by the withdrawal of UNEF on 19 May 1967 (S/7896). In that report he characterized the situation in the Near East as "extremely menacing". The Council met for the first time after this report on 24 May 1967, but took no action.

44. As has already been stated, the Advisory Committee did not make any move to bring the matter before the General Assembly, and no representative of any Member Government requested a meeting of either the Security Council or the General Assembly immediately following the Secretary-General's reports (A/6730 and S/7896). In this situation, the Secretary-General himself did not believe that any useful purpose would be served by his seeking a meeting of either organ, nor did he consider that there was basis for him to do so at that time. Furthermore, the information available to the Secretary-General did not lead him to believe that either the General Assembly or the Security Council would have decided that UNEF should remain on United Arab Republic territory, by force if necessary, despite the request of the Government of the United Arab Republic that it should leave.

PRACTICAL FACTORS INFLUENCING THE DECISION

45. Since it is still contended in some quarters that the UNEF operations should somehow have continued after the consent of the Government of the United Arab Republic to its presence was withdrawn, it is necessary to consider the factors, quite apart from constitutional and legal considerations, which would have made such a course of action entirely impracticable.

46. The consent and active co-operation of the host country is essential to the effective operation and, indeed, to the very existence, of any United Nations peace-keeping operation of the nature of UNEF. The fact that UNEF had been deployed on Egyptian and Egyptian controlled territory for over ten and a half years with the consent and co-operation of the Government of the United Arab Republic. Although it was envisaged in pursuance of General Assembly resolution 1125 (XI) of 2 February 1957 that the Force would be stationed on both sides of the line, Israel exercised its sovereign right to refuse the stationing of UNEF on its side, and the Force throughout its existence was stationed on the United Arab Republic side of the line only.

47. In these circumstances, the true basis for UNEF's effectiveness as a buffer and deterrent to infiltration was, throughout its existence, a voluntary undertaking by local United Arab Republic authorities with UNEF, that United Arab Republic troops would respect a defined buffer zone along the entire length of the line in which only UNEF would operate and from which United Arab Republic troops would be excluded. This undertaking was honoured for more than a decade, and this Egyptian co-operation extended also to Sharm el Sheikh, Ras Nasrani and the Strait of Tiran. This undertaking was honored although UNEF had no authority to challenge the right of United Arab Republic troops to be present anywhere on their own territory.

48. It may be pointed out in passing that over the years UNEF dealt with numerous infiltrators coming from the Israel as well as from the United Arab Republic side of the line. It would hardly be logical to take the position that because UNEF has successfully maintained quiet along the line for more than ten years, owing in large measure to the co-operation of the United Arab Republic authorities, that Government should then be told that it could not unilaterally seek the removal of the Force and thus in effect be penalized for the long co-operation with the international community it had extended in the interest of peace.

49. There are other practical factors relating to the above-mentioned arrangement which are highly relevant to the withdrawal of UNEF. First, once the United Arab Republic troops moved up to the line to place themselves in direct confrontation with the military forces of Israel, UNEF had, in fact, no further useful function. Secondly, if the Force was no longer welcome, it could not as a practical matter remain in the United Arab Republic, since the friction which would almost inevitably have arisen with that Government, its armed forces and with the local population would have made the situation of the Force both humiliating and untenable. It would even have been impossible to supply it. UNEF clearly had no mandate to try to stop United Arab Republic troops from moving freely about on their own territory. This was a peace-keeping force, not an enforcement action. Its effectiveness was based entirely on voluntary co-operation.

50. Quite apart from its position in the United Arab Republic, the request of that Government for UNEF's withdrawal automatically set off a disintegration of the Force, since two of the Governments providing contingents quickly let the Secretary-General know that their

contingents would be withdrawn, and there can be little doubt that other such notifications would not have been slow in coming if friction had been generated through an unwillingness to comply with the request for withdrawal.

51. For all the foregoing reasons, the operation, and even the continued existence of UNEF on United Arab Republic territory, after the withdrawal of United Arab Republic consent, would have been impossible, and any attempt to maintain the Force there would without question have had disastrous consequences.

APPENDIX VIII

UNITED NATIONS SECURITY COUNCIL RESOLUTION 242 (1967), PRINCIPLES FOR A JUST AND LASTING PEACE, NOVEMBER 22, 1967.*

The Security Council

Expressing its continuing concern with the grave situation in the Middle East,

Emphasizing the inadmissibility of the acquisition of territory by war and the need to work for a just and lasting peace in which every State in the area can live in security,

Emphasizing further that all Member States in their acceptance of the Charter of the United Nations have undertaken a commitment to act in accordance with Article 2 of the Charter,

1. Affirms that the fulfilment of the Charter principles requires the establishment of a just and lasting peace in the Middle East which should include the application of both the following principles:

    (a) Withdrawal of Israeli armed forces from territories occupied in the recent conflict;

    (b) Termination of all claims or states of belligerency and respect for and acknowledgement of the sovereignty, territorial integrity, and political independence of every State in the

---

* *Resolutions and Decisions of the Security Council,* 1967, *Security Council, Official Records,* 22nd year, United Nations, New York, 1968.

area and their right to live in peace within secure and recognized boundaries free from threats or acts of force;

2. Affirms further the necessity
    (a) For guaranteeing freedom of navigation through international waterways in the area;
    (b) For achieving a just settlement of the refugee problem;
    (c) For guaranteeing the territorial inviolability and political independence of every State in the area, through measures including the establishment of demilitarized zones;
3. Requests the Secretary-General to designate a Special Representative to proceed to the Middle East to establish and maintain contacts with the States concerned in order to promote agreement and assist efforts to achieve a peaceful and accepted settlement in accordance with the provisions and principles in this resolution;
4. Requests the Secretary-General to report to the Security Council on the progress of the efforts of the Special Representative as soon as possible.

APPENDIX IX

UNITED STATES SENATE: RESOLUTION 155, CONSTRUCTION OF NUCLEAR DESALTING PLANTS IN THE MIDDLE EAST, DECEMBER 12, 1967.*

Whereas the security and national interests of the United States require that there be a stable and durable peace in the Middle East; and

Whereas the greatest bar to a long-term settlement of the differences between the Arab and Israeli people is the chronic shortage of fresh water, useful work, and an adequate food supply; and

Whereas the United States now has available the technology and the resources to alleviate these shortages and to provide a base for peaceful cooperation between the countries involved: Now, therefore, be it Resolved, That it is the sense of the Senate that the prompt design, construction, and operation of nuclear desalting plants will provide

---

* U. S. Senate, Congress 90, Session 1, Committee on Foreign Relations, *Hearings on S. Res. 155, Construction of Nuclear Desalting Plants in the Middle East*, Washington, D. C., 1967.

Appendixes

large quantities of fresh water to both Arab and Israeli territories and, thereby, will result in:

(1) new jobs for the many refugees;
(2) an enormous increase in the agricultural productivity of existing wastelands;
(3) a broad base for cooperation between the Israeli and Arab Governments; and
(4) a further demonstration of the United States efforts to find peaceful solutions to areas of conflict; and be it further

Resolved, That the President is requested to pursue these objectives, as reflecting the sense of the Senate, within and outside the United Nations and with all nations similarly minded, as being in the highest national interest of the United States.

APPENDIX X

UNITED STATES PERMANENT DELEGATE TO THE UNITED NATIONS, ARTHUR J. GOLDBERG'S SPEECH ON THE MIDDLE EAST CRISIS, MAY 24, 1967.*

The United States strongly supported the request by Canada and Denmark last evening for an immediate meeting of the Security Council. We did so out of our grave concern over the sharp increase of tension between Israel and her Arab neighbors, since the Secretary-General's departure, and out of our belief that the Secretary-General should be accorded all possible support in the difficult peace mission on which he is now embarked.

When the Secretary-General announced his intention to undertake this critically important journey, my Government immediately gave him our full backing. We agreed with his assessment of the gravity of the situation when he said on May 19, in his report to the Council that "the current situation in the Near East is more disturbing, indeed, I may say more menacing than at any time since the fall of 1956."

We, like others in the Council, would normally have awaited a further report from the Secretary-General before convening a meeting of the Council.

* *New York Times,* 25 May 1967.

185

However, since the Secretary-General made his report—indeed, in the two days since he departed for Cairo—conditions in the area have taken a still more menacing turn because of a threat to customary international rights which have been exercised for many years in the Gulf of Aqaba.

This has led us to the belief that the Council, in the exercise of its responsibilities, should meet without delay and take steps to relieve tension in the area.

In his report to the Council, the Secretary-General correctly singled out two areas as "particularly sensitive". One was the Gaza Strip. The other was Sharm el-Sheik, which stands at the entrance to the Gulf of Aqaba.

The position of the United States on these matters was publicly stated yesterday by President Johnson, and I shall not take the time of the Council to reiterate what he explicitly said.

We are well aware, of course, of the longstanding grievances, some of them of many years standing, in all sides of this complex dispute. Whoever is familiar with the area knows that, regrettably, these underlying problems are not going to be resolved tomorrow.

The cause of peace which we here are pledged to serve will not be advanced by raking over the past or by attempting overambitiously to settle the future.

Our objective today should be much more limited—but nonetheless of crucial importance under present circumstances. It should be to express full support for the efforts of the Secretary-General to work out a peaceful accommodation of the situation.

Accordingly, we should call upon all states to avoid any action which might exacerbate the already tense situation which prevailed when the Secretary-General departed on his mission.

Judging from what we heard in this morning's meeting, there should be no difficulty in obtaining the agreement of all members for this course of action by the Council.

And surely it is the plain obligation of the parties, as members of the United Nations committed to the cause of peace, to assure that there is no interference with existing international rights which have long been enjoyed and exercised in the area by many nations. Such interference would menace the mission of the Secretary-General and could abort his efforts to work out a peaceful accommodation.

We are fully aware, as are all the members of the Council, of the long-

Appendixes

standing underlying problems in the area. But no problems of this character can be settled by warlike acts.

The United States' opposition to the use of aggression and violence of any kind on any side of this situation over the years, is a matter of record.

As our actions over many years have demonstrated, and as President Johnson reaffirmed in his statement yesterday: "The United States is firmly committed to the support of the political independence and territorial integrity of all the nations in the area. The United States strongly opposes aggression by anyone in the area, in any form, overt or clandestine."

My country's devotion to this principle has been demonstrated concretely—not only in the Suez crisis, where we stood against old allies, but consistently through the years.

In fact, in the most recent debate in this Council involving this area, we made very clear the United States' commitment to the solution of all problems of the area by exclusively peaceful means and by recourse to the armistice machinery.

Mr. President, only two days ago many of us here had occasion, during the debate on the peace-keeping question in the General Assembly, to speak of the vital interest which all powers, great and small alike, share in maintaining an impartial international instrument of stability—an instrument which, when danger and discord arise, can transcend narrow self-interest and put power at the service of peace.

That instrument is the United Nations; and above all it is this Security Council, with its primary charter responsibility for the maintenance of international peace and security.

The view is sometimes stated that the smaller powers, because they are most vulnerable, are the real beneficiaries of United Nations' efforts to maintain the peace, whereas the great powers "can take care of themselves." My country does not accept this view.

Nobody questions the vital interest of the smaller powers in this activity; indeed they have manifested that interest time and time again by their votes and their contributions. But neither should anybody suppose that the exercise by the United Nations of its responsibility for the maintenance of international peace and security does not serve the basic interests of the great powers also.

Great Powers have both interests and responsibilities in this matter—and the greater the power the greater the responsibility.

In this spirit, Mr. President [Liu Chieh of Nationalist China], I am authorized to announce that the United States, both within and outside the United Nations, is prepared to join with all the other great powers—the Soviet Union, the United Kingdom and France—in a common effort to restore and maintain peace in the Near East.

Mr. President, all must join in the search for peace: the Secretary-General, the Security Council and the great powers. Both separately and together, let us work in this common cause which so vitally affects our own interests and those of all the world.

APPENDIX XI

THE PERMANENT DELEGATE OF THE SOVIET UNION TO THE UNITED NATIONS, NIKOLAI T. FEDORENKO'S SPEECH ON THE MIDDLE EAST CRISIS, MAY 24, 1967.*

A situation giving rise to anxiety from the view point of the interests of peace and international security has been taking shape in the Near East in recent weeks. After the armed attack by Israeli forces on the territory of the Syrian Arab Republic on April 7 this year, Israel's ruling circles continued aggravating the atmosphere of military psychosis in this country.

Leading statesmen, including Foreign Minister Eban [Abba Eban of Israel], openly called for large-scale Israeli "punitive" operations against Syria and the striking of "a decisive blow" upon her.

The Defense and Foreign Policy Committees of the Knesset on May 9 granted the Government powers for military operations against Syria. Israeli troops, moved to the frontiers of Syria, were alerted. Mobilization was proclaimed in the country.

It is quite clear that Israel could not act in this way if not for the direct and indirect encouragement it had for its position from certain imperialist circles which seek to bring back colonial oppression to Arab lands. These circles regard Israel in the present conditions as the main force against Arab countries which pursue an independent national policy and resist pressure from imperialism.

Israeli extremists apparently hoped to take Syria by surprise and deal a blow at it single handed. But they miscalculated. Showing solidarity with the courageous struggle of the Syrian people who are upholding their independence and sovereign rights, Arab states—the United Arab Re-

* *New York Times,* 25 May 1967; *Izvestia,* 25 May 1967.

Appendixes

public, Iraq, Algeria, Yemen, Lebanon, Kuwait, Sudan and Jordan—declared their determination to help Syria in the event of an attack by Israel.

The United Arab Republic, honoring its allied commitments for joint defense with Syria, took steps to contain the aggression. Considering that the presence of United Nations troops in the Gaza area and the Sinai peninsula would give Israel in this situation advantages for staging a military provocation against Arab countries, the U.A.R. Government asked the United Nations to pull out its troops from this area. A number of Arab states voiced their readiness to place their armed forces at the disposal of the Joint Arab Command to repel Israeli aggression.

As is known, the Soviet Government warned the Government of Israel in connection with the April 7 armed provocation, that it will bear the responsibility for the consequences of its aggressive policy. It appears that a reasonable approach has not yet triumphed in Tel Aviv. As a result, Israel is again to blame for a dangerous aggravation of tension in the Near East.

The question arises: What interests does the State of Israel serve by pursuing such a policy?

If they calculate in Tel Aviv that it will play the role of a colonial overseer of the imperialist powers over the peoples of the Arab East, there is no need to prove the groundlessness of such calculations in this age when the peoples of whole continents have shaken off the fetters of colonial oppression and are now building an independent life.

For decades the Soviet Union has been giving all-round assistance to the peoples of Arab countries in their just struggle for national liberation against colonialism, and for the advancement of their economy.

But let no one have any doubts about the fact that should anyone try to unleash aggression in the Near East he would be met not only with the united strength of Arab countries but also with strong opposition to aggression from the Soviet Union and all peace-loving states.

It is the firm belief of the Soviet Government that the peoples have no interest in kindling a military conflict in the Middle East. It is only a handful of colonial oil-monopolies and their hangers-on who can be interested in such a conflict. It is only the forces of imperialism, with Israel following in the wake of their policy, that can be interested in it.

The Soviet Government keeps a close watch on the developments in the Near East. It proceeds from the fact that the maintenance of peace and security in the area directly adjacent to the Soviet borders meets the vital interests of the Soviet peoples.

With due account taken of the situation, the Soviet Union is doing and will continue to do everything in its power to prevent a violation of peace and security in the Near East and safeguard the legitimate rights of the peoples.

APPENDIX XII

SOVIET PREMIER ALEKSEI N. KOSYGIN'S SPEECH AT THE EMERGENCY SPECIAL SESSION OF THE U.N. GENERAL ASSEMBLY ON JUNE 19, 1967.*

Mr. President, distinguished delegates:

Representatives from almost all states of the world have gathered for the emergency special session of the United Nations General Assembly to consider the grave and dangerous situation which has developed in recent days in the Middle East and which arouses deep concern everywhere.

True enough, no hostilities are being waged there at this moment. The fact that there has been a ceasefire is a certain success of the peace-loving forces. It also does considerable credit to the Security Council, though it failed to discharge fully its obligations under the United Nations Charter. The aggression is continuing. The armed forces of Israel occupy territories in the U.A.R., Syria and Jordan.

As long as the Israeli troops continue to occupy the seized territories, and urgent measures are not taken to eliminate the consequences of the aggression, a military conflict can flare up any minute with a new intensity.

That is exactly why the Soviet Union took the initiative in convening an emergency session of the General Assembly. We are gratified to note that many states supported our proposal. Thus they displayed their awareness of the dangers with which the situation is fraught and manifested their concern for the consolidation of peace.

The General Assembly is confronted with a responsible task of adopting decisions that would clear the way toward the restoration of peace in the Middle East. This task concerns all states irrespective of differences in

---

* *New York Times,* 20 June 1967; *Pravda,* 20 June 1967.

Appendixes

social or political systems, philosophical concepts, irrespective of geography and alignment with this or that grouping. It can be solved only if the multiple and complex nature of today's world does not push into the background the common objectives that join states and peoples together, and above all, the need to prevent military disaster.

What question is now uppermost in the minds of all peoples? We believe that all the participants in the General Assembly will agree that all nations are concerned above all about the problem of how to avoid this disaster.

No nation wants war. Now-a-days nobody doubts that if a new world war starts it would inevitably be a nuclear one. Its consequences would be fatal for many countries and peoples of the world. The more far-sighted statesmen from various countries, outstanding thinkers and scientists warned of this from the first day nuclear weapons came into existence.

The nuclear age has created a new reality in questions of war and peace. It has vested in the states a far greater responsibility in all that pertains to these problems. This cannot be called in question by any politician, any military man, unless he has lost the capacity for sensible thinking—all the more so in that military men can imagine the aftermath of a nuclear war better than anyone else.

However, the practice of international relations abounds in facts which show that certain states take quite a different approach. Continuous attempts are undertaken to interfere in the internal affairs of independent countries and peoples, to impose on them from outside political concepts and alien views on social order.

No stone is left unturned to breathe a new life into military blocs. The network of military bases, those strongpoints of aggression flung far and wide all over the world, is being refurbished and perfected. Naval fleets are plying the sea thousands of miles from their own shores and threaten the security of states in entire areas.

Even in those cases when the aggravation of tension or the emergence of hotbeds of war danger is connected with conflicts involving relatively small states, not infrequently it is the big powers that are behind them. This applies not only to the Middle East, where aggression has been committed by Israel backed by bigger imperialist powers, but also to other areas of the world. . . .

If the events in the Middle East are analyzed, the conclusion will unfailingly be made that the war between Israel and the Arab states . . .

did not result from some kind of misunderstanding or inadequate understanding of one another by the sides.

Nor is this just a local conflict. The events that took place recently in the Middle East in connection with the armed conflict between Israel and the Arab states should be considered precisely in the context of the general international situation.

I would not like to go into details, but basic facts have to be mentioned in order to give a correct assessment of what has happened.

What were the main features in relations between Israel and the Arab countries during the past year? Those were the continuously increasing tension and the mounting scale of attacks by Israeli troops against one or another of its neighbours.

On Nov. 25, 1966, the Security Council censured the Government of Israel for a carefully planned "large-scale military action" against Jordan in violation of the United Nations Charter, and warned that if such actions were repeated the Security Council would have to consider "further and more effective steps as envisaged in the Charter."

Israel, however, did not wish to draw a lesson.

Last April 7, Israeli troops staged an attack against the territory of the Syrian Arab Republic. This was a large-scale military operation involving planes, tanks and artillery. Following this, Israel provoked new military incidents on its border with Jordan.

At the time, a number of states warned Israel once more that it would be held responsible for the consequences of the policy it was pursuing. But even then the Israeli Government did not reconsider its course. Its political leaders openly threatened 'broader military actions against the Arab countries'. The Prime Minister of Israel made it clear that the April armed attack on Syria was not to be the final measure and that Israel itself would choose the methods and the time for new similar actions. On May 9, 1967, the Israeli Parliament empowered the Government of Israel to carry out military operations against Syria. Israeli troops began to advance to the Syrian borders and mobilization was effected.

At the time, information started to come to the Soviet Government, and I think not only to us, that the Israeli Government planned to strike a swift blow against Syria at the end of May with the aim of smashing it and then to transfer hostilities to the territory of the United Arab Republic.

When the war preparations had entered the final stage, the Government of Israel suddenly began to pronounce, both confidentially and publicly,

Appendixes

assurances of its peaceful intentions. It declared that it did not intend to begin hostilities, and did not want conflict with its neighbors. Literally several hours before the attack on the Arab states the Minister of Defence of Israel swore that his Government was seeking a peaceful settlement. 'Let diplomacy work', this Minister said at a time when Israeli pilots had already received orders to bomb the cities of the United Arab Republic, Syria and Jordan. What unprecedented perfidy!

On June 5, Israel launched war against the United Arab Republic, Syria and Jordan. The Government of Israel violated the U.N. Charter, the norms of international law and demonstrated that all its peaceloving declarations were utterly false.

Everyone knows what followed.

I shall remind you here, at the headquarters of the United Nations Organisation, only of how brazenly the aggressor ignored the demands of the Security Council for an immediate cease-fire.

On June 6, the Security Council proposed that all hostilities should end as a first step towards the restoration of peace. Israel expanded operations on the fronts.

On June 7, the Security Council established a deadline for the termination of hostilities. Israeli troops continued their offensive and Israeli aircraft bombed peaceful Arab cities and villages.

On June 9, a new categorical demand was issued by the Security Council for a cease-fire. Israel ignored this, too. The Israeli army opened an offensive against the defence lines of Syria aimed at effecting a breakthrough to Damascus, the capital of this state.

The Security Council had to adopt yet another, and its fourth, decision, a number of states had to sever diplomatic relations with Israel and give a firm warning that sanctions would be applied, before the Israeli troops stopped hostilities. The major part of the territory of the Arab states, which is now practically under Israeli occupation, was seized after the Security Council had adopted the decision on the immediate termination of hostilities.

There is irrefutable proof to show that Israel bears the responsibility for unleashing the war, for all who suffered from it and for its consequences.

But if anyone needs further evidence that the war in the Near East was unleashed by Israel and that Israel is the aggressor, Israel itself has provided the proof. It is impossible to explain in any other way the refusal of the Israeli Government to support the Soviet Union's proposal to convene an emergency session of the U.N. General Assembly. If the Government of Israel felt no guilt before the nations of the world, it would not fear our discussion and the decisions which the General Assembly is bound to adopt.

Israel has no arguments to justify its aggression. Its attempts to justify itself—like those of its advocates to whitewash its policies and actions—based on declarations that the attack on the Arab states was a forced step, that allegedly, the other side left Israel no other course of action, are all false.

If Israel had claims against its neighbors, it should have come here, to the United Nations Organisation, and sought a peaceful settlement here, as it is authorized by the U.N. Charter. After all, Israel claims the right to use all the rights and privileges which accrue from being a member of the United Nations Organisation. But rights cannot exist without responsibilities.

More and more information is pouring in on the atrocities and violence being committed by the Israeli aggressors on the territories they have seized. What is happening on the Sinai Peninsula, in the Gaza area, in the western part of Jordan, and on Syrian territory occupied by Israeli troops, recalls the monstrous crimes committed by the fascists during World War II. The indigenous Arab population is being ousted from Gaza, Jerusalem and other areas. As in its time, Nazi Germany appointed Gauleiters in the regions it had occupied, so the Israeli Government is setting up an occupational administration in the territories it has seized and appointed its military governors there.

The Israeli troops are razing villages and destroying hospitals and schools. Civilians are being left without food and water, or any means of subsistence. The shooting of POWs and even women and children has been reported and ambulances with wounded have been burned.

The United Nations Organisation cannot ignore these crimes. The Security Council has already approached the Government of Israel with the demand that the preservation, safety, and well-being of the inhabitants in the region it has seized be guaranteed. This resolution in itself is an indictment of the aggressor. The United Nations Organisation must force Israel to respect international laws. Those organising and carrying out crimes on the occupied territories of the Arab countries must be severely punished.

True to its principle of assisting victims of aggression, of supporting peoples who are fighting for their independence and freedom, the Soviet

Appendixes

Union has come out strongly in defence of Arab states. We warned the Government of Israel, both before the aggression began and during the war, that if it decided to take upon itself the responsibility of unleashing a military conflict, it would have to pay in full measure for the consequences. We still firmly adhere to this stand.

There must be no political zigzags when we speak of war and peace and of defending peoples' rights. Of course, in order to settle one or another problem, states sometimes outline several possible ways. But in problems like this, which the emergency session of the General Assembly is now considering, there exists no alternative for a resolute condemnation of aggression, and of those forces behind it, no alternative for the elimination of the aftermath of aggression. Otherwise it is impossible to end aggression, to discourage those who would care to launch such ventures in the future.

One may ask, why does the Soviet Union take such a resolute stand against Israel? No, gentlemen, the Soviet Union is not against Israel, but against the aggressive policies which are being conducted by ruling circles of that state.

Throughout the 50 years of its existence, the Soviet Union has treated all nations—big and small—with respect. Every nation has the right to create its own independent national state. This is one of the main principles of the policy the Soviet Union pursues.

It was this that determined our attitude towards Israel as a state when in 1947 we voted for the decision of the UNO to create on the territory of Palestine, a former British colony, two independent states—one Jewish and one Arab. Guided by this principle, the Soviet Union established diplomatic relations with Israel.

While supporting the right of nations to self-determination, the Soviet Union condemns, just as vigorously, attempts by any state to conduct an aggressive policy in relation to other countries—a policy of seizing foreign lands and enslaving the people living there.

What policy does the state of Israel pursue? Unfortunately, throughout the major part of its history, the ruling Israeli circles have conducted a policy of seizure and expanding their territory at the expense of the territories of the neighbouring Arab states, and ousting or even destroying the indigenous population of those lands.

It was so in 1948-1949, when Israel forcibly seized a considerable part of the territory of the Arab state, which was to be set up according to the U.N. decision. About a million people were driven out of their native land and doomed to hunger, suffering and poverty. All these years these people have lived like exiles, deprived of their motherland and means of subsistence. The acute problem of the Palestine refugees, which resulted from the policies of Israel, remains unsettled to this day, and tends constantly to aggravate tension in that area.

The same occurred in 1956, when Israel took part in the aggression against Egypt. At that time its troops invaded Egyptian territory as they have done now. At that time, too, Israel tried to retain the areas it had seized, but had to retreat beyond the armistice line under the powerful pressure brought to bear on it by the United Nations Organisation, by the majority of its members.

The members of the United Nations Organisation are well aware that throughout the years that followed, Israel has been committing acts of aggression against the United Arab Republic, Syria and Jordan. There has been no other issue about which it has been necessary to convene the Security Council so often, as that of conflicts between Israel and the Arab states.

As we can see, the aggressive war unleashed today by Israel against the Arab countries is a direct continuation of policies which the ruling extremist circles have imposed on their country throughout the entire existence of the Israeli state. It is against this aggressive policy that the Soviet Union has acted firmly and consistently, along with the other socialist and all peaceloving states. It is the duty of the United Nations Organisation to force Israel to submit to the demands of the nations. If UNO fails to do this, it will be failing to fulfil its highest duty, in the name of which it was created, and faith in the Organisation will be undermined.

Israel can establish its place among the nations of the world only by taking the path of peace, by abandoning its aggressive policies towards its neighbors.

We would not be consistent or fair in appraising Israel's policy, if we did not say with complete certainty, that, in its actions, Israel enjoys support from certain imperialist circles outside the country. More than that, these influential circles have made statements and indulged in practical activities which the extremists in Israel could interpret only in one way— as a direct encouragement to commit acts of aggression.

How else, for example, can we estimate the fact that on the eve of the Israeli aggression, a plan was being hurriedly worked out in the U.S.A. and Great Britain—and which was widely reported in the press—on est-

Appendixes

ablishing an international naval force to bring pressure to bear on the Arab states? How else can we estimate the military demonstrations of the U.S. Sixth Fleet off the shores of the Arab states and the increase in British naval and air forces in the Mediterranean and in the Red Sea area, or the stepped-up deliveries of modern armaments and ammunition for the Israeli army? . . .

At present, the extremely bellicose circles in Tel Aviv are declaring that their seizure of Arab territories provides them with—as they brazenly state—the basis for making new demands on the Arab countries and nations. An unbridled anti-Arab propaganda campaign, supported by the press of certain Western countries, is being carried on in Israel. The force of arms is being lauded, new threats are being made against neighboring countries, and it is being said that Israel will not heed any decisions, not even those adopted by the present session of the U.N. General Assembly, if they do not conform to its demands.

The aggressor is in a state of intoxication. Plans devised long before to reshape the map of the Near East, are being brought to the fore. The Israeli leaders are declaring that Israel will not leave the Gaza area, or the western banks of the Jordan River. They are declaring that Israel intends to retain under its control the entire city of Jerusalem and say that, should the Arab countries not submit to Israeli demands, Israeli troops will simply remain where they are now.

What is the attitude of the governments of the U.S.A. and Great Britain to the Israeli claims? For all practical purposes, in this case, too, they are taking the stand of encouraging the aggressor. How else can the aggressor interpret their position in the Security Council which hampered the adoption of a proposal on the immediate withdrawal of the Israeli troops behind the armistice line? Declarations of support for the political independence and territorial integrity of the Near Eastern countries so lavishly made by the U.S. representatives can have meaning only if those who utter them reject in no uncertain way the territorial claims of the aggressor and favour the immediate withdrawal of his troops.

By putting forward a programme of annexation, Israel completely loses all sense of reality and embarks on a very dangerous path. Any attempts to consolidate the results of aggression is bound to fail. We are confident that the United Nations will reject attempts to impose a settlement on the Arab peoples that might jeopardise their legitimate interests or humiliate them. Territorial conquests, if they were recognised by various states, would only lead to new and perhaps bigger conflicts while peace and security in the Near East would remain an illusion. Such a situation cannot be permitted to arise, and one can rest assured that this will not happen. Attempts to consolidate the fruits of aggression will in the long run rebound against Israel and its people.

By occupying U.A.R., Jordanian and Syrian territories, Israel is continuing to throw out a challenge to the United Nations and all peace-loving states. Therefore the main task of this Assembly is to condemn the aggressor and to take measures for the immediate withdrawal of Israeli troops beyond the armistice line. In other words, the task is to clear all the territories of Arab countries of the Israeli invaders.

The Israeli aggression has resulted in paralysing the work of the Suez Canal, an important international waterway which has been transformed by the invaders into a front line.

The Soviet Union voices a categorical demand that the Israeli troops be immediately removed from the shores of the Suez Canal and from all occupied Arab territories.

Only the withdrawal of Israeli forces from the areas they have seized can change the situation in favour of a detente and the creation of conditions for peace in the Near East.

Is it not clear that unless this is done and the Israeli invaders evicted from the territory of Arab states, there can be no hope of settling other unsolved problems in the Near East?

Those who unleashed the war against the Arab states should not cherish hopes that they will gain advantages from this.

The United Nations, called upon to serve the cause of preserving peace and international security, must use all its influence and all its prestige to end aggression.

In its demand to condemn aggression and withdraw troops from the seized territories of the U.A.R., Syria and Jordan, the Soviet Government proceeds from the necessity to maintain peace not only in the Near East. It should not be forgotten that there are many regions in the world where there are bound to be those eager to seize foreign territories, where principles of territorial integrity and respect for the sovereignty of states are far from being honored. If Israel's claims are not rebuffed today, tomorrow new aggressors, big or small, may attempt to overrun the lands of other peaceful countries. . . .

There is another important aspect of the aggression perpetrated by Israel. The point is that this aggression was aimed at toppling the existing regimes in the U.A.R., Syria and other Arab countries, which by their determined struggle to strengthen their national independence and make progress have evoked the hatred of the imperialists and the solidarity and support of the peoples which have embarked on the path of independent development. Therefore, to permit the actions of Israel against the Arab states to go unpunished would mean opposing the cause of national liberation of peoples and the interests of many states of Asia, Africa and Latin America.

The Soviet Union does not recognise Israel's seizure of territories. True to the ideals of peace, freedom and independence of peoples, the Soviet Union will undertake all measures within its power, both in the United Nations and outside it, to eliminate the consequences of aggression and promote the establishment of a lasting peace in this region. This is our firm and principled course. This is our joint course together with other socialist countries.

On June 9, the leaders of Communist and Workers' Parties and governments of seven socialist countries declared their full and complete solidarity with the just struggle of the states of the Arab East. Unless the Government of Israel ceases its aggression and withdraws its troops beyond the armistice line, the socialist states "will do everything necessary to aid the peoples of the Arab countries to deal a firm rebuff to the aggressor, to safeguard their legitimate rights, to quench the hotbed of war in the Near East and restore peace in that region."

No state, however far removed from the area of the aggression, can remain aloof from the problem which is being discussed by the present emergency Session. The problem concerns war and peace. In the present tense international situation hours or minutes can settle the fate of the world. If the dangerous developments in the Near East, South-East Asia or any other place where peace is being violated, are not halted, if conflicts are permitted to spread, the only possible outcome today or tomorrow will be a big war, and no single state will be able to remain on the sidelines.

No state or government, if it is genuinely concerned about peace and the prevention of a new war, can reason that if some event takes place far from its borders it can regard it with equanimity. Indeed it cannot. A seemingly small event or 'local wars' may grow into big military conflicts. This means that every state and government should not only refrain from all actions that would bring about new complications, it must do all it can to prevent any aggravation of the situation, especially the emergence of hotbeds of war. Should they appear, however, it must try and quench them. This should be stressed especially in connection with the recent events in the Near East which have greatly complicated the already complex and dangerous international situation.

The Arab states, which fell victim to aggression, are entitled to expect that their sovereignty, territorial integrity, legitimate rights and interests, that were violated by the armed attack, will be restored in full and without delay. We repeat that this means, first of all, the withdrawal of Israeli forces from the occupied territories. This is the crucial question today, without which there can be no detente in the Near East.

Elimination of the consequences of aggression also means restitution of the material damage inflicted by the aggressor upon those attacked and whose lands were occupied. The Israeli troops and aircraft destroyed homes, industrial projects, roads and transport facilities in the U.A.R., Syria and Jordan. Israel is in duty bound to reimburse the full cost of all it destroyed and to return all captured property. It is in duty bound to do this within the shortest possible time.

Can the General Assembly measure up to the tasks that face it, can it cope with them? Yes, it can. The General Assembly should say its weighty word in favour of justice and peace.

The Soviet Union and its delegation are ready to work together with other countries, whose representatives have assembled in this hall. They are ready to work together with all other states and delegations in order to attain this aim.

Much depends on the efforts of the big powers. It would be good if their delegations also found a common language in order to reach decisions meeting the interests of peace in the Near East and throughout the world.

Guided by the lofty principles of the United Nations Charter and the desire to eliminate the consequences of aggression and restore justice as quickly as possible, the Soviet Government submits the following draft resolution to the General Assembly:

The General Assembly,

stating that Israel, by grossly violating the United Nations Charter and the universally accepted principles of international law, has committed a premeditated and planned aggression against the United Arab Republic, Syria and Jordan, has occupied a part of their territory and inflicted great material damage upon them,

noting that in contravention of the resolutions of the Security Council on the immediate cessation of all hostilities and a cease-fire of June 6,

Appendixes

June 7 and June 9, Israel continued to conduct offensive military operations against the afore-said states and expanded the territory it had seized,

noting further that although at the present time hostilities have ceased, Israel is continuing to occupy the territory of the U.A.R., Syria and Jordan, thus failing to halt the aggression and throwing out a challenge to the United Nations and all peace-loving states,

regarding as inadmissible and illegitimate the presentation by Israel of territorial claims to the Arab states, which prevents the restoration of peace in the area:

1. Resolutely condemns Israel's aggressive actions and its continuing occupation of a part of the territory of the U.A.R., Syria and Jordan, which constitutes an act of recognised aggression;

2. Demands that Israel should immediately and unconditionally withdraw all its forces from the territory of the afore-said states to positions beyond the armistice lines, as stipulated in the general armistice agreements, and should respect the status of the demilitarised zones, as prescribed in those armistice agreements;

3. Also demands that Israel should restitute in full and within the shortest possible time all the damage inflicted by its aggression upon the U.A.R., Syria and Jordan, and their nationals, and should return to them all seized property and other material assets;

4. Appeals to the Security Council to undertake, on its part, immediate and effective measures to eliminate all the consequences of the Israeli aggression.

The Government of the Soviet Union expresses the hope that the General Assembly will make a decision that will be effective in ensuring the inviolability of the sovereignty and territorial integrity of the Arab states, the restoration and consolidation of peace and security in the Near East.

The convening of the General Assembly emergency Session is a fact of great international significance. Should the General Assembly prove incapable of reaching a decision in the interests of peace, this will be a heavy blow to the expectations of mankind regarding the possibility of settling major international problems by peaceful means, by diplomatic contacts and negotiations. No state, which is genuinely concerned about the future of its people, can fail to take this into consideration.

All peoples must feel assured that the United Nations is capable of achieving the aims proclaimed in its Charter, and of safeguarding peace on earth.

Index

Abadan, 4
Abba Eban, 92, 103, 117, 135, 149
Afghanistan, 20
Africa, 40, 56; East, 78; North, 125
Afro-Asian Peoples' Solidarity Movement, 28
Al Fatah, 87-89, 131, 134, 140
Algeria, 33
Algerian Nationalists, 24
American Aid, 61, 84; Assistance, 50; Diplomats, 5; Forces, 53, 54; Policy, 49, 69, 85, 128; Oil Companies, 5
Anglo-American, 24; Aid, 25
Anglo-Egyptian, 15, 22
Anglo-French, 35-37, 40, 41, 47
Anglo-Iranian Oil Crisis, 4, 5
Ankara, 84
Aqaba, Gulf of, 41, 92-95, 98, 102-107, 111, 121, 146
Arab, 23, 36, 44, 71, 73, 78, 79, 99, 104, 110, 115, 117, 120, 128, 129, 131, 136; Command, 99; Communist Parties, 28; Countries, 6, 45, 75, 96, 102, 105, 106, 116, 142; Governments, 72, 95, 135, 138, 139, 145, 146; Interests, 100; Israeli War, 9, 73, 96, 97, 110, 112, 140; League, 16, 19; Legion, 8, 50; Liberation Movement, 66; Nationalism, 21, 42, 67, 74, 80; Nationalist Aspirations, 6; Nations, 41, 74, 130; Refugees, 10, 11, 68, 134, 138, 139; Socialism, 80, 84; States, 7, 8, 10, 12, 17, 19, 37, 47, 51, 56, 57, 62, 68, 71, 80, 81, 114, 119, 122, 124, 127, 128, 130, 133, 134, 136, 137, 141; Summit Conference, 72, 119; World, 42, 44, 47, 48, 51, 56, 64, 65, 69, 72, 75, 89, 110, 113, 114, 119, 133, 143
Arafat, Yasir, 140
Ardahan, 3
Armistice Agreements, 9
Arms, 22-24; Deal, 23; Race, 62, 68, 146; Shipments, 22
Asia, 40, 56
Aswan Dam, 24, 25, 26, 27, 28, 30, 32, 76

203

Index

Asyut University, 31

Baghdad, 28, 53; Pact, 18, 19, 20, 22, 44, 47, 49, 53, 56, 57, 74
Baker, Howard H., 73
Balkans, 3
Beirut, 50
Belgrade, 69
Berlin, 111
Bernadotte, Count Folke, 9
Black Sea, 3
Bosphorous, 3
Bowles, Chester, 70
Britain, 17, 25, 32, 34, 36, 37, 42, 48, 53, 63
British, 1, 7, 35, 41, 45, 47, 108; Forces, 53, 54; Paratroops, 53
Brezhnev, Leonid, 77, 79
Bulganin, 20

Cairo, 26, 27, 28, 69, 75, 81, 97, 101, 132, 150; Radio, 14
Canal Zone, 22
Cambodia, 128
CARE Program, 43
Castro, Fidel, 69
Ceasefire, 41, 42
CENTO (Central Treaty Organization), 57, 83
Chamoun, Camille, 52, 53
China, Communist, 21, 25, 26, 48, 78, 79, 143; Nationalist, 25
Chou en-lai, 79
Christian Science Monitor, 97
Churchill, Randolph, 96, 97
Cold War, 2, 15, 18
Colonial Powers, 17
Communism, 16, 51, 52
Congo, 69

Congress, U.S., 4, 46
Cotton, 21; American, 25; Egyptian, 21, 25; Prices, 21
Cuba, 111
Curtis, Senator Thomas B., 13
Cyprus, 84
Czechoslovakia, 8

Daily Telegraph, 34
Dardanelles, 3, 96
Dayan, Moshe, 149
Department of State, U.S., 59, 61, 128
Dulles, John Foster, 17, 18, 23-27, 32-34, 41, 51, 83
Dutch Shell, 5
Dutton, Frederick G., 61, 66

East, 20
Eban, Abba, 92, 103, 117, 135, 149
Eden, Anthony, 24, 33, 39
Egypt, 8, 14-17, 19-30, 32-35, 37, 39, 41-44, 47, 49, 51, 52, 56, 58, 60, 61, 67, 71, 75, 78, 89, 90, 92, 93, 101-107, 112, 115, 127, 128, 149
Egyptian economy, 27; people, 27
Eisenhower Doctrine, 46-48, 49, 51, 52, 53, 55
Eisenhower, Dwight D., 33, 37, 42, 45, 50, 53, 58, 61, 62, 72
Electrical energy, 24
England, 35
Eshkol, Levi, 98, 125
Europe, 16, 35, 41; Eastern, 143; Markets, 21; Western, 21, 39, 40, 55, 123

Farouk, King, 15

204

Index

Fedayeen, 87, 88, 133-136, 141, 145
Federenko, Nicholas T., 110
Fertilizer Plant, 24, 29
France, 3, 14, 17, 24, 32, 34-37, 40, 42, 44, 48, 62, 63, 129
French, 1, 33, 35, 41, 45, 47; Petroleum, 5
Frankel, Max, 106
Fulbright, Senator J. William, 12

Gaza Strip, 14, 22, 41, 92, 136
Glassboro, 121
Glenn, Milton W., 65
Golan Heights, 136
Goldberg, Arthur S., 110, 120
Great Britain, 3, 14, 18, 24, 32, 33, 37, 40, 44, 62, 129
Great Powers, 51, 54
Greece, 3, 4, 5
Gruening, Ernest, 58, 65
Gulf, Arabian, 132
Gulf of Aqaba, 41, 92-95, 98, 102-107, 111, 121, 146

Hammarskjold, Dag, 62
Hanoi, 132
Heykal, Hassanein, 149'
Hitler, 140
Humphrey, Hubert H., 43
Hudson, Noel, 98
Hungary, 36, 42
Hussein, Ahmed, 26
Hussein, King, 49, 50, 90

Immigration, Jewish, 10
International Bank for Reconstruction and Development (IBRD), 25, 58

International Communism, 46, 49, 50
International Peace, 4
Iran, 2, 3, 5, 15, 18, 20, 31, 47, 57, 82-85; Shah of, 4, 5, 82, 84
Iraq, 8, 15, 18, 19, 28-30, 47, 49, 51, 52, 55-57
Iron Ore, 24
Ismailia, 35
Israel, 6-10, 12-15, 19, 22-24, 35-37, 39, 41, 42, 49, 58, 60-65, 68-74, 81, 87-92, 94-105, 108, 110-114, 116-121, 124-140, 145, 146, 149, 150
Izmir, 85

Jarring, Gunnar, 129
Javits, Senator Jacob, 12, 65
Jerusalem, 136, 146
Jet Fighter Planes, 125, 126
Jewish,
 Leaders, 7, 67; Liberation Movement, 66; State, 7, 8; Voters, 124
Johnson, Lyndon B., 70, 71, 103, 106, 120, 121, 125
Johnston, Eric, 72
Jordan, 8, 14, 49-55, 71-73, 88-90, 94, 99, 134; River, 71-73; Valley, 71

Kabul, 20
Kars, 3
Kassim, Abdel Karim, 52, 53, 55, 56
Keating, Kenneth, 61
Kennedy, John F., 12, 60, 64-69; Administration, 66, 69, 70

Index

Khrushchev, Nikita, 20, 53, 74-76
Korea, 16
Kosygin, Alexei, 77, 79, 81, 101, 113, 116, 121
Kremlin, 45, 81, 113, 114
Kurdish Republic, 2
Kuwait, 56

Lake Tiberias, 88
Latin America, 123
Lebanon, 8, 47, 50-55, 57, 71, 72, 88
London, 35, 37, 39

Mason, Edward, 70
Mediterranean, 3, 50, 52, 103
Meir, Golda, 137
Montreux Convention, 3
Metal Industry, 29
Middle East, 1-3, 5, 6, 9, 14-21, 23-24, 28-31, 34, 36, 37, 40, 42, 44-49, 51, 54-56, 58, 59, 61, 64-69, 72, 74, 75, 77-81, 87, 89, 96, 100, 103, 107, 112, 114, 117, 118, 120-123, 127-131, 134, 136-137, 139, 141-144, 146, 148; Communist dominance, 4; Emergency Committee, 40
Middle East Defence Organization (MEDO), 17
Missiles,
  Ground-to-Air "Hawk", 64, 68
  Ground-to-Ground, 64, 68
  Polaris, 122
  Surface-to-Air, 64, 127, 149
Moscow, 2, 5, 16, 20, 22, 23, 27-30, 48, 57, 69, 76, 81, 84, 85, 111, 115, 131, 143, 150

Mossadegh, Mohammed, 4, 5

Napoleon, 140
Naguib, General Mohammed, 15
Nasser, Gamal Abdel, 15, 19, 21-28, 32-36, 42, 57-62, 65, 69, 75, 89, 91, 92, 94, 96-99, 101-103, 106-108, 110-115, 128, 133, 145
Near East, 66, 96
Negev Desert, 72
Netherlands, 106
New York Times, 91, 106, 126, 139
Nile, 24, 26
Nixon, Richard M., 39, 126-128
Nolte, Richard H., 93, 97
North Atlantic Treaty Organization (NATO), 6, 16, 17, 74, 84
Northern Tier, 18, 19

Oil, 40, 41
  concessions, 2
  Middle Eastern, 123
  monopolies, 54, 81, 106; resources, 53

Pakistan, 18, 20, 57
Palestine, 7, 9, 11, 66; Liberation Movement, 78, 131; Liberation Organization, 134; Refugees, 9, 12, 131
Paris, 35, 37, 39
Partition Plan, 13
Pentagon, 53
Persian Gulf, 15, 78, 81
Planes, Jet Fighter, 125; Phantom Jet Fighter, 125, 126; Skyhawk Jet Fighter, 126

Index

Port Said, 35, 61
Power Vacuum, 45, 47, 141

Refugee resettlement, 10
Riyad, Mahmud, 93, 134
Rogers Plan, 148
Rogers, William, 148
Russia, 16, 20, 22, 26, 37, 42, 43, 48, 51, 76, 96, 101, 113, 115-117, 119, 140
Russian, 4, 5, 15, 24, 28, 29, 39, 49, 69, 78, 79, 96, 97, 102, 106, 108, 111, 113, 115, 130, 141; penetration, 23

Saudi Arabia, 15, 18, 56, 94
Scott, Gavin, 140
Scott, Senator, 12
Sea of Galilee, 71
Second World War, *see under* World War II
Senate Foreign Relations Committee, 12, 23
Sharm-el-Sheikh, 92, 94, 98, 136
Shepilov, 26
Sinai, 35, 39, 58, 64, 92, 95, 102, 112, 132, 133, 145
Soviet Union, 1, 3-8, 15, 17-22, 26-31, 35-37, 39, 42-48, 54-57, 60, 69, 73-85, 88-91, 95-104, 106, 108, 110-119, 127, 129-131, 141-148; Middle Eastern Policy, 2, 74; Soviet Aid, 69, 77; Soviet Arms, 35, 78, 110; Soviet Bloc, 26, 57, 62; Soviet Cultural Activities, 31; Soviet Economic Assistance, 81; Soviet Government, 20, 26, 72, 97

Stalin, 2, 85
Steel Mill, 24; Plant, 77
Straits, 3; of Tiran, 92, 94-96, 98-100, 103, 107, 112
Strauss, Lewis L., 73
Sudan, 16
Suez Canal, 14, 27, 32-37, 41, 58, 62, 119, 132, 146, 149, 150
Suez Crisis, 42, 45, 48, 55, 59, 123, 137
Superpowers, 74, 129, 130, 133, 144, 146

Taft, Senator, 11
Tanganyika, 69
Tanks, 63, 90; Patton, 90
Technical Assistance, 58
Teheran, 84
Tel Aviv, 35, 37, 39
Third World, 81, 143
Totalitarian regimes, 4
Tripartite Declaration, 14
Truman Doctrine, 2, 46
Truman, Harry S., 4, 7
Turkey, 2-6, 16-18, 31, 47, 51, 57, 74, 82, 84, 85

U Thant, 92, 93, 98, 135
United Arab Republic (UAR), 51, 52, 58, 60-65, 70, 71, 75-77, 81, 94, 95, 98, 99, 114, 115, 133, 134, 150
United Nations, 2, 3, 8, 10, 14, 32, 44, 54, 57, 100, 102, 110; Emergency Force (UNEF), 39, 92-94, 96, 98, 137; Peacekeeping Force, 41, 42, 146; General Assembly, 6, 7, 9, 12, 39, 53, 94, 116, 120, 121; Re-

Index

lief for Palestine Refugees (UNRPR), 9; Relief and Works Agency for Palestine Refugees (UNRWA), 9, 10, 11; Security Council, 9, 52, 88-90, 93, 113, 129, 134, 137

United States, 1-9, 11, 12, 14-26, 31-34, 36, 39, 40-55, 57-70, 73, 74, 79, 80-81, 84, 86, 88, 92, 94, 95, 99, 100, 103-106, 110-112, 114, 117-120, 122-124, 126-130, 141-148; Aid, 66; Assistance, 65, 66; Department of State, 59, 61, 149; Government, 23, 43, 45, 55, 90, 102, 103, 125, 150; Oil Companies, 123; Sixth Fleet, 50, 52

Vacuum, 44, 47, 141
Venkataramani, M. S., 40

Vietnam, 99, 107, 111

Washington, 5, 23, 25, 34, 35, 55, 105, 149
Washington Post, 97
West, 2, 15, 16, 18, 20, 21, 23, 27, 30, 34, 47, 48, 78, 81-84, 86, 98, 100, 114, 120
West Germany, 90
Western Alliance, 46
Western Hemisphere, 40, 123
Western,
  Maritime Powers, 106, 112
  Powers, 3, 5, 17, 48, 55, 72, 88, 92
World War II, 1, 2, 5, 6

Yemen, 18, 28, 30, 60, 78

Zionist Pressure Groups, 124